How Socialist East Germany's Elite Turned Capitalist

HOW SOCIALIST EAST GERMANY'S ELITE TURNED CAPITALIST

Gerhard Schnehen

Algora Publishing
New York

Library of Congress Cataloging-in-Publication Data:

Names: Schnehen, Gerhard, 1949- author.
Title: How socialist East Germany's elite turned capitalist / Gerhard
    Schnehen.
Description: New York: Algora Publishing, [2021] | Includes
    bibliographical references. | Summary: "When East and West Germany
    re-united, the world was amazed - but this great moment should have been
    foreseen. East Germany, the GDR, was not transformed by a
    counterrevolution from the outside; the leadership was always capitalist
    at heart. The author shows how they were undermining the socialist
    foundations even in the 1950s, as soon as Stalin died"— Provided by
    publisher.
Identifiers: LCCN 2021023234 (print) | LCCN 2021023235 (ebook) | ISBN
    9781628944433 (trade paperback) | ISBN 9781628944440 (hardcover) | ISBN
    9781628944457 (pdf)
Subjects: LCSH: Germany (East)—Economic conditions. | Germany
    (East)—Economic policy. | Capitalism—Germany (East)—History.
Classification: LCC HC290.78 .S358 2021 (print) | LCC HC290.78 (ebook) |
    DDC 330.943/1087—dc23
LC record available at https://lccn.loc.gov/2021023234
LC ebook record available at https://lccn.loc.gov/2021023235

Printed in the United States

TABLE OF CONTENTS

SETTING THE SCENE 1

PREFACE 3

PART ONE: BEFORE THE 1963 'ECONOMIC REFORM' 9

1. The Prevention of Democratic Change in East Germany
   after World War II 9
   Ulbricht's group and the new Berlin administration 9
   Ulbricht disbands the anti-fascist committees 14
   Top administrative positions handed over to reactionary forces 17
   Leading positions in industry and commerce given to the old German bourgeoisie 19
   Veteran communists and anti-fascists excluded from leading positions 22
   The suppression of the workers' council movement 23

2. The Role of the Soviet Military Administration in Germany (SMAD) 30
   Introduction 30
   Origins and development of SMAD 30
   The SMAD under Army-General Vasily Sokolovsky 35

3. The Foundation of the GDR on October 7, 1949 37

4. Stalin's Diplomatic Initiative in March/April 1952 41

5. "Accelerated Construction of Socialism" — the Second Party Conference
   of the Socialist Unity Party 43

6. The 17th of June, 1953 48

The triggers of the workers' rebellion	48
The deeper roots	52
The uprising and the violent suppression	55
Time Line, June 17 in East Berlin	55
Ulbricht's political survival thanks to Khrushchev's putsch against Beria	58
Khrushchev's coup	60
Ulbricht's purge	60
Was the 17th June an "imperialist provocation"?	64
7. The New Character of the Socialist Unity Party after the June Events	65
8. First Steps Towards the New Economic System	68
9. The Events Preceding the Building of the Berlin Wall	71
10. The Building of the Berlin Wall on August 13, 1961	74
11. "De-Stalinization"	78
12. A Former Nazi — Ulbricht's First Choice for the "Economic Reform"	79
13. Final Preparations	81
PART TWO: THE "NEW ECONOMIC SYSTEM OF PLANNING AND LEADERSHIP" (NÖSPL)	83
1. Disregard for the Law of Central Planning	83
Principles of central planning	83
The basic laws of building socialism must be observed, or else!	85
The three main tasks of NÖSPL and the socialist facade	87
The factual ending of central planning	88
2. Profit as Regulator of Social Production	91
The new emphasis on profit	91
The role of profit in building socialism	92
What was Lenin's stance?	93
3. The Realization of Profit through the Market	95
4. Means of Production Becoming Commodities	98
5. The New Banking and Credit System	102
6. The Reform of Industrial Prices	105
The denunciation of Stalin	105
A closer look at the law of value	107
New price fixing	107
The consequences	110
7. Self-financing	111
8. Concentration and Centralization of Capital	112
9. The New Premium System	115
10. The Abolition of the State Monopoly on Foreign Trade	117
11. Influx of Foreign Capital	120
12. The Sector "Commercial Coordination" (KoKo)	124

Origins, status and the role of the "Stasi"	124
The backers	127
The methods	128
Human trafficking	130
KoKo and Wandlitz	131
13. Debt Policies	135
The socialist principle of freedom from debt	135
The GDR's policy of debt accumulation	136
Was the GDR free of debts under General Secretary Ulbricht?	140
Honecker's ambitious spending programs	141
International finance capital silently colonizes the GDR	144
14. A New Capitalist Class	146
What are classes?	146
Was there still any "people's property"?	147
The new capitalists: "capital personified"	148
The members of the new GDR bourgeoisie	151
The new composition of the GDR bourgeoisie	151
15. The GDR Working Class — An Exploited Class	153
16. The Consciousness of the GDR Working Class	154
17. The GDR State — An Instrument of the New Ruling Class	157
PART THREE: THE END OF THE ULBRICHT ERA	161
1. The plot to get rid of Walter Ulbricht	161
2. The reasons for Ulbricht's removal: The economic crisis in the GDR in 1970	162
3. The "Prague Spring"	165
4. The Polish rebellion	166
5. Honecker's "Main Task"	167
Honecker's price freeze and spending programs	167
The consequences	168
SUMMARY AND CONCLUSIONS	175
APPENDIX I. CHRONOLOGY OF THE GDR'S FINAL TWENTY YEARS	185
APPENDIX II. DOCUMENTS	205
Document 1. The political legacy of Anton Saefkov	205
Document 2. Honecker seeks early release from prison	205
Document 3. The penitentiary director recommends his release	206
Document 4. Did Ulbricht install a Gestapo spy into the German anti-fascist resistance fighters during the Spanish Civil War?	206
Document 5. "Anti-fascist" Eric Mielke was in the pay of the OSS	208
Document 6. Stalin's views on a post-war Germany	209
Document 7. The "anti-fascist" Walter Ulbricht disbanding the anti-fascist committees in Berlin	210

Document 8. Ulbrich tells Dimitrov how he dealt with "illegal" German anti-fascists   211

Document 9. Pieck asks Soviet General Serov to send German POWs home to assist Ulbricht's mission in Berlin   211

Document 10. The 1946 internal crisis of the Socialist Unity Party   212

Document 11. A Soviet officer complains about shortcomings in the democratization effort in the new East German administration   213

Document 12. The dismissal of General Tulpanov   215

Document 13. Order no. 1, Marshal Zhukov appointing himself chief of SMAD   216

Document 14. Zhukov keeps large amounts of German treasure for himself   217

Document 15. Goodwill telegram by the Communist Party of the Soviet Union sent to the Second Party Conference of the SED   219

Document 16. The Soviet leadership (Malenkov/Beria) sharply criticizes the policy of the SED Politburo   220

Document 17. Ulbricht speaks to rebellious workers   222

Document 18. The unconstitutional arrest of Justice Minister Max Fechner   224

Document 19. Ulbricht praises the 20th Congress   225

Document 20. Ulbricht settles the score with Stalin   225

Document 21. Human trafficking in the GDR   226

Document 22. Schalck's decorations for "outstanding services"   227

Document 23. Schalck's connections to West German intelligence   228

Document 24. The GDR selling off its cultural heritage   229

Document 25. Werner Krolikovsky on the GDR economy   230

Document 26. Two Schürer documents (1989) on the GDR's impending insolvency   232

Document 27. Former Stasi officer Ralf Opitz describing the corrupt lifestyle in Wandlitz   234

4. HOW ANTI-FASCIST WAS THE GERMAN DEMOCRATIC REPUBLIC?   237

Setting The Scene

After World War II, Germany was in ruins, a heap of rubble. The western part was occupied by the Americans, the British and later also by the French armies, and the East by the Soviet Army. Although the Soviet Union insisted on treating Germany as a single entity at the Potsdam Conference of the Big Powers in July of 1945, the Western powers soon steered towards carving the country in two. That way, they could integrate their occupied zones into the Western alliance and start the Cold War to roll back communism.

To make this happen, in September 1949 a separate West German state, the Federal Republic of Germany, was created by the United States, and soon afterwards the German Democratic Republic (GDR) came into being, leading to decades of strife in a divided Germany: one part belonging to the Western bloc and NATO, and the other to the Eastern alliance, the Warsaw Pact. The Germans themselves were never asked if they were in favor of such a scenario. Whole families were torn apart, and in the summer of 1961, things got even worse when a separation wall was built right through Berlin. The Berlin Wall split apart a thriving city of four million inhabitants. Again, the Germans were not asked if they wanted this. They were victims of Big Power politics, the Cold War and an unpopular regime.

This book traces developments in East Germany in the decades after the end of World War II. The socialist political and economic model established in the GDR was soon mishandled by the leaders, and capitalism was restored under the guise of a "modern socialism." Again, at no point in time were the Germans living there asked if they were in favor of such models.

In 1989, the GDR was about to collapse; state bankruptcy was imminent. The people took to the streets in massive demonstrations, bringing down a deeply unpopular pseudo-socialist regime. East Germany became part of West Germany in 1990, but again the grandiose promises made to them that they would soon be living in a thriving and prosperous state were broken.

The following chapters look at the who's, the how's and the why's of this transformation and the consequences.

PREFACE

In dealing with GDR historiography, one is confronted with two paradigms.

On the one hand, there is the ordinary GDR-bashing exercised by Germany's neo-liberal and anti-communist media and intellectuals who consider the other German state to have been an Unrechtsstaat, a police state without any legitimacy, with no freedoms whatsoever, with a dilapidated infrastructure and a ruined natural environment. This is the usual line of thought of the German mainstream; it's been hammered into the brains of the Germans for decades on end and is regularly repeated on commemoration days, among them the national holiday of October 3, when the two German states became reunited. An avalanche of "documentaries" is regularly produced to mark the occasion and poured out over TV viewers to make them believe how bad the GDR was and how the poor East Germans suffered under a totalitarian regime before they finally won their freedoms and their right to join West Germany, to pay in Deutschmarks and to live in a paradise of wealth, freedom and democracy.

On the other hand, there are still those "on the left" who feel very strongly in favor of the former GDR, about their old auntie GDR — the poor and innocent victim of the "counter-revolution" instigated by West German agencies, politicians and media. Even today, these nostalgic-minded people still call the East German state "the greatest achievement of the German working class." They keep telling us that the second German state had been a truly socialist, anti-imperialist and anti-fascist state with no unemployment, good housing, cheap rents and prices, free medial care, an efficient educational system, with no Nazis in leading government positions — something the Federal Republic could only dream of. "The GDR was the better Germany!"

In the 2013 book *Walter Ulbricht*, the long-time leading politician of the GDR is remembered by people who lived through the 40 years of the GDR's existence, old witnesses, GDR veterans and functionaries, who proudly testify that this man was a great socialist leader, a wise statesman, deeply humane, that he loved children, listened attentively to the everyday problems of ordinary working people and that he was a German "patriot," as the editor Egon Krenz calls him in his introduction.

Between these two extremes virtually nothing exists. Almost nobody has tried to analyze the GDR from a principled Marxist point of view to find out what went wrong in this allegedly "socialist" state. Almost nobody has made a thorough attempt to apply tried and tested principles of Marxist analysis — principles that were still held high in the old Soviet Union.

The USSR, in its primary stage (not in its later, degenerated one), provided enough evidence that a socialist economy and society can be built successfully if one follows these principles and that a fair, just and stable society without exploitation can be created and that this society proved to be far superior to that in the West — culturally, socially, militarily or economically speaking. But let's put aside principles for a moment: neither has anybody made an attempt to look at the GDR without being influenced by these two schools of thought, looking behind the two curtains of propaganda raised both in the West and in the East and trusting solely their own reasoning to get closer to the truth. Why not put aside prejudices and ideologies once and for all and attempt to apply objective reasoning? Why not think and work independently? Why not simply collect facts, connect the dots, put together the pieces of the puzzle, then look at the whole picture and only then draw conclusions? It is not that difficult. This should be the primary task of historians, should it not?

It seems only natural and obvious to look at the German Democratic Republic from a point of view of how a truly socialist society can be erected and use the valuable experiences gathered in Stalin's Soviet Union, and to find out how this society can defend itself against all attempts to destroy it from within and from without. But the GDR leaders did not do that. They ruined socialism, thereby bringing about their own demise.

But the problem is this: For a very long time, Stalin and the old USSR have been vilified and denounced to such an extent that almost nobody dares to refer to the time when socialism was under construction — under construction in record time. Think of the 1930s, when you had the Great Depression in the West and the Great Building Site in the East, stretching from Belarus in the West to Vladivostok in the East. Nobody wants to be called a "Stalinist" anymore; nobody, especially in academia, risks being given this title which could end their career in no time. Everybody seems to "know" that Stalin was a "dictator and a tyrant" and the Soviet Union at that time a "totalitarian state" and nothing but a huge "Gulag."

But we should neither be guided by fear nor by prejudice. Fear blurs the mind and prejudice leads thinking into the wrong direction. If we want to gain a deeper understanding about why the GDR collapsed, we have to ask ourselves the following questions.

How comes it that the USSR under Stalin proved to be so successful and powerful, even succeeding in defeating the most modern army at that time, the Deutsche Wehrmacht and its many allies, and how comes it that the ruined and burnt down country could be rebuilt in record time after the war, in the face of aggressive US imperialism which already possessed the "bomb" and even created its own nuclear arsenal? How was it possible that the USSR could become a superpower and a fortress of socialism and peace within a historically very short period of time, in the twenties and thirties? And on the other hand: how was it possible that the GDR under Ulbricht and Honecker became so crisis-prone from the moment it left Stalin's Soviet Union behind and joined Khrushchev's noisy bandwagon of sabotaging socialism in the mid-fifties?

If such an analysis is done in detail, one begins to comprehend that the GDR was bound to collapse and become a victim of international imperialism sooner or later, that this was the inevitable outcome of the way the leading GDR politicians were acting over many years. If you ignore the laws of building socialism — and there are such laws — then they make themselves felt and come back at you through the back door. And that is what happened in the GDR, but also in other "socialist" East European countries and in the Soviet Union itself. In the end, the GDR leaders lost complete control over their country, especially over the economy, and were swept away by a powerful popular movement they and their children nowadays call "counterrevolution" or a "manipulated mass movement."

If we want to understand why the GDR disappeared from the political scene, it is by no means sufficient to just repeat the same old story that the "defeat," as some nostalgic people call it, was only caused by the powerful "counterrevolution" organized by Western agencies who manipulated the East Germans in a sort of "color revolution." It is necessary to analyze the whole long process of degeneration that preceded this "defeat," that paved the way for 1989.

Those who initiated this process, this process of sabotage and wrecking of socialism, leading to the restoration of capitalism in the GDR, were the real counter-revolutionaries who did the preparatory work, so that later the fruits of their sabotage could be reaped by Big German Money, by Deutsche Bank and all the other greedy corporate predators and oligarchs residing in West Germany and elsewhere. But the East German leaders did not do that intentionally and willfully! They wanted to reap the fruits of restoring capitalism for themselves. In their blindness and social isolation they thought they could stay in power forever. In 1989, when their house of cards collapsed, they lost all these illusions, had to leave the political arena and some even went to prison in West Germany.

This is what happens to those who have no understanding of the laws of history, which are rooted in the economy.

In my analysis I have tried to look at the whole process of degeneration in detail, from the time before the foundation of the GDR to the time thereafter, putting the main pieces of socialist sabotage and deformation together and coming to the final conclusion that capitalism had been restored in the GDR even before the country collapsed in 1989.

One last word: What can we learn from this process of creeping socialist degeneration and gradual transformation into capitalism, when thinking of other allegedly "communist" societies and economies in existence today? Here, Chinese so-called communism comes to mind, where a different process of deformation has been taking place for a very long time now. It is urgently necessary to analyze the Chinese "model of socialism" as well. By the way: those people who still call themselves communists and who lauded the GDR when "socialism" (in fact a version of capitalism) still existed there, today are among those praising the Chinese "road to socialism" or Chinese "communism." You still find them in the German Communist Party, but also in Maoist groupings and elsewhere. They harbor the same illusions about "socialism" and are trying to tell us that China is still a socialist country, and it is stunning to discover that they refuse to analyze this Chinese model just as they have never been willing to look into what really happened in the "socialist" GDR.

I would hope to find people who are willing to do such an analysis based on solid Marxist principles. The outcome, in my opinion, would probably be the following: China is not "communist," has never been, just the facade is communist. Chinese "communism" is a modern model of authoritarian capitalism. Meanwhile, the Western globalist elites under the chairmanship of the World Economic Forum (chaired by the China-fan Klaus Schwab) and the World Health Organization are also apparently now hard at work to copy and to introduce this model into our Western societies under the pretext of fighting the Covid-19 pandemic — at least elements of it.

Here, too, it is equally necessary to look behind the facade, to question the false labels and to never trust the outer appearance. This is still a hypothesis, but I believe it will be possible to verify it. A lot of work needs to be done in that respect.

PART ONE: BEFORE THE 1963 'ECONOMIC REFORM'

1. The Prevention of Democratic Change in East Germany after World War II

Ulbricht's group and the new Berlin administration

According to Marxist principles, socialism can only be built in a country where the working class, together with other sections of the population being exploited by finance capital, such as the intelligentsia, the petty bourgeoisie, the peasantry or small and medium-sized businesses, plays the leading role in overcoming the super-rich elites, also called the ruling class.

In the long run, the working class can only stay in power if the old state machine of the exploiting class has been completely dismantled and a new popular state apparatus, serving the interests of the vast majority of the people, the 99%, has taken its place, which can then serve the interests of the people.

However, the ruling class cannot be toppled and socialism cannot be built if the old state machine remains in place. That is why Lenin wrote, "The state apparatus created by the ruling class must be destroyed."[1] Without destroying the old state machine, the liberation of the working class, the vast majority of the people in modern societies, is impossible.

---

[1] J. W. Stalin, *Über die Grundlagen des Leninismus, Fragen des Leninismus*, Berlin, 1946, p. 84, Stalin quoting Lenin; Stalin on Leninism.

After the end of World War II, conditions in Germany were favorable for completely smashing the old state machine. The victorious Soviet Union had completely overcome Nazi aggression and defeated Nazi Germany almost on its own. In April of 1945, the Soviets had entered the capital, Berlin, before the other allied forces, the American and British army, were able to reach the city. The international balance of power had dramatically changed in favor of progressive, anti-fascist, democratic and socialist forces.

Thus, it was an exceptionally good opportunity to get rid of the old German state apparatus, which essentially had been serving German finance capital. The Eastern part of the country was occupied by the Soviet Red Army. The German ruling class, which had brought the Nazis to power in 1933, had almost completely lost its Prussian state machine and was economically and politically weakened; however, it was not completely wiped out.

By the end of the war, in early May of 1945, Berlin was in ruins and there was little left of the old state and administrative structures. This was the time to establish completely new democratic and anti-fascist structures in the very heart of Germany with the help of the Soviet Army and German anti-fascists and also other democratic forces who had resisted the Nazi regime. This would have provided a solid base for building real working-class democracy and later maybe even socialism under the leadership of tried and true German Communists and anti-fascists.

Shortly before the end of the war and Nazi Germany's capitulation, the 'Ulbricht Group' (two groups altogether, to be more precise) arrived in Berlin on a plane from Moscow. It seemed that the German Communist Party leadership under Wilhelm Pieck and Walter Ulbricht would soon take advantage of these favorable circumstances and start rebuilding the German state and administration in line with the principles of thoroughgoing democratization, also adopted at the Potsdam Conference by the Allied Powers in July 1945.

Ulbricht's group had been trained since the beginning of 1944 in Moscow to be prepared to take power in East Germany; they were closely linked to the former chairman of the dissolved Communist International, the Bulgarian born Georgi Dimitrov, but not to Stalin. Were these people genuine and selfless revolutionaries who would enthusiastically seize the unique opportunity to put an end to the political rule of German finance capital and the German aristocracy, or were they driven by other motives?

It soon became obvious that these so-called Communists would do everything possible to safeguard their own interests and those of the old entrenched German bourgeoisie, who were in an even weaker position than after their first big defeat in the First World War in 1918. In early 1945, when Nazi Germany had capitulated to the Allied Powers, the remnants of their class rule had neither social-democratic helpers such as Ebert, Scheidemann or Noske, nor armed militias at their disposal as they did the first time around, when they made ample use of the terrorist "Freikorps" to nip in the bud the victory of the German November Revolution (1918–1919). Now they were also partly on the run toward the Western part of Germany controlled by the American and British armies, leaving the capital Berlin behind them, and also most of their properties, their land and factories.

The Leipzig-born Walter Ulbricht, being in charge of these groups of Communists, who had spent the time of the war in a Moscow hotel called 'Luxe,' immediately ordered his people to find "reliable" figureheads and managers in Berlin to rebuild the destroyed city administration. Whom did they come up with? Conservatives like Arthur Werner and Andreas Hermes, who were soon entrusted with the top positions in the Berlin city administration. Often someone from Ulbricht's group was put in second place as a deputy. Werner, an ex member of the Nazi party, became the first mayor of Berlin.

But Ulbricht was not completely independent: he had a superior in Moscow named Dimitrov, the former leader of the Communist International, who saw to it that his underling sent regular progress reports on how things were developing in Berlin in the early months after the end of the war. These letters are documented in the appendix. They prove that these German Communists, if we can call them that, by no means relied on true anti-fascists and resistance fighters who had spent many years in Nazi concentration camps or in prison and had risked their lives on numerous occasions during the Nazi tyranny, who had even made concrete plans for a new and democratic Germany after the end of the Nazi era.

What was materializing ran counter to Stalin's ideas for a new Germany. Stalin did not appoint the participants of the Ulbricht group (this was Dimitrov's job). On June 7, 1945, a dissatisfied Stalin told Dimitrov that now...

an anti-fascist parliamentary regime should be established and that the Communist Party proposes a bloc of anti-fascist parties with a common platform.[2]

Two days later, Dimitrov met again at a "conference with German comrades (Pieck, Ackermann, Ulbricht, Sobotka) about their forthcoming work as leaders of the German CP in Berlin."[3]

Did they discuss Stalin's suggestion that the German Communists should propose a 'bloc of anti-fascist parties with a common platform'? No, they did not. According to Dimitrov's diary entries:

> We refined the German text of the party appeal. We added the following passage about confiscation of major landowners' and Junker estates: 'It stands to reason that these measures do not apply in the slightest to land ownership and farming activities by the Großbauer' [large farmer].[4]

So Dimitrov and his German friends discussed the founding of the German Communist Party in Berlin, again adding a strange passage to safeguard the interests of big German farmers. Stalin, on the other hand, had proposed not to found political parties early, but wanted the Germans to form an anti-fascist bloc to establish a democratic parliamentary regime, which the German Communists should then also join. Obviously, this was not to the liking of Pieck, Ulbricht and others who later became the top politicians in East Germany.

Nothing came of Stalin's idea to create a broad anti-fascist bloc, including all those who had resisted German fascism — at home and abroad in exile. Instead, the anti-fascist groups and alliances that had mushroomed soon after the collapse of the Nazi regime in early 1945 were immediately banned by Ulbricht and his followers (also see: Wolfgang Leonhard's report, document 4 in the appendix. The young Leonhard belonged to Ulbricht's group, but later left it).

Two years later in 1947, a representative of the Soviet Military Administration in Germany (SMAD) came to the following conclusion:

> The apparatus is democratic and new, but only in theory. As far as the personnel, the leading personnel, the political officials, is concerned, it is still the old established Prussian bureaucracy. You see, we have a contradiction here in the German administration: there is a tiny minority of old and experienced anti-fascists, but

---

[2] Ivo Banac, ed., *The Diaries of Georgi Dimitrov, 1933–1949*, New Haven & London, 2003, p. 372

[3] Ibid.

[4] Ibid., pp. 372f.

they have not learned to govern yet and very often they have been trained by veteran Prussian civil servants...[5]

The Soviet official whose task was to oversee the political process in Berlin had this to say:

> Through the armed forces and, as a result of denazification, the fascist state apparatus has been smashed, however, this 'most democratic administrative body in the entire history of Germany' as we are being told, there is, as it turns out, a strong tendency towards sabotaging democratization, and they have acted not democratically in a number of cases and are trying to ignore the orders of the SMAD by all means possible.[6]

The SMAD official especially deplores the fact that even some members of the Socialist Unity Party (a merger between Communists and Socialists in Berlin) "are hiding behind the provincial parliaments and state governments when we demand something."[7]

He also regrets that representatives of 'monopolists' — the old German grande bourgeoisie, that is — had been extremely successful in pulling all strings "from behind the scenes and [kept] preserving their old ties to West German cartels."[8]

He deplores the lack of capable "leading cadres of anti-fascists, so that in many positions you have rather suspicious and often untrained people."[9]

The Soviet SMAD official categorically demanded that Directive No. 201 of the Supreme Chief of the Soviet Military Administration be put into effect to thoroughly purge the state apparatus of hostile and antidemocratic elements, and he also emphasized Stalin's order to heed the mood of the masses, to encourage their initiative, to foster the development and support for public organizations of working people and to take orders seriously.

The question is this: How could it happen that two years after the war, neither the German Communist Party nor the Socialist Unity Party was able to achieve the important goal of thoroughly democratizing the German public sector, including already-nationalized enterprises, and

---

[5] Rolf Badstübner, Wilfried Loth, eds., *Wilhelm Pieck — Aufzeichnungen zur Deutschlandpolitik 1945–1953,* Berlin, 1994, notes on German policies, document 48, undated manuscript, late August/early September 1947, ZPA NL 36/734, Bl. 347-362, p. 164. ZPA= Central Party Archive.

[6] Ibid., pp. 162f.

[7] Ibid., p. 163.

[8] Ibid., p. 165.

[9] Ibid.

to staff the leading positions there with genuine and committed anti-fascists and proven democrats in order to create a new state apparatus?

The answer to this question lies in the fact that the Ulbricht-Pieck group of German "Communists" were neither true democrats nor Communists at all, but a group of political opportunists who had no interests in a thorough sweep-up of the state machine. Their main concern was to conquer the key positions and staff them with like-minded people and followers and to establish their own rule together with remnants of the old Prussian reactionary state under the guise of anti-fascism.

As mentioned already, it was not the "almighty dictator Stalin" who was responsible for putting together this group of alleged Communists. We have evidence that it was Georgi Dimitrov and Wilhelm Pieck who nominated the members of this spurious. They were both high officials of the Executive Committee of the defunct Communist International, dissolved by Stalin in early 1943. Dimitrov had been its leader since 1934. After the war they worked in tandem to pick the participants of the group, which is evidenced by a document according to which Pieck only informed Stalin at a meeting in the Kremlin on July 6, 1945, about the group's final composition. The candidates, all of them close friends of Pieck and Ulbricht, were also meant to be members of the new "Central Committee" of the Moscow wing of the German Communist Party. So Stalin was faced with a fait accompli. At that time the group had already been working clandestinely for a full month. Later Stalin nominated two of his own people for Germany: the anti-fascist Rudolf Herrnstadt, who had worked for the Soviet Army in Warsaw during the war as an undercover agent, and Wilhelm Zaisser, who took part in the Spanish Civil War ("General Gomez").

Ulbricht disbands the anti-fascist committees

As has already been mentioned, shortly before and immediately after the war a great number of anti-fascist committees were founded to take part in the political process at a time when the Nazi tyranny was already collapsing. They had different names like "People's Committee," "National Committee for a Free Germany" and the like, and were often led by those heroic anti-fascists who had actively resisted the Nazis even in the numerous concentration camps where they were risking their lives as members of various resistance groups. Many of these groups were destroyed by the Nazis especially, after the failed attack on Hitler's life on July 20, 1944 when a group of military men around General Stauffenberg planted a bomb next to Hitler during a meeting. Hitler was only slightly wounded.

One of the younger members of Ulbricht's group, Wolfgang Leonhard, later described these anti-fascist committees as "a genuine grass roots movement which was enormously active."[10]

The German authors Borsdorf and Niethammer in their book *Zwischen Befreiung und Besatzung* (between liberation and occupation) quote the example of the Leipzig 'Anti-fascist Committee' with 4,500 resistance fighters in the city alone. Many of the members of the Leipzig committee had joined the movement soon after the liberation of the Buchenwald concentration camp.

But instead of giving support to these numerous groups and their enthusiasm, their unbounded energy, their initiatives and great spirit, and using them to build a new anti-fascist and democratic German state and incorporating them into the Ulbricht group by giving them leading positions and responsibility, Ulbricht and his people did the exact opposite. One of Ulbricht's first comments regarding the committees on his arrival in Berlin in April of 1945 was the following, if we can believe Wolfgang Leonhard:

> These groups are infected with Nazis; they're a cover for Nazis who are trying to disrupt the effort of democratization.[11]

Ulbricht tells his underling Leonhard, in his early twenties at the time, to immediately disband these 'Nazi groups':

> Tomorrow you'll go there again and you'll tell them to stop their activities. We do not need these committees.[12]

But the young co-worker Leonhard has his doubts as to what Ulbricht told him:

> Soon I was convinced that these people were no 'Nazis in disguise' but honest comrades anti-fascists.[13]

Leonhard was all the more dumbfounded about his Communist boss's attitude since the directives given to his group in Moscow in the spring of 1945 had been of a completely different nature:

---

[10] Wolfgang Leonhard, *Die Revolution entlässt ihre Kinder*, Cologne, 1955, the revolution releases its children, p. 414.

[11] Ibid., p. 389.

[12] Ibid., p. 393.

[13] Ibid., p. 390.

I was all the more astonished, as only some weeks later measures were taken in Berlin which blatantly contradicted the instructions given to us.[14]

What then was the nature of these directives given to the Ulbricht group shortly before their departure in Moscow? One of them read as follows:

As soon as German organizations are allowed, it would be reasonable to create a broad anti-fascist and democratic mass organization called 'Bloc of a Fighting Democracy.'[15]

This was completely in line with Stalin's ideas. Stalin had told Dimitrov in the already mentioned meeting in the Kremlin that this was the best way forward in creating a German anti-fascist and democratic state serving the majority of the German people. But instead of creating such a broad-based coalition of fighters for real German democracy, starting in the occupied city of Berlin, where thousands of highly motivated anti-fascists had already set to work before the Ulbricht group had even arrived, and uniting these various groups of Communists, Socialists, Social Democrats, progressive Christians and the like, Ulbricht gave out orders to liquidate them as soon as possible, against Stalin's explicit directives.

But the former Comintern leader Georgi Dimitrov seemed to be in favor. In a progress report to Dimitrov, Ulbricht wrote:

The spontaneously created CPG offices [offices of the German Communist Party not linked to Ulbricht and Pieck's Moscow group — author], the People's Committees, the Committees Movement for a Free Germany and those of the 20th of July, which had previously been working underground, are now raising their head. We've closed all these offices and told the comrades to join us to assist our work in the town and in the city councils.[16]

The Ulbricht-Pieck group, which had seized control of the old Communist Party of Germany at a party conference with the help of leading officials of the Communist International near Moscow in October 1935, was not prepared to tolerate the newly established anti-fascist groups. They were also keen on suppressing the newly set up Communist groups who stood in the tradition of the old German Communist Party founded by Karl Liebknecht and Rosa Luxemburg in

---

[14] Ibid., p. 335.
[15] Ibid., p. 334.
[16] Gerhard Keiderling, ed, ‚Gruppe Ulbricht‘ in Berlin, April bis Juni 1945, Berlin, 1993, Ulbricht's group in Berlin, p. 320.

1919. These rival Communists who had actively resisted the Nazis during 12 long years of a life-and-death struggle in concentration camps and who had not collaborated with the Nazis there, were obviously considered competitors challenging the Ulbricht people.

Small wonder that the above-mentioned Soviet official was highly dissatisfied with the German democratization effort which, after two years of work had come next to nothing. The obvious reason: the most active anti-fascists who were really interested in denazification and democratization of Germany had been sidelined.

Only a small group of experienced anti-fascists followed Ulbricht's appeal to assist him rebuilding the administrative bodies in Berlin.[17]

Many of those who were kept out were soon driven into resignation and passivity. Ulbricht and his group, skillfully assisted and instructed by Dimitrov in Moscow, had successfully liquidated the anti-fascist movement; and right-wing conservative politicians like Ferdinand Sauerbruch and Arthur Werner, who had both collaborated with the Nazis, were put into top positions in Berlin to make sure that no substantial change as to the character of the state apparatus could occur. Sauerbruch, an enthusiastic Nazi follower, became Ulbricht's new health official. From now on these people were usually referred to as 'anti-fascists' or 'resistance fighters' to cover up their Nazi past.

Top administrative positions handed over to reactionary forces

Immediately after their arrival, the Ulbricht group set to work to recruit conservative and former Nazi people for the top posts in the Berlin administration. According to Wolfgang Leonhard, Ulbricht soon issued the following guideline for this purpose:

> It is necessary that the regional authorities are adequately staffed. We do not need communists as mayors, maybe one in Wedding or Friedrichshain [Berlin districts — author]. In the working-class districts they should normally be social democrats; in the bourgeois quarters like Zehlendorf, Wilmersdorf or Charlottenburg...we must put a bourgeois person in charge...[18]

One of Ulbricht's favorites for a top job in the Berlin administration was Andreas Hermes. In the Weimar Republic after World War I, he had been a member of the Catholic Center Party and, at one time, had been Minister for Nutrition. He was found in his villa by one of Ulbricht's lieutenants and was politely asked to become the new city councilor

---

[17] Rolf Badstübner, Wilfried Loth, eds., ibid., p. 164.
[18] Wolfgang Leonhard, ibid., p. 364.

for nutrition. He accepted. But soon he had to pack his bags again. The Soviets demanded his resignation in July 1945, because Hermes had opposed the democratic land reform project.

Another choice was Professor Ferdinand Sauerbruch, Adolf Hitler's personal physician.[19] He was appointed city councilor for health affairs. However, Sauerbruch, too, was soon to be released from his post by the Allied Command for the City of Berlin due to his Nazi past.[20]

Last but not least, Ulbricht could not abstain from making another highly controversial appointment: Heinz Ruehmann, a well-known actor who had been praised by Hitler for his various performances in Nazi movies, became his advisor in cultural affairs, because, according to Ulbricht, he was allegedly 'pro-Soviet' and had 'never acted in any movie for the Nazis'.[21] In fact, Ruehmann had excellent ties to Joseph Goebbels, Hitler's propaganda chief.[22]

Lord Mayor of Berlin became Dr. Arthur Werner, who, if we can believe Mr. Ulbricht, had "never been affiliated to any party whatsoever." However, according to the German historian Harry Waibel, Mr. Werner joined the Nazi party in January 1932, exactly one year before the Hitler putsch.

So it became obvious that Ulbricht, who was closely linked to the former head of the Communist International, Georgi Dimitrov, saw to it that, at least in Berlin, a thorough shake-up of the city administration did not take place, for this would have meant staffing all the top jobs with honest democrats and true anti-fascists — and there were plenty of them waiting in the wings. It maybe true that not all of them were as yet qualified to do these jobs, but they were keen to learn and the Soviets were ready to teach them the ropes.

It was Ulbricht's and Pieck's intention to keep the old-ancient Prussian bureaucracy intact and to cover up this project by appointing a member of their group as a deputy. They did not refrain from even using former members of the Nazi Party, the NSDAP, at a time when nearly everybody who had welcomed the defeat of German fascism after the war was strongly demanding a thorough denazification of the public services (German: Entnazifizierung). The Potsdam conference of the

---

[19] Martha Dodd, *Meine Jahre in Deutschland, 1933–1937. Nice to see you, Mr. Hitler!* Frankfurt/M, 2005, p. 233

[20] Allgemeine Zeitung Berlin, no. 29, October 12, 1945.

[21] Rolf Krebs, *Der deutsche Film von 1929–1945, Heinz Rühmann, ein Berater?!* In: ,Zeitgeschichte,' October 13, also at: http://www.kinosessel.de/ruehmann1.htm, p.1, quote from: Frankfurter Allgemeine Sonnatagszeitung.

[22] Ibid.

Allied Powers issued decrees to do just that which became law in all the four occupied zones.

To cover up their traces, the duo Ulbricht and Pieck, who had spent the war in a cozy Moscow hotel room and who had never been seriously persecuted by the Nazi regime before they arrived in Moscow, provided certain Nazis, among them a whole series of top Nazi generals, with false 'anti-fascist' testimonies. True anti-fascists, however, who had fought Hitler's tyranny from the very beginning, were seen as spanners in the works and pushed aside.

Leading positions in industry and commerce given to the old German bourgeoisie

What about the top jobs in the nationalized industries in the Eastern part of Germany or those in commerce? Were they at least given to anti-fascists or representatives of the German working classes?

The representative of the Soviet Military Administration to oversee the process of denazification in the Soviet Occupied Area, whom we have met before, says this:

> Secondly, in the nationalized enterprises in a number of cases the old masters or their relatives are still there and it is they who run the show and manage the factories, and they keep up their old networks to the West.[23]

The situation in the management of German corporations under Soviet control, also called SAG, was hardly any different:

> The German leadership of the SAG largely consists of old members of the bourgeoisie; personnel are competent people with a lot of experience. Against the privileges of the technical intelligentsia, even workers' councils are fighting a lost battle.[24]

These SAGs were the 200 most important industrial enterprises in the Soviet Occupied Zone (SBZ) which, between the summer of 1946 and April 1952, were put under Soviet proprietorship to make up for the huge damage in the Soviet Union caused by the Nazi invasion. The Western part of the country was almost completely devastated and burnt down by the German Wehrmacht.

The companies were led by Soviet technicians, but there was also a parallel German management regime. Later, in 1952, when these companies were given back to the Germans, it soon emerged that the

---

[23] Rolf Badstübner, Wilfried Loth, eds., ibid., p. 167.

[24] Rainer Karlsch, *Die Arbeitsverhältnisse in den Sowjetischen Aktiengesellschaften, SAG,* in: Peter Hübner, Klaus Tenfelde, eds., *Arbeiter in der SBZ/DDR*, Essen, 1999, p. 274. Employee-Employer relationship in the Soviet Stock Companies.

company management was again solidly under bourgeois German control, often exercised by people who had mostly belonged to the Nazi party before the end of the war. An inner party analysis conducted by the Socialist Unity Party, the country's leading organization, on the situation in the Thaelmann works in the city of Magdeburg revealed that former Nazis were in charge at all levels. The German news magazine *Der Spiegel* wrote:

> The membership of the former Nazi party NSDAP [National Socialist German Workers' — author] extends to practically all important levels of the enterprise, from the works director, his deputy, the other directors, their assistants, the dispatchers, the wages clerk to the ordinary white-collar worker.[25]

In May of 1958 a workers' brigade of the combine Schwarze Pumpe told the Central Committee of the Socialist Unity Party that the leading personnel of the enterprise was "a concentration of former members of the Nazi party."[26]

Ulbricht himself made sure that former conservative captains of industry and commerce like Peter-Adolf Thiessen and Max Steenbeck were able to retain their former influential positions. Guenter Vyshovsky, former GDR Minister for Industries, tells the story:

> Thiessen used to be director of the Kaiser-Wilhelm-Institute under Hitler. He was one of the most influential representatives of German industrial chemistry and capital. Steenbeck had worked for the Siemens Group. He was technical director there... Bertsch, the former executive director of the Henkel Group, was nominated a member of the "Wirtschaftskommission" [Economic Commission — a leading planning authority in the GDR]. He was cynically called the "red professor," but he was never red![27]

Thiessen joined the Nazi party on March 3, 1925, long before the Nazis came to power. He left the party in 1928 but rejoined them and in 1935 the Nazi leaders appointed him director of the Institute for Physical and Electrical Chemistry at the Kaiser-Wilhelm-Society in Berlin-Dahlem, and he was also given a top job at the Nazi Research Council.[28] In the early seventies, The GDR leaders decorated him with various medals and gave him a doctorate as well.

---

[25] Der Spiegel, May 9, 1994, no. 19, p. 91.
[26] Ibid.
[27] Günter Wyschowsky, in: Theo Pirker et al, *Der Plan als Befehl and Fiktion*, Opladen, 1995, p. 190; the plan: command and fiction.
[28] Olaf Kappelt, *Braunbuch DDR*, Berlin, 1981, p. 386; Brown Book GDR.

Another one of Ulbricht's darlings was Erich Apel who, during the Nazi era, had been on the staff of the Buchenwald-Dora concentration camp, there assisting the terror organization SS. For a while he also took part in developing Hitler's 'wonder weapon,' the V2 missile, in a last-ditch attempt to regain the upper hand in the final stages of the war. SED General Secretary Honecker, in an interview with two journalists, confirmed the fact this way:

> In fact, Erich Apel was active in Peenemuende, where they tried to develop the V1 and 2. Later, Peenemuende was relocated to the Harz Mountains. There at camp Buchenwald —Dora, Apel was one of the people in charge. He didn't have to fear any consequences because of that, since everything was known to us and well documented.[29]

Instead of putting the war criminal Apel behind bars, Ulbricht appointed him chief of the GDR's State Planning Commission, and he was also put in charge of a commission to draw up the plans for the East German economic reform in the early sixties. His economic plans were later approved by the 6th Party Congress of the SED.

A second example: Ulbricht was also instrumental in bringing back to East Germany Guenter Kohlmey who was still held in captivity in the Soviet Union. Kohlmey joined the Nazi party on September 1, 1941 shortly after Hitler had invaded Russia. He served as a Wehrmacht officer in the war. Ulbricht made him general director of a large East German combine and used his expertise for his economic reform plans in the mid sixties.

To sum up:

The leading politician of the team sent to occupied East Germany from Moscow after the end of the war, Walter Ulbricht, staffed the leading positions in the new East German administration, but also in industry and commerce, with conservative forces, even full-blown fascists, who had survived the war and were ready to start a second career in a 'communist'-led Prussian state. He successfully prevented anti-fascists, who been in the anti-Nazi resistance for years, some even for decades, from taking the reins in East Germany, thus helping to circumvent a genuine transition to an anti-Nazi democracy in the Soviet Occupied Zone and in the GDR.

He also needed well-qualified personnel to carry out his favorite project, the economic reform which was designed to restore a basically capitalist or state capitalist economy. These people were welcome in

---

[29] Erich Honecker in: Reinhold Andert, Wolfgang Herzberg, *Der Sturz. Erich Honecker im Kreuzverhör*, Berlin/Weimar, 1990, p. 282. The fall. Erich Honecker cross-examined.

the GDR, and no obstacles were put in their way to prevent them from starting a second career in the "anti-fascist GDR."

Veteran communists and anti-fascists excluded from leading positions

The Socialist Unity Party (SED) was founded in Berlin on April 21–22, 1946. It was a merger between the Ulbricht-Pieck wing of the former Communist Party of Germany, established in 1935 with the help of the leadership of the Communist International (Dimitrov, Togliatti, Manuilsky) and the Social Democratic Party in the Soviet Occupied Zone. Soon Ulbricht and Pieck and their followers occupied the leading positions in the new party, but accepted some well-known social democrats like Otto Grotewohl or Friedrich Ebert (the son of the former president of the German Reich) to join them as co-leaders.

However, only a few months later a severe crisis emerged within the ranks of the young party. Many German communists, who had joined the old Communist Party of Germany established in early 1919 after the German November Revolution, soon after the foundation of the SED complained bitterly that they had been sidelined and excluded from any influence by the leadership. The result was that the party meetings of the SED, especially in the city of Berlin, were often only attended by a handful of functionaries.

In July and October 1946, reports were compiled by a correspondent of the Soviet Information Bureau in Moscow and by the Deputy Chairman of the Political Department of the SMAD pointing out that there was growing dissatisfaction among formerly active communists who had become members of the SED.

Prominent anti-fascists filed complaints to the Soviet officials in Berlin that the SED leaders would not allow them to occupy leading positions. On the one hand there was a lot of talk that active members were urgently needed to assist with the reconstruction of the city, but on the other this category of anti-fascist cadres apparently was not welcome. They also deplored that the leading party bosses did not have close ties to the Berlin population but preferred to stay away from the masses and sought protection by the Soviet military stationed in the Berlin district of Karlshorst. One of the authors of the report did not mince his words:

Some of them complained that certain leading officials led a privileged life in luxury at a time when the majority of the people were suffering from hunger and distress.[30]

Later, the SED's leading politburo officials went a step further and settled in the remote village of Wandlitz, near Berlin, where they indulged in hunting activities and had a dense hedge installed around their property to keep out the prying eyes of the East German population. A detachment of the Soviet army was stationed nearby. So the first traces of corruption were already visible shortly after the war.

The suppression of the workers' council movement

Apart from the mighty anti-fascist movement which had gained enormous momentum all over Germany, including in the Western part, after the collapse of the Nazi regime, there was another popular movement to be liquidated by the Ulbricht group, a movement directly linked to the East German working class. This was the movement of workers' councils and played an important role between 1945 and 1948 in the Soviet Occupied Zone. But it suffered the same fate as the anti-fascist movement. In the official GDR history and school books this movement was never mentioned.

How did it start?

On July 5, 1945, an article was published in the official journal of the Ulbricht group under the heading of "What kind of a representation do we need in the enterprises?"[31] The writer made a plea to disband all workers' councils and all anti-fascist factory committees which had emerged spontaneously in a great number of enterprises. Instead, a new type of 'genuine' representations should be established as a substitute. The new breed he called "betriebliche Gewerkschaftsausschüsse" (shop floor union committees). The writer, most probably one of Ulbricht's minions, argued:

After the crushing of the fascist state apparatus by the Red Army, anti-fascist factory committees and in some enterprises provisional workers' councils have emerged... As soon as a trade union leadership has been established, it will replace these workers' councils or anti-fascist committees. Since, up to now, there has been no legal basis for

---

[30] Report of the Deputy Chariman of the Political Department, I. F. Filipov, *Die sozialistische Einheitspartei Deutschlands; The Socialist Unity Party of Germany*, October 9, 1946, in: Hermann Weber, Ulrich Maehlert, eds.,*Terror. Stalinistische Säuberungen 1936–1953*, Paderborn, 1998, p. 323.

[31] Deutsche Volkszeitung, 1st year, no. 20, July 5, 1945, p. 2.

---

the creation of such councils and committees, the only organs of the workforce remain the shop floor trade union committees.[32]
—The independent workers' councils were simply declared illegal.

This was a heavy blow to the anti-fascist committees and factory councils which could have developed into power organs of the working class at a later stage. Their ideas were based on the experience of the anti-fascist struggle of leading German communists and resistance fighters, many of whom with close ties to the former Communist Party of Germany which was banned by the Nazis in 1933. But they had carried on clandestinely, in some cases even inside concentration camps.

Where are the origins of these councils to be found?

The activists were mainly members of the German Communist Party (KPD) who were not directly affiliated to the Moscow communists. They were organized in various underground anti-Nazi groups, and some of them had even laid out their ideas for a post-Hitler Germany in manifestos and platforms.

One of these groups was the Saefkow-Jacob-Baestlein group of dedicated communists. In early 1944 they developed a platform called 'We communists and the National Committee for a Free Germany.' There factory councils are given an essential role for a democratic new beginning in a post-fascist era:

> In all factories do not elect representatives of your interest but your power organs; give them armed protection by company militias. Mind this: these departmental representatives, workers' councils; negotiators...should not just be representatives of your interests but your power organs to take decisions on issues of power and authority. People power can only be achieved if the working class instructs its organs of power to rule or to participate in ruling. This is the only path to democracy. If people want to rule, they must be armed! Organize, whether legal or illegal, a company militia, protect and arm your power organs![33]

These proposals from one of the most prominent and active German resistance groups explicitly ruled out any return to the bourgeois Weimar Republic (the political system in Germany between 1919 and 1933). For a great many anti-Nazi resistance fighters who survived Nazi tyranny and the war, the Baestlein group was a main point of reference.

> You Berlin workers should draw your lessons: in a new Germany it is up to the working class to achieve a united front and to approach socialism. As soon as the proletariat constitutes itself as the ruling

---

[32] Deutsche Volkszeitung, ibid.
[33] Gerhard Nitzsche, *Die Saefkow-Jacob-Bästlein-Gruppe*, Berlin, 1957, pp. 201f.

class, everything else is just a matter of how fast we move on. In any event: take your chance, you are on the right track![34]

In many German towns and cities, this platform seems to have been a guideline for clandestine resistance groups, anti-fascist committees or committees for a free Germany.

Those resistance fighters who had stayed behind in Nazi Germany and who had not emigrated or fled the country, wanted genuine workers' representations, real and genuine organs of working class power and not just weak trade union councils which had existed in the Weimar Republic. In short: they wanted the whole thing, they wanted organs of power assisting them to take power one day on a national level, they wanted proletarian rule and not just some fake 'anti-fascist system' presented by the Ulbricht people.

How did Ulbricht react to these proposals? If he was a real communist, he would have welcomed them wholeheartedly. But the worried Walter Ulbricht, now leader of the German Communist Party in Berlin, in a letter to his close friend Wilhelm Pieck in Moscow, wrote:

> We must be aware that the majority of our comrades are sectarian minded and I'd suggest that the composition of the party be changed as soon as possible by recruiting anti-fascists who have proven to be reliable workers. Some comrades only pretend to follow our directives, some have good will, but then again there is this old 'red front' slogan and some, especially in the problem districts of Charlottenburg and Wilmersdorf, even talk about "Power to the Soviets!" or something like that.[35]

Soviet power or something like that! Here Ulbricht shows his true face. In view of this dismal state of affairs in his own party, he arrived at the following conclusion:

> We need a new party to carry out our policy correctly, with new members. Three quarters of our party are useless.[36]

So for this "communist" who, later on, would play the dominant role in East Germany and the GDR, truly revolutionary-minded party members were 'useless' and not only that: they had to be purged from the organization and replaced by 'more reliable workers,' as he put it. Reliable towards whom?

---

[34] Ibid., pp. 202f.

[35] Walter Ulbricht writing to Wilhelm Pieck, Berlin, May 5, 1945, in: Gerhard Keiderling, ed., ibid., pp. 348f.

[36] Ibid., p. 354, Ulbricht writing to Dimitrov on the very same day.

He would not achieve this goal soon, only after the events of June 17th 1953, and with the help of the Soviet military stationed in Berlin.

The Ulbricht-Pieck group had their own agenda for a post-fascist Germany which had been developed in Moscow, hand in glove with Georgi Dimitrov, the former leader of the Communist International. Stalin did not play a role in that. He was occupied with other issues at the time.

If one reads their platform issued in June 1945, soon to become the new program of the German Communist Party, it is striking that there is not much space for any future workers' committees or factory councils, not to mention any "organs of power" as outlined by the Baestlein group which, by the way, was smashed by the Nazis in 1944 with all their participants being beheaded for "treason." Instead there is a lot of talk of a completely different nature: the necessity to develop the private initiative of entrepreneurs, for example:

> The immediate and most urgent tasks on this road are...the completely free development of free trade and private initiative on the basis of private property.[37] Only vaguely, "workers' representations" are mentioned.[38]

Not even a truly democratic land reform is mentioned there: large farmers were to be exempted from land confiscation. Nevertheless, a land reform was actually carried out in the Soviet Occupied Zone: the Soviets insisted on nationalizing the estates of German aristocrats, the Junker class, and gave the land to landless peasants. Estates of more than 100 ha of land were affected.

However, the highly praised "private initiative of entrepreneurs" soon proved to be a complete fiasco: many private company owners had already left the Soviet zone, heading west as soon as the Soviet Red Army approached Berlin, taking the remaining cash with them as well as their leading personnel, and those who stayed behind, had little inclination to take an active part in rebuilding the damaged factories.

At a conference of trade unionists in July of 1945 sharp criticism was voiced against private entrepreneurs. The *Deutsche Volkszeitung* wrote at the time:

> The trade unionists pointed to the complete failure of large parts of the management, on acts of sabotage and the lack of comprehension on the part of big business, such as AEG. On the other hand, the

---

[37] Appeal of the Communist Party of Germany, in: *De Waarheid, Volksdagblad voor Nederlande*, Verlag Volkszeitung Dresden, p. 9.
[38] Ibid.

selfless initiative of ordinary workers and employees was given prominence.[39]

Only a few weeks later it became obvious what the 'private initiative' of German business was worth:

> The spontaneous initiative of the workforce was far superior to the entrepreneurial effort to rebuild the economy. Only after a few weeks this had become obvious and was also recognized by party and trade union officials.[40]

In fact, the working class and their representatives in the enterprises were the very first to set to work and to rebuild the ruined factories. Thus, a key element of the Ulbricht's party appeal had proved to be unrealistic.

But irrespective of these facts and the great initiative shown by the East German workforce, the Ulbricht group demanded the immediate disbandment of the workers' councils and to replace them with their own brand of "representations." Meanwhile, the group had established "The Free German Trade Union Confederation" (FDGB) which was completely dominated by the Ulbricht group. They now played first fiddle in the enterprises. The original representations, which had originated spontaneously, were smashed.

What was the main reason for that?

This genuine movement was not just organized on a shop-floor level but nationwide; as a matter of fact, it was a militant workers' movement, and, what is more: in mid-1946, the first political strikes against Ulbricht and his followers were organized. Here's some background.

Some major private monopolies belonging to Nazi war criminals were nationalized following the referendum of June 30, 1946. Seventy-five percent of the voters in the province of Saxony in East Germany had opted in favor of the expropriation of these companies and for their transfer into public ownership. Immediately after the voting results were out, the newly formed Socialist Unity Party, dominated by the Ulbricht group, decided to ignore the outcome and to hand the firms back to their original owners. The reaction of the people in Saxony was furious and unambiguous: through the workers' councils they organized the first political strike after the war to prevent this from happening.

The strike action met with a popular response in early 1947, when in the Eastern part of Saxony 125 enterprises alone, and in the district

---

[39] *Deutsche Volkszeitung,* year one, no. 39, July 27, 1945, p. 2.
[40] Siegfried Suckut, *Die Betriebsrätebewegung in der Sowjetisch Besetzten Zone Deutschlands, 1945-1948,* Frankfurt/Main, 1982, p. 112; the workers' council movement in Soviet Occupied Germany.

of Bautzen 4,000 employees from 28 works joined the strike. It should remain the only political strike in the entire history of the GDR, apart from the strikes on June 17th, 1953.

At a conference of workers' representatives in the city of Bautzen being attended by 950 delegates a resolution was passed to respect the will of the people and the outcome of the referendum. The participants threatened to organize a general strike if the nationalized companies were given back to their former Nazi owners. Stefan Doernberg:

> The workers demand to respect the will of the people as expressed in the referendum...We demand from the government a clear commitment to preserve the common ownership of the enterprises. If this claim is not met by January 28, we shall call for a general strike.[41]

The provincial government led by the newly founded Socialist Unity Party was impressed and shied away from nullifying the will of the people. This highly successful move showed the growing political consciousness of the Saxon workers, who did not consider the SED their own party. Later, the "socialist" leaders of the GDR claimed that they had respected the referendum from the beginning. However, the strike was never mentioned in GDR historiography. It was declared a non-event.

The desire to prevent more independent actions by the working class was the real reason why the leadership of the SED wanted to disband the workers' councils altogether and declared them illegal. So they conjured up the alternative "trade union committees," being under their control, to break the back of the independent organizations, or at least to keep them in check.

One year later, in 1948, the appointees of the 'Free German Trade Union Confederation,' FDGB for short, held a conference at Bitterfeld in Saxony and passed a resolution to dissolve the independent workers' councils once and for all:

> The federal executive [of the FDGB — author] is charged to take appropriate steps to transfer the representations of workers and employees in factories and in the administration to the leadership of the trade unions in each enterprise, as well as all rights and duties, in accordance with law no. 22 of the Allied Control Commission [a directive passed by the Big Four, the occupying powers earlier on in 1945 — author].[42]

---

[41] Stefan Doernberg, *Die Geburt des neuen Deutschlands*, p. 372, in Siegfried Suckut, ibid., p. 449; the birth of the new Germany.

[42] Siegfried Suckut, ibid., p. 761, document 60: Decision by the FDGB's Bitterfeld Conference to abolish the workers' councils.

Law No. 22 of the Allied Control Commission passed in 1945 did permit elections on a shop-floor level to vote for independent workers' committees, but elections were postponed several times and, later on, only elections for the candidates on the list of the newly established trade union councils were allowed to take place. The turn-out in these fake elections was low, and when the elections were finally arranged in September 1948, only 5% of the members of the FDGB took part.[43]

The sad outcome for the East German working class: till autumn 1989, when the SED regime was bound to collapse, no independent workers' representations on a grass roots level, let alone independent trade unions, were allowed to exist.

The official trade union FDGB under the long-time chairman Harry Tisch did nothing to fight for the interests of the employees. After the demise of the German Democratic Republic, this was freely admitted by leading executives of combines, among them Christa Bertag, chief executive of a large East Berlin combine manufacturing cosmetics. In an interview she said: "The FDGB didn't play any role whatsoever."[44]

The FDGB did not take part in any wage negotiations, either. Wages and salaries were fixed by the state, later by the combine directors; they never called the workers and employees of any enterprise or combine out on strike, as strikes were forbidden. The leaders of the new officially recognized trade union closely collaborated with the directors of enterprises and with the SED politburo, where Harry Tisch, the long-time chief of the FDGB, had a seat for decades on end.

To sum up, leading positions, both in the administrative bodies and in the economy, and in science institutes and elsewhere, were systematically manned with bourgeois personnel and specialists by the Ulbricht group and later by the leadership of the Socialist Unity Party. The movement of workers' councils was smashed because it threatened to become a rival force challenging the predominance of the leading party. The newly founded "Free Trade Union Confederation" (FDGB) was used to break the back of an independent workers' movement with the intent to integrate the East German working class into the new so-called socialist system. It was a tool to discipline the workers and to avoid troubling strikes.

---

[43] Rosenthal/Loeding, *Stadien der Betriebsrätebewegung in der SBZ, eine Skizze*, in: Beiträge zur Geschichte der Arbeiterbewegung, 41st year, March 1999, p. 55, note 163; stages of the workers' council movement in the Soviet Occupied Zone.

[44] Christa Bertag, in Theo Pirker et al, *Der Plan als Befehl und Fiktion*, ibid., p. 244.

2. The Role of the Soviet Military Administration in Germany (SMAD)

Introduction

In the usual historiography dealing with the Soviet Military Administration, the SMAD is always considered to be a unified body or bloc. Controversies within the SMAD are never discussed or even taken into consideration. But if one takes a closer look at the Soviet military stationed in Berlin after the end of hostilities in Berlin, one easily recognizes that there was a power struggle going on right at the center of the command structure: some generals supported Stalin in Moscow and carried out his orders loyally, others sabotaged him and defied them, among them especially Marshals Zhukov and Tulpanov, who were no friends of Stalin at all, but friends of Stalin's rival Khrushchev they were.

The leading figures, among them Marshal Zhukov, General Tulpanov and Marshal Sokolovsky, Zhukov's successor after Stalin recalled Zhukov to Russia for having hidden war bounty from rich Berliners in his dacha near Moscow, often did not abide by the orders handed down to them by the Moscow center where Stalin was still in charge. Not one GDR historian has ever dealt with the fact that generals like Zhukov and Tulpanov, who are always praised by them, were reprimanded for corruption and ordered to quit their jobs. Only recently, documents have been released by the Russian government showing just that.

It has been evidenced by hard facts that some Soviet generals worked hand in glove with Wilhelm Pieck and Walter Ulbricht, the new communist leaders in the Soviet Occupied Zone and assisted and supported them in every way possible. They even housed the German 'communists,' the politburo of the SED, at their base in Karlshorst/Berlin and protected them when the workers of East Berlin threatened to oust them on June 17, 1953. Tanks were used to quell the workers' uprising on that day and 40 people lost their lives.

Origins and development of SMAD

The SMAD administration was established by Order No. 1 in the Karlshorst district of Berlin exactly one month after Nazi Germany's unconditional capitulation. There we read:

> On June 9, 1945, the formation of the SMAD as supreme instrument of power for the Soviet Occupied Zone was officially announced.[45]

---

[45] Stefan Creuzberger, *Die Sowjetische Militäradministration in Deutschland, SMAD, 1945–1949*, Melle, 1991, p. 12.

Strangely enough, this order was not signed by the representative of the Stalin administration or a member of the Central Committee of the Communist Party of the Soviet Union, but just by the Commander-in-Chief of the Soviet Occupation forces, Georgi Zhukov, and only co-signed by General V. V. Kurosov, chief-of-staff of the SMAD.

It is also rather strange that Marshal Zhukov seems to have appointed himself Chief of the Soviet Military Administration. Zhukov:

> For general information, the following announcement is made: ...I was appointed Supreme Chief of the Soviet Military Administration. ... The Supreme Chief of the Soviet Military Administration, Marshal of the Soviet Union, G. K. Zhukov; the Chief-of-Staff of the Soviet Military Administration, Colonel General V. V. Kurasov.[46]

But who exactly appointed him and when? Colonel Kurasov could not have done it as he was a lower rank than Zhukov himself; neither did Stalin or any other official of the Soviet administration or the Central Committee of the Communist Party.

Having captured the top job in Germany, Zhukov then appointed other men like Generals Serov and Sokolovsky and gave them high positions in the SMAD. Stefan Creuzberger, a German historian, notes:

> The directive [Order No. 1 — author] appointed Army General V. D. Sokolovsky First Deputy and Colonel General I. A. Serov Deputy for matters of civil administration.[47]

All these generals later took part in the conspiracy against Stalin and made sure that Nikita Khrushchev — then just an ordinary politburo member — became Stalin's successor.

So from the very start, the leadership of the SMAD stationed in East Germany consisted of high-ranking army personnel, who would go on to play a pivotal role in the liquidation of Stalin and his closest associate, Lavrenti P. Beria — the first in early March of 1953 by poisoning. (Anastás Mikoyan, Khrushchev's closest co-conspirator, openly admitted in a private conversation with the Albanian leader Enver Hoxha that they had tried to get Stalin out of the way by violent means.). The second man was eliminated on the orders of a kangaroo court in late December of 1953.

---

[46] http://www.dokumentArchiv.de/ddr/1945/smad-befehl_nr01.html. Order no. 1 of the SMAD on the organization of the administration of the Soviet Occupying Forces in Germany.
[47] Stefan Creuzberger, ibid.

However, in April 1946, only ten months after his arbitrary self-appointment, Zhukov had to go and was sent back to the Soviet Union:

> Zhukov held office from the foundation of the SMAD on June 9, 1945 until April 9, 946.[48]

> After his recall from Germany he lost his seat in the Central Committee.[49]

The reason being: He had ordered his subordinates to confiscate valuables found in the villas of rich Berliners and ordered to hide them in his Moscow dacha. The Soviet secret service with Victor Abakumov at its head conducted a search one day and found the war bounty, reason enough for Stalin to demote him:

> Stalin did have Zhukov demoted after the war when it was discovered that the Marshal had been stealing German war booty on a grand scale, instead of contributing it to the state..[50]

Secret service chief Abakumov, supported by Beria, even demanded to put Zhukov on trial.

And there was a second reason: at a session of the Supreme Military Council in Moscow at which Stalin was also present, Zhukov, even at this early stage, was accused of having organized a conspiracy. The incriminating evidence was handed over to Stalin by Beria.[51]

Zhukov's successor as Chief of the SMAD was Army General Vasily D. Sokolovsky, who also belonged to the group of conspirators working to oust Stalin and to install Khrushchev.

But let us return to Zkukov's "self-appointment" in June of 1945. Only three weeks after his 'coup,' on June 29, a military council was installed in Germany to cut his wings. From now on he was no longer alone in taking decisions and his predominance was ended. The Stalin confidant Lieutenant-General Fjodor E. Bokov now chaired the council and Zkukov's arbitrariness came to a halt.

Bokov was given powers by Moscow to check and counter-sign all directives of SMAD, making him a counterweight against the anti-Stalin generals.

---

[48] Ibid.

[49] Ibid., p. 34.

[50] Grover Furr, *Khrushchev Lied*, Kettering/Ohio, USA, 2011, p. 95, document here: pp. 363ff, from: Voennie Arkhivy Rossii, 1993, pp. 189–191, also at: http://chss.montclair.edu/english/furr/research/zhukovtheft4648_var93.pdf.

[51] M. I. Semirjaga, *Schukow — oberster Chef der Sowjetischen Militäradministration in Deutschland*, in: *Internationales Leben*, Nr. 42, 1995, p. 78, not 44; Zhukov — supreme chief of the Soviet Military Administration in Germany.

Late in 1946, however, the right-wing generals took their revenge for Zkukov's demotion and succeeded in getting rid of Bokov, arguing that he was completely 'incompetent' and supposedly possessed 'no leadership qualities.' He was then replaced by General Makrov who saw to it that the collective leadership ended and Marshal Sokolovsky, together with his deputy, was again in charge.

Other right-wing heavyweights in the SMAD leadership were General Sergei I. Tulpanov, the head of the powerful Information Department and Vladimir S. Semyonov who became political adviser of the SMAD replacing Deputy Soviet Foreign Minister Andrei E. Vyshinsky who had been ousted only weeks after the foundation of SMAD in 1945. Vyshinsky was a close associate of Stalin.

Thus, after the dissolution of the military council and the successful intrigue against Bokov, all key positions were again under the control of pro Khrushchevite generals.

The next step: Now that the power struggle was won, the leading generals tried to wrest the military administration away from the control of the Moscow politburo to enable SMAD to lead a life of its own. In spite of that, frequent attempts were made by the Moscow center to reverse the trend. The leading staff, however, was not changed and remained in control, at least for the time being.

Late in 1946, the Central Committee of the Soviet Communist Party, still supporting Stalin, ordered an inspection into the dealings of the Information Department and General Tulpanov. The reason: the poor results of the Socialist Unity Party at municipal elections in East Berlin. The general was charged with "incompetence in administrative and organizational matters and...of having failed to lead a forceful election campaign against reactionary elements of the bourgeois parties.[52]

For the time being, he stayed in office, although his resignation was demanded in Moscow. The SMAD leaders then scored another victory for themselves: Mikhail Suslov, a member of the opposition within the Communist Party and a Khrushchevite, was nominated for the post of a SMAD inspector, so that the right-wing generals no longer had much to worry about.

However, in 1949 the tables were turned again: Tulpanov was finally dismissed. He had to return to the Soviet Union and was only allowed to give lectures there.[53]

---

[52] Stefan Creuzberger, ibid., pp. 103f.
[53] Ibid.

What were the reasons for his premature return after only three years in service? A report sent to the Moscow politburo by S. Shatilov, then the deputy chairman of the Political Department of the Soviet Army (GPU), says:

> I ask you to dismiss Major-General Sergei Ivanovich Tulpanov as head of the Information Department of the Soviet Military Administration in Germany and to place him under the Supreme Command of the Political Division of the Soviet Army...Recently, a great number of employees of the Information Department have been charged with espionage and some of them had to be recalled from Germany to return to the Soviet Union for reasons of political unreliability.[54]

As it turned out, Tulpanov had accepted bribes in Germany and had also covered up the shady dealings of some of his subordinates. When suspicions became rife, a search of his residence in East Berlin was ordered:

> Major-General Tulpanov failed to act against any of those being compromised...Feldman, a former employee of the Information Department, who is now in prison, stated that Tulpanov had been involved in criminal acts together with his subordinates... He accepted bribes and a total of 35 books of fascist nature was found in Tulpanov's residence...In the interest of our mission, I deem it appropriate to remove him from his post and not to allow him to return to Germany...Comrades Vasilievsky and Chuikov are supporting the proposal to release Major-General Tulpanov from his duties in the Soviet Military Administration in Germany. Shatilov — September 17, 1949.[55]

The case of General Tulpanov showed that the right-wing predominance of the SMAD administration was on rather shaky grounds as long as Stalin and Beria were in charge in Moscow, and often found out what kind of games were being played in far-away East Germany. The Political Division of the Soviet Army (GPU) at this stage was not yet under the control of Zhukov's and Sokolovsky's anti-Stalin followers. So they had to be very careful or they might risk being removed from their posts and sent back to Russia. After the Tulpanov affair, regular checks were carried out to wipe out corruption at the top echelons of the Soviet Army, especially in Germany.

---

[54] Cold War International History Project: *Report of the Deputy in Command of the GPU of the Soviet Armed Forces to the member of the politburo, Georgi Malenkov, on the dismissal of Tulpanov*, RtsKhIDNI, fond 17, opis 118, delo 567; SAVG Sbornik, pp. 233f.
[55] Ibid.

Marshal Sokolovsky should suffer the same fate as Tulpanov in 1949. He was then replaced by Marshal Chuikov as head of SMAD.

The SMAD under Army-General Vasily Sokolovsky

Alliance North America, a dedicated group of Canadian Marxist researchers, in their analysis *Beria and the Berlin Rising* deal with leading Soviet SMAD generals, but above all with its head, General Sokolovsky, Marshal Zhukov's successor. The study concludes that Sokolovsky, on various occasions, provided useful pretexts for the three Western powers, the United States, Britain and France, to create a separate currency in Berlin as a prelude to divide Germany.

The authors of the study first state that the Americans and the British had decided to create two German states back in 1948:

> There will be two German states. The eastern zone, for the time being, will be surrendered to the Soviets; the western part, however, will constitute a separate state.[56]

The Soviet government under Stalin was strongly in favor of a united Germany and had succeeded in getting the Western allies to sign the Potsdam Agreement in July 1945, guaranteeing a joint administration in Berlin, later to be extended to the whole of Germany.

Contrary to this agreement, the Western powers sabotaged the joint administration right from the start and secretly favored dividing Germany to make the western zones part of their sphere of influence against the Soviet Union. The creation of a separate German currency in the territories under the control of the US, the British and the French was an integral part of these designs, in fact, it was the door opener for these plans.

The official Soviet policymakers resisted strongly and did everything possible to thwart the project. Then Army-General Sokolovsky as head of the SMAD gave the Western powers a valuable pretext to introduce the new currency, the *Deutschmark* (DM for short) in West Berlin:

> Marshal Sokolovsky, the Soviet representative in the Allied Control Commission, made a plea to postpone the next session of the Commission and left the meeting. This was a pretext for US General Lucius D. Clay not having to coordinate the currency plans with his Soviet partners.[57]

---

[56] Alliance! A Revolutionary Monthly: *Beria and the Berlin Rising of 1953*, August 2003, no. 6, citing Carolyn Eisenberg, *Drawing the Line. The American Decision to Divide Germany, 1944–1949*, Cambridge, 1997, p. 363.
[57] Ibid.

But this was not the only gift made by the Soviet general to the Western imperialists. On April 1, 1948, Soviet General Dratvin, without having contacted Moscow, introduced a traffic blockade between the western sectors of Berlin and the rest of the eastern territories which became known as the "Berliner Blockade." This was exactly what the imperialist powers needed to create a climate of confrontation between the Soviets and their allies. From then on there was no need for the Americans to summon the Allied Control Commission anymore.

Alliance North America gave this analysis: This bluff became the biggest propaganda coup: the Berlin airlift was organized.[58]

Now the US representative for Berlin, General Lucius D. Clay, could claim that it was the Soviets who were dividing Germany and intended to establish a separate German state on their territory:' "Thereby the buck was passed to the Soviets as far as the division of Germany was concerned." [59]

Stalin reacted soon: he met with the Western ambassadors in Moscow, Walter Bedell Smith (USA), Frank Roberts (Great Britain) and Yves Chataigneau (France) in order to defuse the explosive situation around Berlin. He proposed the immediate lifting of the blockade under the condition that "talks on a unified Germany would resume."[60]

Under these circumstances, Sokolovsky in his capacity of head of the SMAD again played into the hands of the Western powers and their plans to carve up Germany: "He acted as a saboteur by questioning the concessions made by Moscow."[61]

On July 14, 1948, the official Soviet proposals to resume talks on reunification, as specified in the note of the official Soviet government, were rejected by the West.

Therefore, the Supreme Chief of the SMAD, General Sokolovsky, must be considered an enemy of the official Soviet line on Germany which insisted on adhering as long as possible to a common allied policy on Germany's future and not to provide any pretexts to the imperialists to withdraw unilaterally from the common policy agreed upon at the Potsdam conference in July of 1945.

On March 29, 1949, Sokolovsky was finally dismissed from his post and called back to the Soviet Union. He was one of so many treacherous

---

[58] Ibid., p. 7.
[59] Carolyn Eisenberg, ibid., p. 396.
[60] Ibid., pp. 429f.
[61] Ibid., p. 437.

Soviet generals who shared this fate as long as Stalin was in the driving seat in Moscow. Marshal Chuikov, his deputy, took over.[62]

But Sokolovsky soon recovered from this setback in his military career: on February 21, 1953, he suddenly became Chief-of-Staff of the Soviet Armed Forces. In his study on the mysterious death of Stalin in March the same year, William B. Bland, a British analyst, writes:

> Finally, on February 21 [1953 — author] an important change occurred at the top of the Soviet Army: General Sergei Shtemenko was replaced by Vasily Sokolovsky as Chief-of-Staff of the Soviet Armed Forces...and, at the same time...the body guards of the special forces protecting Stalin were removed.[63]

This meant that two weeks before Stalin's sudden and unexpected death on March 5, 1953, the Soviet General Staff had been taken over by a chief conspirator. Deriabin:

> The conspirators who now controlled state security and the armed forces as well, had finally won the upper hand.[64]

This coup by the conspirators against Stalin, only a fortnight before he died, brought the Soviet Military Administration in Berlin fully under the control of corrupt Soviet military men who wanted Nikita Khrushchev to become Stalin's successor. Under Khrushchev Sokolovsky reached new heights in his career: he served under him as Deputy Defense Secretary and General-Chief-of-Staff of the Red Army until 1960.[65]

3. The Foundation of the GDR on October 7, 1949

On September 20, 1949, a separate West German state was created in the provincial town of Bonn, uniting the three zones occupied by the Americans, the British and the French, with Konrad Adenauer, the former mayor of Cologne and an old separatist, becoming the first Chancellor of the *Federal Republic of Germany*, also called FRG.

The official Soviet bulletin commenting on this step by the Western allies of the USSR says:

---

[62] Stefan Creuzberger, *Die sowjetische Besatzungspolitik und das politische System der SBZ*, Weimar, 1996, p. 30; the Soviet policy of occupation and the political system of the Soviet Occupied Zone.

[63] William B. Bland, *The Doctors' Plot and the Death of Stalin*, London 1991, p. 16. http://ml-review.ca/aml/BLAND/DOCTORS_CASE_FINAL.htm, citing P. Deriabin, *Watchdogs of Terror*, no place, 1984, p. 325.

[64] Pjotr Deriabin, ibid., p. 326.

[65] http.//www.dhm.de/lemo/html/biografien/SokolowskiWassilij_D.

> The foundation of a separate government for the western zones by the Western allies of Germany must be regarded as the culmination of the policy of dividing Germany, which has been carried out over the past few years by the government of the United States, Great Britain and France in contravention of the Potsdam Agreement which constituted a binding commitment to work towards a united Germany and to contribute towards creating a democratic and peaceful German state together with the Soviet Union.[66]

On August 14th, elections for the first West German Bundestag were held and the conservative Christian Democratic Union (CDU), the successor organization of the Catholic Weimar Center Party (Zentrum Partei), was declared the winner. With only a very slight margin, Konrad Adenauer became the first chancellor of the Federal Republic of Germany.

On October 7, only two or three weeks later, the German Democratic Republic was founded — as a "provisional government" according to a law passed by the German People's Council (Deutscher Volksrat). No general elections had taken place. The leadership of the Socialist Unity Party, with Wilhelm Pieck, Otto Grotewohl and Walter Ulbricht at its head, were wise enough to 'postpone' them for a year. When the year was over, no elections were held.

Stalin did not attend the festivities to celebrate the new East German state, but he sent a telegram to Wilhelm Pieck, the declared president of the new state, using the following words: "Long live and thrive a united, independent and peaceful Germany!"[67]

Stalin did not welcome the foundation of the GDR, but insisted on his plans to create a unified Germany. He regarded the new entity a provisional arrangement, as a "first step towards a united, democratic and peaceful Germany."[68]

For Stalin a peaceful, neutral and unified Germany was more important than a separate East German state. Quite different the attitude of the leaders of the Socialist Unity Party: they could not wait to create a separate entity, thus playing into the hands of the Western imperialists who sought to weaken Germany as soon as possible and divide it, drawing West Germany into the new NATO alliance which was founded on April 4, 1949.

Stalin wanted to keep the German question open as long as possible. On August 2, 1948 he had a conversation with the ambassadors of the

---

[66] Archiv der Gegenwart, *Deutschland 1949–1999*, digital library, Berlin, 2004, pp. 1,049f.
[67] Ibid., p. 1,121.
[68] Congratulatory message by Joseph V. Stalin, in: Archiv der Gegenwart, ibid.

three imperialist powers. He stressed that "the Soviet Union would not be provoked to install a new government in East Germany."[69]

On December 18 the same year, Stalin met with the leaders of the Socialist Unity Party in the Kremlin for talks on Germany's future. He clearly rejected a 'socialist course' in East Germany, any 'economic plans' and referred to the Potsdam Agreement treating Germany as a unified country. Wilfried Loth in his book on Ulbricht writes:

> In December 1948 Stalin again stressed the following sequence of events which had been his political guideline since 1945: first unification and peace, first the implementation of the Potsdam Agreement, then everything else. For Stalin German division was by no means a foregone conclusion, and the idea to integrate the eastern part of Germany into the camp of people's democracies was not on his mind.[70]

On January 31, 1947 the SED leaders Pieck, Ulbricht and Grotewohl, who had come to Moscow for talks, were told by him in no uncertain terms that a united Germany was necessary to counteract the influence of Anglo-American corporations in Europe:

> England and America are afraid of Germany's rise, they fear competition on the international markets. America wants to control the global markets, wants to set monopoly prices unilaterally, and when it has reached its goal, it wants to get rid of unemployment at home. Anything that speeds up Germany's rise, German foreign trade, they reject. The Soviet Union, however, wants the opposite. If reparations hinder Germany's rise, they could be shelved.[71]

On this occasion, Stalin also outlined in great detail the political strategy of the Western allies to the East Germans:

> The English, Americans and French want federalism as this means a weak Germany that should not have any influence on world markets, no foreign trade, therefore no central government, no central administration. The Soviet concept is the opposite...[72]

Therefore, in Stalin's opinion, no hasty steps should be taken to deepen the rift between East and West. The doors for a later peaceful German reunification should be kept open as long as possible.

These were clear guidelines for the Kremlin guests. But did the East Germans take them to heart? The answer is a clear-cut no. They

---

[69] Rolf Badstübner, Wilfried Loth, eds., ibid., p. 259.
[70] Wilfried Loth, *Stalins ungeliebtes Kind*, München, 1996, p. 146; Stalin's unloved child.
[71] Rolf Badstübner, Wilfried Loth, eds, ibid., pp. 113f.
[72] Ibid., p. 112.

did not take them to heart but ignored them. And, what is more: they were supported by none other than General Tulpanov, whom we have already met — the bald chief of the Soviet Information Department in East Berlin. The proof is found in a speech dated March 8, 1948, in Berlin, in which he outlined his own strategy. It was completely different from Stalin's political line. Tulpanov:

> A divided Germany into two parts, which are developing along the lines of different laws, has become a fact.[73]

And what is more: he also demanded 'faster political development in the Soviet Occupied Zone.'[74]

After the foundation of the FRG and shortly before that of the GDR the East Germans again went to Moscow to get Stalin's approval for the creation of their own state. But Stalin did not want to see them! He kept them waiting in Moscow so that the guests had to contact other members of the politburo and held talks with them, among them also Nikita Khrushchev and his close ally Anastás Mikoyan. Wilhelm Pieck only speaks of 'other leaders' in his notes on the visit lasting 12 days, from September 16–28, but we can safely say that Khrushchev and Mikoyan were present.[75]

Pieck's notes do not mention any meeting with Stalin.

On October 7, the GDR was established nonetheless, and only two days later, the designated president, Wilhelm Pieck, gave a speech in front of an enlarged politburo meeting in the party headquarters, saying:

> This is a very serious moment we find ourselves in, maybe the most serious in the life of our party. But it is a certain triumph as well — a triumph of our endeavors, a great success. We are aware that this success was made possible because we had the support of the Soviet government and especially that of Comrade Stalin.[76]

Pieck was well aware that no meeting with Stalin had taken place in the Kremlin on the issue of the GDR in late September; only meetings with other members of the politburo of the Communist Party of the

---

[73] Ibid., p. 216, document 56, notes of Tulpanov's speech on May 8, 1948, Central Party Archives of the SED, NL No. 36/735, pp. 54ff.

[74] Ibid.

[75] Ibid., pp. 314/315, *Wilhelm Piecks Aufzeichnungen zur Deutschlandpolitik 1945–1953*, document 83; notes on German policies.

[76] Vierteljahreshefte für Zeitgeschichte, 39th year 1991, bulletin 1, p. 169, *Die Entscheidung zur Gründung der DDR*, Dokument II, stenografische Niederschrift über die erweiterte Parteivorstandssitzung der SED im Zentralhaus der Einheit; the decision on the foundation of the GDR, minutes of the enlarged politburo meeting, Sunday, October 9, 12:00.

Soviet Union. But he conveniently told the delegates that he also had Stalin's support!

Pieck no doubt played on the high regard for Stalin among some members of his own politburo and for the authority of the Soviet government in general and used it for his own purposes, his own political designs and ambitions, or to put it more bluntly: he lied to them to persuade his comrades to establish a separate East German state as soon as possible, with him as president.

Wilfried Loth describes the unholy alliance between the SED leaders and the anti-Stalin SMAD officials this way:

> In practice, the program of the Ulbricht and Tulpanov people was to establish a dictatorship of cadres on the basis of the Soviet military might. As this might was only present in the Soviet Zone, the division of Germany was deepened at the same time.[77]

The Soviet government under Stalin never recognized the GDR as a state diplomatically. Only on March 25, 1954 the new leaders of the Soviet Union who had come to power by a military coup in 1953, recognized the GDR as a state. On September 29, 1955, a state treaty was concluded between the GDR and the USSR.[78]

4. Stalin's Diplomatic Initiative in March/April 1952

Even after the formation of the two German entities in September and October of 1949, the Soviet government under Joseph Stalin spared no effort to overcome the new problems in connection with the division of Germany. Stalin adhered to his goal of creating a united, independent, neutral, democratic and peaceful German state. Only with such a sovereign state could a peace treaty be concluded, and only this way the heightened tensions in the very heart of Europe between the western imperialist and aggressive states on the one hand and the peace loving Soviet Union and its allies on the other could be diminished.

The USSR that bore the brunt of the Second World War and had the highest number of casualties — 27 million people died during the war! — needed peace to rebuild the destroyed country, especially its western part. Only in a stable and peaceful environment could the USSR be safely rebuilt and could the socialist system thrive again.

---

[77] Wilfried Loth, ibid., p. 135.

[78] http://bio.bwbs.de/bwbs_biografie/Brandt/Anerkennung_der_ DDR_durch_die_ Sowjetuni.

The proof that Stalin or the Soviet government in Moscow during his reign, was prepared to give up the 'provisional' East German state and to help build a neutral and demilitarized Germany can be found in the diplomatic initiative he launched in the spring of 1952, also known as 'Stalin's notes'.

Stalin's first note, dated March 10, 1952, which included a draft for a peace treaty, says:

> 1. Germany is reconstituted as a unified state. Thereby, the division of Germany is ended and the united Germany gets the chance to develop as an independent, democratic and peaceful state. At the same time, all foreign military bases on German soil are liquidated.
>
> ...
>
> 4. In Germany all democratic parties and organizations must develop freely.[79]

In the "economic fundamentals" outlined in Stalin's note, no mention is made of socialism:

> No restrictions should be imposed on a peaceful German economy aiming at raising the people's living standard.[80]

No doubt, this would have been a capitalist, not a socialist Germany, but one that was demilitarized after two devastating wars and no longer posed a threat to the Soviet Union.

The wings of the strong American imperialism which had emerged very strong from World War II and its expansionist ambitions also in Europe had to be cut first — at least in the center of Europe. West Germany's integration into the NATO alliance had to be avoided at all costs.

> The Western powers immediately rejected the offer as well as the West German puppet government in Bonn who called it a Soviet propaganda trick.

In the Soviet answer to the negative response of the West, Stalin even offered to organize free all-German elections without delay.[81] The four powers should monitor the election process.

There can be no doubt that the result of such free all-German elections would have been the political demise of the SED leaders Pieck.

---

[79] Heinrich von Siegler, *Wiedervereinigung und Sicherheit Deutschlands, 1944–1963*, volume one, Bad Godesberg, 1967, p. 42; reunification and German security.

[80] Ibid.

[81] Norbert Podewin, *Ulbrichts Weg an die Spitze der Macht*, Hefte zur DDR-Geschichte, no. 49, Berlin, 1998, p. 21; Ulbricht's rise to power.

Grotewohl and Ulbricht and their relinquishing the helms of power in East Germany. The proof:

> At the municipal elections in East Berlin in the fall of 1946 only 29.9% of the electorate voted for the Socialist Unity Party. The Social Democrats scored 43.8% and the conservative Christian Democrats 18.4%.[82]

This was the last time the Social Democrats were allowed to take part in East Berlin elections. Stalin had insisted on their participation in a conversation with the East German leaders in Moscow. So at an all-German election the SED would not have received more than 15% of the votes, if at all.

Stalin's proposal to organize free elections all over Germany would have led to the removal from office of the East German party leaders and the Socialist Unity Party would have become an opposition party in the German Bundestag, the German parliament.

This scenario had to be avoided at all costs, as far as Ulbricht & Co. were concerned. For the down-to-earth politician Stalin, however, peace and stability in Central Europe weighed more than the ambitions of certain party leaders once appointed by the former leader of the Communist International, Georgi Dimitrov.

5. "Accelerated Construction of Socialism" — the Second Party Conference of the Socialist Unity Party

To boycott Stalin's policy on Germany and the Potsdam Agreements, treating Germany as a unified entity, the GDR leaders at a party conference of the SED arbitrarily proclaimed the "accelerated building of socialism" in the GDR. This project, not even broadly discussed at a party congress, should then lead to the massive exodus of East Germans to the West — among them thousands of workers, peasants and even members of the Socialist Unity Party and their youth organization, the Free German Youth (FDJ).

The conference took place in the Werner Seelenbinder Halle in East Berlin, lasting from July 9–12.

The main report was given by Walter Ulbricht, lasting a full eight hours. Originally, the subject of his speech was to be 'The new tasks of how to achieve a peace treaty, the unity of Germany and national reconstruction.' This subject was agreed upon by the politburo on March

---

[82] Stefan Creuzberger, *Die sowjetische Besatzungsmacht und das politische System der SBZ*, ibid., p. 94.

3.[83] But surprisingly enough, Ulbricht gave a completely different speech. His biographer, Norbert Podewin writes:

> On the eve of the conference first the politburo held a meeting; after that the Central Committee met. This session only lasted 45 minutes. Ulbricht read out a prepared draft resolution to the members. He said: 'I'm sorry, but we didn't have time enough to make copies of the draft, so I'm just reading it out to you.'[84]

What he then read out to the astonished members of the Central Committee was the real subject of the marathon speech which he would later present to the party conference, the draft resolution included. The main point of the draft resolution was this:

> The Party Conference states that in the German Democratic Republic and in Berlin the social and economic development has greatly progressed so that it is in the interest of the working class and all working people to start building socialism.[85]

This resolution, well prepared in advance, was Ulbricht's and Pieck's own 'intellectual property.' So it can be safely said that some other people, closely connected to them, may have assisted them in drafting it. Ulbricht could neither speak nor write proper German; he had enormous problems with German grammar and spelling.

The duo even duped their own politburo, as it had passed a completely different resolution: one that was in line with Stalin's policy on Germany, on how to achieve a peace treaty, German unity, etc. In other words: they showed complete disregard for their own comrades sitting on the politburo.

During his long speech Ulbricht also used an old trick developed by the Soviet Trotskyites during the time when the Soviet opposition was still strong. The method was first developed by Karl Radek in early 1934: he praised Stalin to the skies, although, in reality, he was a staunch enemy of his:

> Long live our wise teacher, he who carries the banner of peace and progress of the world...[86]

Like the Trotskyites in the USSR in the thirties, he whipped up the personality cult around Stalin to cover up his own real intentions. All in all, he mentioned Stalin's name 35 times in his address to deceive the

---

[83] Rolf Badstübner, Wilfried Loth, eds., ibid., p. 399, note 8.
[84] Norbert Podewin, Hefte zur DDR-Geschichte, no. 49, Berlin, 1998, p. 24; GDR history booklet.
[85] Ibid.
[86] *Protokoll der Zweiten Parteikonferenz der SED*, ibid., p. 158.

delegates, to make them believe that Stalin and he himself stood shoulder to shoulder on the issue of building socialism in the GDR.

The delegates then rose and enthusiastically gave him a standing ovation for minutes on end. Some of them had tears in their eyes. The old dream of socialism in Germany was about to come true.

Eleven years later, when Stalin was dead and the Khrushchevites were in power in Moscow, the same Ulbricht saw no more need to praise "the wise Stalin, our teacher..." On the contrary: now he had become a "terrorist." Ulbricht said, in his speech to the delegates of the Sixth Party Congress in Berlin in January of 1963:

> And we the members and leaders of the Communist Party of Germany also had to suffer under Stalin's methods of terror. And if some people want to know more about it: our politburo made a firm stand against Stalin's methods and were supported by many Soviet comrades, but above all by Comrade Dimitrov.[87]

But in 1952, at a time when the Second Party Conference was meeting, Stalin was still alive, was still at the helm of the USSR and enjoyed a tremendous popularity and authority worldwide and also among many of Ulbricht's own comrades. The shrewd tactician could not dare to criticize Stalin at the risk of his own reputation.

One week before the conference, Ulbricht even wrote a personal letter to Stalin to get his last-minute go-ahead for his project of 'building socialism in the GDR.' He asked for his approval to "lead the working class and the toilers on to the path of socialism."[88]

Moscow's response reached the party officials only one day before the conference started. The word 'socialism' was not mentioned even once. Instead, the Central Committee of the CPSU expressed its...

> strong conviction that the working class and all working people of Germany will achieve their goal of creating a united, independent, democratic and peaceful Germany.[89]

No Soviet delegation was sent to Berlin.

What is the difference between Stalin's stance and the decisions taken by the 2nd Party Conference? Weren't they both socialists or even communists? Was there a difference at all?

---

[87] Carola Stern, *Ulbricht — eine politische Biografie*, Cologne, 1964, p. 312, note 17; Ulbricht — a political biography.

[88] Norbert Podewin, *Hefte zur DDR-Geschichte*, ibid., p.22.

[89] Begrüßungsschreiben des ZK der KPdSU, B an die 2. Parteikonferenz der SED, in: *Einheit*, 7th year, August 1952, no. 8, p. 706; congratulatory message of the Central Committee of the CPSU to the 2nd Party Conference of the Socialist Unity Party of Germany.

The answer is a clear-cut yes. There was a huge difference; they were worlds apart.

Whereas Stalin and the Central Committee of his party stressed the need for restoring Germany's unity to avoid integrating the Federal Republic into NATO and turning it into an anti-communist and armed-to-the-teeth bulwark against the USSR, the SED leaders wanted to deepen the rift between the two German states even further to secure their hold over 17 million Germans. To achieve this goal, the party conference also adopted a resolution on dissolving the existing administrative structures in the GDR and to create new ones. The former German provinces, also called Länder, were dissolved and 14 new districts (Bezirke) created instead, causing a huge amount of unnecessary bureaucracy.

The SMAD leaders, who were hostile to Stalin as we have seen on numerous occasions, had been informed of the step beforehand and given their go-ahead. When the SED leaders met with Stalin in the Kremlin in April, this subject was not even discussed, but Pieck raised it at a meeting with General Chuikov, the new head of the SMAD, on May 7: "Reorganization of GDR: no objections; some districts too large."[90]

This again shows that the SMAD pursued their own foreign policy independent of the Moscow center and assisted the GDR leaders in their plans to deepen Germany's division which was also in the interest of the Western allies, the United States, Britain and France.

Whereas Stalin in his note of March 1952 speaks of the "development of a peaceful German economy," the SED party conference dominated by Walter Ulbricht and his followers in the politburo demanded a resolute "construction of socialism as a fundamental task."

Whereas Stalin in his note to the Western alliance speaks of raising the living standard of the German people, the Party Conference demands "cutting social spending and a reduction in consumption to finance the new armed forces" — an estimated 1.5 billion marks project.[91]

Whereas Stalin was basically in favor of having collective farms, he stressed that nobody should be forced to join them; the SED leaders, however, were in favor of forcing small and medium-sized farmers to stop farming their private plots and making them join the collective farms more or less by force.[92]

This is Stalin on collectivization:

---

[90] Rolf Badstübner, Wilfried Loth, eds, ibid., p. 403.
[91] Norbert Podewin, *Ulbrichts Weg an die Spitze der Macht*, ibid., p. 28.
[92] Ibid., p. 32.

As long as the peasants are not convinced of the superiority of collective property you have no way to increase the number of cooperatives. If the existing cooperatives prove beneficial to the peasants, then the other peasants will also follow you.[93]

Did the eager GDR leaders listen to Stalin's advice? How did the East German peasants react to enforced collectivization? Did they like that?

Only a few months after the decision taken by the 2nd Party Conference, a growing number of people turned their backs on the GDR and tried to settle in West Germany. Here are the numbers:

1952:   165,571
1953:   120,531 (only Jan–Mar)[94]

The population drain, however, was not reason enough for the SED leaders to revise their unrealistic project of accelerated construction of socialism and to think twice. On the contrary: a huge flow of directives to carry out the decisions and resolutions of the conference ensued, often remaining unconfirmed by the Central Committee.[95]

What happened next?

Not surprisingly, the first serious supply shortages emerged. The reason being: many small and medium-sized farms were abandoned. Their owners preferred to "go West" instead of remaining in the East. They had no intention of joining the collective farms, and they knew that they could be forced to do so one day.

This again resulted in cuts in social spending on the part of the administration, and the working class was hardest hit:

Special benefits for workers who were in jobs detrimental to health and with a big work load were cut; single working mothers lost their monthly day off; special fares as well as travel allowances were also cut.[96]

Now the GDR judiciary had to deal with all sorts of petty crime, with people, who in their predicament, had committed a minor theft or other little offenses and were given harsh sentences because of that.

Then a great event had to be prepared. Walter Ulbricht, the First Secretary of the SED, was to mark his 60th birthday on June 30, 1953 and expensive preparations were made by the party cadres to celebrate it. At

---

[93] Enver Hoxha, *With Stalin. Memoirs*, Tirana, December 1979, p. 210.

[94] http://wilsoncenter.org/index.cfm?topic_id=1409&fuseaction=va2. document&identify..., memorandum of General Vasily Chuikov et al to Georgi Malenkov (Politburo of the CPSU), March 18, 1953, p. 1.

[95] Norbert Podewin, *Ulbrichts Weg an die Spitze der Macht*, ibid., p. 27.

[96] Ibid., p. 33.

the same time, work quotas were raised sharply by a full 10% on average — the straw that would break the camel's back. The events of June 17th were looming large.

6. The 17th of June, 1953

The triggers of the workers' rebellion

As has already been said: an ever growing number of East Germans turned their backs on the new state and its economy, moving west: [97]

	1951	1952	1953 (Jan–May)
Blue-Collar	27,173	35,300	17,784
White-Collar	12,098	22,022	13,156
Small Farmers	1,250	4,022	7,555
Intelligentsia (physicians, teachers, writers)	2,062	3,044	2,498
Others (petty bourgeoisie, bourgeoisie)	57,214	70,613	78,302

Lavrenti Beria, the new Soviet Minister of the Interior after Stalin's death in early March, 1953, presented similar figures on May 6, pointing out that during the first three months of 1953 alone the wave of emigration to the West had reached a new peak. Among the emigrants were almost 2,000 members of the Socialist Unity Party.[98]

These official Soviet figures clearly show that the dissatisfaction with the social, economic and political situation in the GDR was rampant — even among workers, the section of the population which the SED leaders pretended to represent most.

On May 28, ten days after the memo written by the Soviet Control Commission was sent to the Moscow leadership, the politburo of the Socialist Unity Party and the GDR Council of Ministers decided to raise the work norms by at least 10%. The Soviet Control Commission, by the way, was the new name of the SMAD. The official justification was "to

---

[97] Memo of SMAD leader General Chuikov, ibid.
[98] Memorandum of L. P. Beria presented to the Presidium of the CPSU, May 6, 1953, SVRA file 3581, vol. 7, in:

Yale University Press, New Haven, 1997, p. 157.

take all necessary steps to put an end to the misuse in the field of work norms...and to raise those of importance by at least 10% by June 1, 1953.[99]

The official East German trade union (FDGB) welcomed the measure. In the journal *Tribüne* the trade union leadership gave their unequivocal approval of the step, which was especially hitting the working class and cutting their living standard.

> On the morning of June 16, the new issue of the trade union magazine is distributed among construction workers in the Stalin Alley in East Berlin. Shortly afterwards, some 300 angry construction workers march in the direction of the seat of the East German government to talk to Mr. Grotewohl and Mr. Ulbricht, the then most influential leaders of the GDR. They carry only one big banner with them, bearing the following slogan, "Construction workers demanding lower work norms!"[100]

That was the only banner they were carrying, but they were also shouting other slogans. When passing the biggest department store in East Berlin, the HO-Warenhaus, they shouted:

"HO macht uns k-o!" (HO is knocking us out!)[101]

This way the protesters were pointing to the recent price increases for meat and other consumer goods, such as bread, cakes and pastries, by which the working class and most disenfranchised sections of the population were particularly hit. Even Kurt Gossweiler, an advocate of the GDR system and a staunch supporter of Ulbricht, wrote in his diaries that the measures led to a "sharp decrease in the living standard, especially of the working class and the poorest sections of our population."[102]

But according to Professor Gossweiler this was not Ulbricht's fault at all. The former 'criminal' GDR trade minister Mr. Hamann and 'his gang' were to blame.[103]

The government had lifted the price freeze on consumer goods on April 20, which caused a sudden and sharp increase in food prices.

The working class was indeed the victim of the measures taken: to receive the same wage as before, the workers now had to raise their work performance, and, at the same time, the purchasing power of their wages dropped due to the new prices.

---

[99] Arnulf Baring, *Aufstand in Ostdeutschland vom 17. Juni 1953*, Berlin, 1972, pp. 21F; uprising in East Germany on June 17, 1953.

[100] Wolfgang Kraushaar, *Die Protest-Chronik, 1949–1959*, vol. II, 1953–1956, Hamburg, 1996; the protest chronicle.

[101] Ibid., p. 796.

[102] Kurt Gossweiler, *Die Taubenfußchronik oder Die Chruschtschowiade, 1953 bis 1964*, Munich, 2002, p. 30; pigeon-foot chronicles and Khrushchevism.

[103] Ibid.

What happened next?

Right in front of the government seat (the 'House of Ministries') the following verbal exchange took place between Fritz Selbmann, the Minister for the Iron and Steel Industry, and the small group of protesters.

Selbmann: 'Dear Colleagues...'

Protesters: 'We aren't your colleagues.'

S.: 'I'm a toiler like you!'

P.: 'You're nothing but a rogue and a traitor of the workers!'

S.: 'Workers — look at my hands!' (The minister stretches out his arms, making a dramatic gesture)

P.: 'Your hands are mighty plump!' ...

Selbmann was booed and hissed. The protesters only wanted to talk to Ulbricht. There was a small table in front of the building and a woman climbed up on it and start asking for Ulbricht and Grotewohl, but they are not there. Then, a construction worker in his white overall jumped up on the table, trying to make a speech:

'Dear Colleagues,

The Nazis kept me in a concentration camp for five years. I'm not afraid of risking ten more years in prison here with them bastards if it is for the cause of freedom!' (applause)

He then summed up the main demands of the protesters: lower work norms, lower prices, no punishment for the speakers at the demonstration. Another worker then climbs onto the table, positioning himself close to the minister and pushing him aside:

'Nobody is interested in your talk. This is a people's uprising. The government must learn from its mistakes and bear the consequences. We demand free and fair elections!'[104]

After this exchange, Selbmann leaves the "debate table" and enters the government building, while outside an ever -growing number of people is gathering.[105]

Kraushaar chronicled the events like this:

After a moment of indecision, another worker suggests to wait for Ulbricht and Grotewohl for 30 more minutes and, should they fail to turn up by then, to march through the working-class districts and call for a general strike. The others seem to agree and again voices of 'down with the government!' are heard and slogans

---

[104] Wolfgang Kraushaar, ibid., pp 787f.
[105] Ibid., also see photo on page 799.

of 'Spitzbart, Bauch und Brille sind nicht des Volkes Wille!' are heard. After half an hour of waiting, the crowd leaves, forming a protest march.[106]

By the way: Spitzbart (goatee), Bauch (belly) and Brille (glasses) refers to the trio of leading GDR officials. Ulbricht wore a goatee, Pieck had a substantial belly and Grotewohl was never seen without his glasses.

This no doubt was a spontaneous uprising of a section of disgruntled and deeply frustrated East German workers (construction workers, hard working men). The fact that they had only one large banner with them shows that there was no organization or apparatus behind them. They had no official representation anymore after the smashing of the works council movement; and the official trade union, which was left, stood firmly behind the decision to raise work norms and consumer prices.

Right from the start of the workers' rebellion, the SED leaders tried to blame 'provocateurs' and 'imperialist agencies' for the events:

> The politburo calls on the workers to rally around the Party and the Government and to unmask the hostile provocateurs who are trying to sow disunity and confusion among the working class.[107]

Soon the "hostile provocation" becomes a "fascist provocation" instigated by "special agencies" in West Berlin and, still later, a carefully planned plot by "Western imperialist circles" and their tool, West Germany, is blamed to destroy the GDR according to a premeditated plan also called "Plan X."

The truth, however, is that the real provocateurs were those who had extended the working day and who had removed the freeze on consumer prices, thus sparking the protests in their early stages.

As the workers of the GDR no longer had a lobby to press their demands, a delegation of the protesters entered the building of Radio RIAS Berlin in the western sector of the city, asking to transmit their agenda. The main demands were as follows:

1. Wages must be paid according to the previous work norms;

2. Immediate reduce the cost of living;

3. Set up free and confidential elections;

4. No punishment for the protesters and their speakers.[108]

Soon afterward, these demands were repeated by the radio station on the hour, making sure that everybody in the whole republic heard them.

---

[106] Ibid., pp. 797f.

[107] Ibid., p. 798.

[108] Ibid., p. 799.

The deeper roots

In mid-1953, the presidium (formerly politburo) of the Communist Party of the Soviet Union held a meeting on the political situation in the GDR. East Germans were fleeing the country in ever growing numbers. After the meeting, the leading politicians of the GDR, Ulbricht, Grotewohl and Pieck, were summoned to Moscow for urgent discussions. Fred Oelßner accompanied them as their interpreter. But Pieck did not attend the meeting, due to "health issues," as he said.

In the Kremlin the three Germans were given a document titled 'Measures to Stabilize the Political Situation in the German Democratic Republic.' Later the SED leadership called it 'The New Course' or sometimes 'The Beria Plan.'

This document stated the main reasons behind the serious problems of the country:

1. The project "accelerated construction of socialism" as decided upon by the 2nd Party Conference;

2. The fact that the farming cooperatives [LPGs] were not established on a voluntary basis, prompting many farmers to slaughter their live-stock, to leave their fields or to cross into West Germany. About 500.000 hectares of land was left uncultivated, causing severe food shortages;

3. The accelerated construction of heavy industries;

4. Petty interference in the affairs of small traders and craftsmen;

5. Repressive measures against the Protestant Church, etc. [109]

On the basis of this analysis, the Soviet government told the GDR delegation in no uncertain terms to take the following steps as soon as possible:

1. Desist from 'ultra-left' concepts, especially the 'accelerated building of socialism';

2. Dissolve those agricultural cooperatives which were created on a compulsory basis;

3. Create 'machine tractor stations' [MTS] like the ones in the USSR to supply small farmers with the necessary agricultural machinery they otherwise would be unable to afford, thereby strengthening the alliance between workers and peasants;

4. Allow small private capital in trade and industry to stimulate the economy and to keep people from leaving;

5. Slow down the development of the heavy industries;

---

[109] Karl Schirdewan, *Aufstand gegen Ulbricht*, Berlin, 1995, p. 178; rebellion against Ulbricht.

6. Refrain from the policy of 'naked administrating' [giving orders and bossing around rather than consulting and explaining] and try to achieve better results by working together with the masses. Avoid creating a disconnect from the people.

7. Don't interfere in with religious clerics;

8. Work harder to achieve a united Germany and the conclusion of a peace treaty.[110]

Georgi Malenkov and Lavrenti Beria were in charge of the Soviet government at this time, shortly after Stalin's death. Khrushchev had not yet become First Secretary of the CPSU; that only happened in September.

After the joint session with the Soviet leaders, the SED leaders were asked to comment. Their first statement was rejected out of hand, as it was considered completely inappropriate The second, which was still not considered appropriate, was grudgingly accepted.

Ulbricht and Grotewohl said that they were only prepared to accept "in principle" the Soviet proposals for a so-called New Course in their country. In particular, they did not want to take back the 10% increase in work norms by which the working class was most affected. Alliance North America writes on this:

Although the Ulbricht leadership of the SED resisted, it had to make some retreat. However, it refused to make any retreat on the 10% work increase for the working class. In fact, they were confirmed on June 13.[111]

But it is doubtful whether the CPSU Politburo knew at all about the rise in work expectations set by the SED leaders on May 28 — just one week before the crucial meeting in the Kremlin. No mention of it is made in the official document. The document can be found here, in the appendices.

The only social group not benefiting from the "New Course" was the GDR working class. Thus, not surprisingly, the working class became the strongest and most outspoken group in the June rebellion. The bourgeoisie, the middle class and the intelligentsia largely stayed away, watching the unfolding events from the sidelines:

It is quite odd that the so-called bourgeoisie is keeping quiet and that it is the workers who are staging the protests, who turn their

---

[110] Ibid., pp. 178ff.

[111] Alliance North America, *Beria and the Berlin Rising*, in: Alliance! A Revolutionary Monthly, no. 6, August 2003, p. 7, also here: http://ml-review.ca/aml/PAPER/AUGUST2003/berlinBeria1953.html.

backs on the Party and demand that the SED bosses who do not want to accept the workers' demands must go.[112]

What, then, were the underlying causes of the uprising?

The main reason prompting the rebellion of the East German workers was the seemingly "ultra-left" policy of "accelerated construction of socialism" which was arbitrarily imposed on the country, indeed on the SED itself, by Walter Ulbricht and Wilhelm Pieck. The conditions for such a "socialist strategy" did not exist in the country at all. No country-wide discussion had taken place and no referendum on the introduction of socialism had been organized either. Another reason: the party leaders' insistence on increasing work time, on cutting social spending and rising consumer prices — even after the Moscow meeting which had tried to calm things down and to stabilize the situation in the country.

Thus, the events of June 17th were a foregone conclusion.

Some people argue that Ulbricht's increase in work norms was intended to provoke the workers and to discipline them afterwards, maybe also with the help of the Soviet army. A former member of the politburo of the SED, who was later forced to give up his seat, wrote in his memoirs:

> The administrative increase in work norms was a time bomb...It was on June 15, and we were having a meeting of the Secretariat, the last one of the kind. Then suddenly an instructor came who had been in Berlin-Friedrichshain joined us. He informed us that people were quite ready to go on strike and that many intended to demonstrate the next day to get the work norms back down. Then Ulbricht, who was very agitated as always in those days, smashed his fist on the table and shouted at the top of his voice: 'No way! We shall not beat a retreat!'[113]

According to Schirdewan it seems that Ulbricht, whose position in the politburo was very shaky at the time, insisted on the measures taken as he wanted to provoke a power struggle, being well aware that the leaders of the Soviet military and the Soviet Control Commission were on his side. And the Soviet generals also seem to have already taken military steps to intervene in the conflict. Probably the rock-solid alliance between the SED leaders and the anti-Stalin generals in Berlin-Karlshorst, as well as his awareness that they were prepared to use even tanks against the demonstrators, made Ulbricht so confident and unyielding.

---

[112] Udo Wengst, *Der Aufstand des 17. Juni 1953 in der DDR*, in: Vierteljahreshefte für Zeitgeschichte, 41st year, 1993, no. 2, p. 383; the uprising of June 17, 1953 in the GDR.
[113] Karl Schirdewan, ibid., p. 51.

The uprising and the violent suppression

At 10 a.m. on Wednesday, June 17, the protests were in full swing. At this time, the Central Committee members of the Socialist Unity Party were meeting on Wilhelm Pieck Street (a street named after the GDR president) to discuss the worsening situation.

Hermann Axen, the chief of the Propaganda Department of the SED and one of Ulbricht's staunchest supporters, made the following public statement:

> The agencies of the enemy in West Berlin are attempting to disrupt the forthcoming understanding between the two German states by sending fascist provocateurs. Behind all this are the Americans who intend to sabotage the imminent rapprochement between the Soviet Union and the other Allied Powers. The imperialist agencies in West Berlin must be held responsible for this and bear the consequences.[114]

In other words: the public was made to believe that the uprising was not a genuine protest of the working class against the deteriorating living conditions but was the work of imperialist agencies based in West Berlin, using fascist provocateurs. Thus it seemed justified to suppress the rebellion by force in an 'anti-fascist manner'.

Time Line, June 17 in East Berlin

10:00
Barricades that were erected by the police to protect the government buildings are set on fire.

11:00
Demonstrators march through the Brandenburg Gate (dividing East and West Berlin), carrying the German national flag: black, red and gold.

11:45
On Marx-Engel's Square 50,000 people have gathered — the biggest gathering in the history of the GDR. Soviet tanks which have been on standby since early morning are now trying to disperse the crowd. One demonstrator is squashed by a tank. He is the first victim of the Berlin rising. Immediately afterwards, a wooden cross is put up to mark the spot where he was killed.[115]

---

[114] Wolfgang Kraushaar, ibid., citing Hermann Axen.
[115] Ibid., p. 808.

12:00

The demonstrators succeed in pushing back the police cordon in front of the government building. Soviet tanks step in, using machine gun fire. The main government building is now protected by 15 tanks and a great number of armored cars.[116]

12:30

The Soviet city commander, Major-General Pavel Dibrova, is in charge of the tank deployment. The East German police, also called People's Police (Volkspolizei), is unable to control the protesters. Demonstrators are walking arm in arm towards the tanks. A loudspeaker van appeals to the Soviet military in Russian language 'not to shoot at German proletarians!'

13:00

Dibrova declares a state of emergency and imposes a 9 p.m.–5 a.m curfew.

All gatherings of more than three are forbidden. The state of emergency lasts almost a month; it is only lifted on July 12.

13:30

Some protesters are marching towards the police headquarters. In chorus they appeal to the them to join them. When they refuse, the building is stormed, the guards disarmed and their weapons destroyed. A police car is overturned and put on fire, whereupon Soviet infantry is called in. With its help the demonstrators are pushed back in the direction of the sector boundary to West Berlin.

15:00

A convoy of Soviet trucks with women and children is leaving Berlin. They are the women and children of high-ranking members of the GDR government and the politburo.

The area of Karlshorst, where members of the SED politburo live side by side with Soviet generals, is surrounded by tanks and anti-aircraft batteries.

16:00

All larger demonstrations have now been dissolved.

18:00

Radio Berlin transmits Otto Grotewohl's announcement that the 10% increase in work norms has been canceled.

---

[116] Ibid., p. 807.

The following day, protests all over the GDR continue. Everywhere the Soviet military has to intervene to restore law and order and to protect the GDR government from the people's wrath. Despite the collapse of the uprising, the struggle continues in major factories and many workplaces for several weeks on end.

Mike Dennis wrote:

> For example, strikes and protests were organized against the imprisonment of colleagues involved in the uprising. Demands were made for improvement of working conditions, work organization and housing. And strong protests were leveled at the lack of democracy at the workplace and the arbitrary methods of trade union officials.[117]

Forty people died during the rebellion.[118]

The German sociologist Helmut Mueller-Enbergs sums up the protests this way:

> The unrest spread in large parts of the GDR. In more than 383 factories strikes occurred, approximately 333,000 employees taking part — among them 275,000 steelworkers. Even though this figure may seem low, industrial centers and former strongholds of the Communist Party of Germany [KPD] and the Social Democratic Party [SPD], such as Leipzig, Bitterfeld, Magdeburg and Berlin, were affected. 58,000 workers downed their tools in the center of Bitterfeld alone; 45,000 in the center of chemical industries around the cities of Merseburg, Leuna and Buna.
>
> The strikers' movement was largely spontaneous and not directed from the outside or staged, though there were some attempts of infiltration. Soviet military commanders imposed a state of emergency in 167 out of a total of 217 districts of the GDR. According to a report by the Ministry of State Security there were 157 strikes, 82 demonstrations, 49 'fascist provocations' and 22 attempts to free prison inmates.[119]

Karl Schirdewan, a former member of the SED politburo and no friend of Ulbricht, adds:

> It must also be said that some people were even carrying posters of Ernst Thaelmann [the former leader of the German Communist

---

[117] Mike Dennis, *German Democratic Republic. Politics, Economics and Society*, London and New York, 1988, p. 24.

[118] http://www.si.edu/index.cfm?topic_id=1409&fuseaction=library.document&id=441, Christian Ostermann,
Working Paper no. 11, *The United States, the East German Rising of 1953 and the Limits of Roll Back*, citing Marshal Sokolovsky's report on the events.

[119] Helmut Müller-Enbergs, *Der Fall Rudolf Herrnstadt*, Berlin, 1991, p. 203; the case of Rudolf Herrnstadt.

Party from 1925 to 1933 — author]. They were mostly angry people and, of course, there were also some who were hostile.[120]

One day after the uprising, on June 18th, Ulbricht issued guidelines for his party members about how to confront the general public, saying that all this had been the sinister work of "fascist provocateurs":

> On the morning of June 18, Ulbricht also decided how to explain all this to the population...He tried to point out that 'it was a fascist provocation.'[121]

Ulbricht's political survival thanks to Khrushchev's putsch against Beria

Did Ulbricht, the chief architect and perpetrator of a failed policy in East Germany, have to resign?

One is tempted to believe that even for the Soviet generals this man who had proved to be so enormously incompetent, heavy-handed and unpopular, who was almost completely disconnected from the working class, who had made all these disastrous mistakes — leading even to hunger and despair in some parts of the population — was no longer acceptable as leader of the GDR. And as regards the Moscow leadership, wasn't it high time to get rid of this bureaucrat [the words of the former leader of the German Communist Party Ernst Thaelmann — author] who believed to be able to govern solely by decree and to replace him with someone of the politburo who had a better understanding of the situation in East Germany and of the everyday problems the GDR population? And there were indeed people in the Party like Rudolf Herrnstadt and Wilhelm Zaisser who stood in opposition to Ulbricht and his followers and were ready to take over. But astonishingly, Ulbricht survived the crisis unscathed and emerged in an even stronger position than before the crisis. Ulbricht kept his post as First Secretary of the SED until 1971. He remained the most powerful political figure in the GDR for 18 more years!

How can this phenomenon be explained?

The opposition against Ulbricht blared forth in a headline on June 25, one week after the rebellion of the East German working class, when Rudolf Herrnstadt — member of the SED politburo and editor-in-chief of the party paper *Neues Deutschland* (New Germany) — demanded Ulbricht's resignation:

---

[120] Karl Schirdewan, ibid., p. 53.
[121] Andrea Görldt, *Rudolf Herrnstadt und Wilhelm Zaisser*, Frankfurt/Main, 2002, p. 280.

The first meeting of the commission [on how to implement the "New Course" as demanded by the Soviet leadership — author] must have taken place on June 25. Grotewohl, Ulbricht, Zaisser and I took part...The meeting didn't last very long...In connection with my proposal to dissolve the Party Secretariat, I said to Walter Ulbricht: 'Wouldn't it be better if you gave up your leading position in the party apparatus? ... I knew that the majority of the politburo wanted Ulbricht to resign as General Secretary. [122]

A fortnight later, on July 7, the vote against Ulbricht was taken.

Out of 13 comrades who were present...only two were still in support of Ulbricht remaining General Secretary: Matern and Honecker.[123]

The condemnation of Ulbricht and his handling of the East German crisis was almost unanimous. Politburo member Elli Schmidt is reported to have said, "Without Walter Ulbricht, [there would have been] no 17th of June![124]

At the same meeting, Wilhelm Zaisser, the Interior Minister of the GDR, proposed Herrnstadt as the new General Secretary. Zaisser's assessment of Ulbricht's legacy was blunt:

My proposal is Herrnstadt because he is closer to the masses than we are. My proposal is no ideal solution. In my opinion: Walter Ulbricht is responsible for the course adopted at the 2nd Party Conference more than we are. His line is naked administrating, wrong education of cadres, etc. This has corrupted the Party, and with this attitude the 'New Course' cannot be made. Therefore, he must be kept distant from the party apparatus. The apparatus in Ulbricht's hands is a catastrophe for the 'New Course'.[125]

Suddenly, Ulbricht and Grotewohl announce that they have to leave the meeting, saying that they have to catch a flight to Moscow very early in the morning. So the remaining members are left to themselves. No formal resolution to oust Ulbricht can be passed. Later, with the two gone, an informal vote is taken against Ulbricht, but it is not binding for the Party. This rescues the shrewd General Secretary from being thrown out.

---

[122] Nadja Stulz-Herrnstadt, citing her father in: *Rudolf Herrnstadt, Das Herrnstadt-Dokument*, Reinbek/Hamburg, 1990, pp. 105f; the Herrnstadt document.

[123] Ibid., pp. 126f.

[124] Ibid., p. 128.

[125] Andrea Görldt, ibid., p. 333, citing Martin Krämer, *Der Volksaufstand vom 17. Juni 1953 und sein politisches Echo in der Bundesrepublik Deutschland*, Bochum, 1996, p. 137; the people's uprising on June 17, 1953 and the political reverberations in the Federal Republic of Germany.

Khrushchev's coup

On June 26, 1953, nine days after the events in East Berlin, Soviet Minister of the Interior Lavrenti Beria, who had drafted the 'New Course' for the GDR, was arrested by some members of the Soviet army under the command of Georgi Zhukov, the former head of SMAD, and by Kirill Moskalenko, a Soviet air force general — right in the middle of a joint meeting of the CPSU presidium and the Central Committee. Never before in the history of Soviet socialism had such a thing happened! Beria was accused of 'espionage' for a Western power, of "Titoism," sexual misconduct, rape of young girls, of betraying GDR socialism and "other crimes." Together with six of his Georgian confidants, among them the former ambassador to Nazi Germany, Vladimir Dekanosov, he was tried in late December the same year by a military court, found guilty and executed immediately after the verdict together with his comrades.

But to this day, we can't be absolutely sure about this version of the events, as major documents have not been declassified yet.

According to a different version, Beria was shot by a special task force at his home as much as ten days before the meeting took place. Beria's son Sergo later wrote in his memoirs:

> There are at least six different versions of the arrest and death of my father: Khrushchev himself provided several variants. In one of them the principal role is played by Zhukov. The effect is all the better. Hero of the Soviet Union Zhukov arresting Beria! Many years later, Zhukov, to my great surprise, asked to see me. 'I've no reason to lie to you,' he said. 'I took no part, direct or indirect, in the arrest of your father'... My father was shot at our home. They killed him then and there, and it took ten days to assemble the Plenum, so that everyone might have time to realize that he was dead.[126]

With Beria out of the way, Khrushchev and his followers gained the upper hand in the top decision-making body of the USSR, and in September 1953 they elected him First Secretary of the Communist Party.

Needless to say, this coup was completely illegal and a blatant breach of the Soviet constitution adopted in 1936.

Ulbricht's purge

Only a few hours after they left the night-time meeting of the SED politburo on July 7, Ulbricht and Grotewohl were indeed en route to Moscow.

---

[126] Sergo Beria, *Beria — my Father. Inside Stalin's Kremlin*, London, 1999, pp. 269 and 271.

Two days later, on July 9, they informed their politburo colleagues of Beria's arrest and his alleged 'crimes.' They claimed that Khrushchev, Molotov and others had given them verbal reports of what had actually happened in the Kremlin and also another document by the CPSU presidium. Then Otto Grotewohl read out the document to the astonished listeners. It outlined "Stalin's and Beria's abuses of power," the "neglect of collective leadership" under Stalin, his "arbitrariness," and so forth.

At the following meeting of the politburo Ulbricht and his supporters, among them Matern and Honecker, went on the offensive and created 'the Herrnstadt-Zaisser' case. Andrea Görldt has noted that: "It cannot be excluded that Ulbricht had the backing for creating the 'Herrnstadt-Zaisser case by one member of the triumvirate."[127]

The term "triumvirate" refers to the new leadership of the CPSU in Moscow after the liquidation of the Soviet Interior Minister Beria. We have reason to believe that Nikita Khrushchev, an old friend of Ulbricht from his days in Moscow during his exile, had promised to give him and his followers the necessary backing against his rivals.

Now Ulbricht was no longer being accused of mismanagement of the economy, "naked administrating," "corruption," etc., but his two most outspoken opponents who had demanded his resignation were now all of a sudden in the dock. They were accused of having organized a "conspiracy," of having "split the Party," in order to "seize power" for their own good. Herrnstadt was also reproached for having "capitulated" when the workers' rebellion took place on June 17; he had allegedly "shown traces of social democracy," etc. The second, Wilhelm Zaisser, was charged with a "lack of vigilance" during those critical days.

Zaisser was Minister of the Interior at the time of the protests and did not want to use force against the demonstrators. Later, both Zaisser and Herrnstadt were booted out of the politburo and the Party and were sent into exile. They were no longer allowed to return to Berlin. Herrnstadt got a job in the city archives of Merseburg; Zaisser died an untimely death. He is said to have suffered a "heart attack" in 1958.

Another victim of Ulbricht's purges was Max Fechner, former Minister of Justice — one of the few social democrats in the SED politburo. What was his "crime"?

In an interview he gave on June 17th, he told the striking workers that they shouldn't be afraid of being punished. This was in line with the GDR's own constitution passed in 1949 where the right to go on strike was still guaranteed. He was arrested, put in jail and denounced as an

---

[127] Andrea Görldt, *Rudolf Herrnstadt und Wilhelm Zaisser*, ibid., p. 338.

'enemy of the Party and the state.' He was sentenced to eight years in prison.

In 1956 Fechner was granted an early release and even readmitted to the Central Committee. The two others, however, were never rehabilitated, not even under Ulbricht's successor Honecker. Both were communist celebrities: Herrnstadt had worked for the Soviet Intelligence Service in Warsaw during the war for nine years and Zaisser had been a commander of an International Brigade during the Spanish Civil War in 1936–39.

When pensions for "fighters against fascism" were later introduced, Ulbricht issued a special order not to give one to his rival Herrnstadt.[128] Herrnstadt died on August 28th 1966 after a long illness. He suffered from a grave lung condition. Only two obituaries were permitted to be published in the newspapers. The local newspaper *Freiheit* (Freedom) in the city of Halle wanted to describe him as an "upright communist" in the obituary notice. Soon the editors were told by the center in East Berlin that the word "communist" was inappropriate for this person. It should correctly read "upright person."[129]

Thus Herrnstadt was not only stripped of his pension but, post mortem, also of having been a communist.

Ulbricht had also accused his main rivals of having played into the hands of those who wanted to 'restore capitalism'.[130]

So the very same person who later set to work to organize the restoration of capitalism in the GDR under the label of 'New Economic System of Planning and Leadership' exactly ten years earlier had accused his greatest rivals of wanting to restore capitalism! We will deal with this issue later in more detail.

After the collapse of the GDR, Eric Honecker, Ulbricht's successor in 1971, was interviewed. He told his two interviewers, Andert and Herzberg, that something rather strange occurred one day in 1953. It explains Ulbricht's bitter enmity towards Zaisser and may be another important reason why he was purged from the Party. Honecker called attention to Walter Ulbricht and the Slánsky trial in Prague:

> Zaisser himself was linked to the Soviet Cheka so that we had to be very vigilant after the death of Stalin in 1953. We prevented

---

[128] Jürgen Kuczynski, *Ein linientreuer Dissident, Memoiren 1945–1989*, Berlin, 1994, p. 8; a loyal dissident.

[129] Helmut Müller-Enbergs, ibid., pp. 344F, document 17.

[130] Norbert Podewin, *Walter Ulbricht. Eine neue Biografie*, Berlin, 1995, p. 353, citing Ulbricht's speech at the 15th Plenum of the SED on July 24, 1953.

a meeting with Zaisser at the airport of Schoenefeld. Two Beria people turned up who wanted to do their business in the GDR together with some others who had already arrived. We sent them back soon.[131]

Then the two interviewers asked him: What did the two Beria people want from Zaisser?

Honecker:

It was about Hungary and the Czechoslovak Republic, it was about the Slánsky trial. It was about Ulbricht. There was the danger that he could be drawn into the trial like other General Secretaries at the time. But we were lucky enough to prevent that from happening. It was after the death of Stalin.[132]

The two 'Beria people' were no non-entities, but his two deputies who were sent to Berlin to investigate Ulbricht's possible involvement with the American spies Herman and Noel Field. They had been exposed as foreign agents at the Slánsky treason trial in late 1952.[133]

Slánsky, the then General Secretary of the Communist Party of the Czechoslovak Republic, was sentenced to death for having committed high treason against his country. It turned out that Noel Field's brother, Herman Field, who also was a US spy, had ties to some members of the SED politburo as well, among them Franz Dahlem, a close friend of Ulbricht. Dahlem had admitted these ties to the American spy. Honecker in the interview:

We could clearly see what was going to happen with these Beria people...So they were sent back and Zaisser was deposed and replaced by Wollweber and Walter Ulbricht stayed in power.[134]

So there had indeed been plans to get rid of Ulbricht as long as Beria had a say in Moscow. Khrushchev's putsch, organized with the help of high-ranking Soviet generals, among them Marshal Zhukov, rescued the embattled General Secretary in Berlin and allowed him to keep his top job for almost two more decades. After his chief rivals were removed, Ulbricht's position in the Party was stronger than ever before.

This explains the 'phenomenon' that a seemingly incompetent leader, semi-illiterate, speaking with a squeaky voice and strong regional accent,

---

[131] Reinhold Andert, Wolfgang Herzberg, *Der Sturz,* Berlin and Weimar, 1991, p. 231; the fall.

[132] Ibid., p. 232.

[133] Also see: Prozess gegen die Leitung des staatsfeindlichen Verschwörer-Zentrums mit Rudolf Slánsky an der Spitze, Prague, 1953; trial against the leadership of the Slánsky conspiracy.

[134] Ibid., p. 232.

who was ridiculed and despised by the East Germans, could survive and rule the country until 1971. Finally, one of his long-time allies, Eric Honecker, deposed him with the consent of Leonid Brezhnev, the then leader of the Soviet Communist Party.

Was the 17th June an "imperialist provocation"?

As has been shown, the country-wide strikes, riots and demonstrations on June 17th, 1953, were protests provoked by the anti-working class policy of the chiefs of the Socialist Unity Party. Whereas the increase in consumer prices was rolled back and ration cards for the intelligentsia were restored, the 10% increase in work norms was not; it was only rescinded when the protests were already under way. This was also a rebellion against a deeply unpopular regime, claiming to be 'socialist' through and through. The rebellion, which spread like a wildfire in only two days, showed that the majority of the population in the GDR distrusted the regime and wanted free, confidential and fair elections to get rid of it. They had been promised that elections would take place one year from the foundation of the GDR in October 1949 — a promise on which the GDR leaders had reneged.

As to the question of whether all this was an "imperialist provocation," the observer Mike Dennis had this to say:

> Before they had time to concoct the legend of D-Day, the SED leaders had admitted their responsibility. The 14th Central Committee meeting on 21st of June had declared: 'If the masses of the workers do not understand the Party, then the Party is guilty, not the workers!'...And three days later, Otto Grotewohl confessed: 'We're guilty of the conditions which led up to it.'[135]

So at least Grotewohl, the social democrat, had shown some traces of self-criticism, but the others had not.

The protests were spontaneous, not the result of a premeditated "color revolution" as has been recently claimed by some people in defense of the GDR. It can't be denied, though, that there were some attempts from outside to infiltrate the workers' protests when the demonstrations were already under way. But this does not change the essential character of the uprising. There were indeed rioters and provocateurs, setting buildings on fire, who were sent in from West Berlin agencies. But how could ordinary construction workers, who had started the uprising peacefully, prevent this from happening without having any organizational strength whatsoever?

---

[135] Mike Dennis, ibid., p. 26.

The city commander of the Western powers in West Berlin even sealed off the Western sectors from the East to prevent provocateurs from entering East Berlin and joining the movement, and a demonstration of support planned by the Social Democratic Party in West Berlin was forbidden.

The CIA director in West Berlin, Henry Hecksher, who had asked the US embassy to arm the protesters in East Berlin, was soon brought back into line. The Eisenhower administration in Washington D.C. needed two German states at this point in time to hasten the integration of West Germany into the NATO alliance. A united Germany was not in the interest of the Western powers, and the Soviets were not ready yet to allow a united Germany to become a NATO state, as was later the case under General Secretary Mikhail Gorbachev.

The 17th of June was not an 'imperialist provocation' but was made to look like one by the Ulbricht people to divert attention from the real causes and their own responsibility.

7. The New Character of the Socialist Unity Party after the June Events

Zaisser, Herrnstadt and Fechner were not the only ones to be purged from the politburo and the Central Committee; other critics of Ulbricht and his policy suffered a similar fate.

Let's first take a closer look at the changes that occurred in the politburo in the mid-fifties.

In 1950, at the Third Party Congress of the SED, the following persons had Permanent seats: Franz Dahlem, Friedrich Ebert, Otto Grotewohl, Hermann Matern, Fred Oelßner, Wilhelm Pieck, Heinrich Rau, Walter Ulbricht, Wilhelm Zaisser. Candidates: Anton Ackermann, Rudolf Herrnstadt, Eric Honecker, Hans Jendretzky, Eric Mückenberger, and Elli Schmidt.[136]

Four years later (at the Fourth Party Congress), Permanent members were Ebert, Grotewohl, Matern, Oelßner, Pieck, Rau, Schirdewan, Stoph and Ulbricht. Candidates: Honecker, Leuschner, Mückenberger, Neumann, Warnke[137]

The changed composition of the politburo before and after the purges is striking. All the outspoken critics of First Secretary Ulbricht —

---

[136] Hermann Weber, ed., *Der deutsche Kommunismus. Dokumente*, Cologne/Berlin, 1963, p. 650.

[137] Ibid.

Herrnstadt, Zaisser, Ackermann, Schmidt, Jendretzky — were gone. The only moderate critic who survived the shake-up was Mr. Rau. New faces were admitted, or co-opted rather, such as Neumann, Stoph, Schirdewan, Leuschner, and Warnke — all of them supporters of Ulbricht, with the possible exception of Karl Schirdewan who later became a fierce critic; and in 1958 he was purged too.

When exactly did the purges begin?

When the last wave of strikes had died down in mid-July of 1953, the SED leaders gave orders to shake up all party organizations. Carola Stern wrote,

> In all party organizations political screenings of all party officials and members as to their attitude during the rebellion occurred....

> One of the victims was Adalbert Hengst who had been nominated Central Committee member only the year before. The reason for his ousting: he had read out the protesters' demands in public, using the radio station of the shipyard of Warnov on June 17.[138]

For a future career in the SED, the candidates' acting on June 17 was made a touchstone.[139]

Mike Dennis presents the following table on SED membership from 1946 through to 1986:

Date	Membership total
April 1946	1,298,415
June 1948	ca 2, 000,000
July 1950	ca 1,750,000
September 1953	ca 1,230,000
December 1957	1,472,932
December 1961	1,610,769
June 1971	1,909,859
April 1981	2,043,697
April 1986	2,304,121

Sources: Zimmermann, 1985, p. 1185; Fricke, 1986b, p. 629[140]

So there was a steady rise in party membership throughout the years, but with one notable exception: from 1950 onwards the figures came down, reaching a low in the fall of 1953.

---

[138] Ibid., p. 163.
[139] Ibid.
[140] Mike Dennis, ibid., p. 80.

What had happened? Ehrhardt Neubert may be right in saying that after the June events, many hundreds were expelled from the party.[141]

And some historians may be even closer to the truth, when speaking about a comprehensive purging of the party apparatus:

> Of those members who were elected to the provincial SED party organizations in 1952 more than 60% resigned; of the first and second district party secretaries even more than 70%. In September 1953, the SED politburo criticized that of the 1,2 million members many were passive...and some even 'hostile elements.' By mobilizing 150 to 200 thousand 'party activists,' a new momentum was expected for the party. [142]

In fact, the social composition of the whole party changed, as historian Weber points out:

> Whereas in May 1947 47.9% of the members were manual workers, this share came down to only 39.1% in 1954.[143]

This is roughly confirmed by Mike Dennis, citing figures for the year 1961: "In 1961, for example, workers represented only 33.8% of total party membership."[144] An inner party analysis of the SED conducted in 1954 also concluded that 25.8% of the members had a Nazi background.[145]

So the doors of the party were now wide open for former supporters of the Nazi party, Hitler's NSDAP.

Thus there is substantial evidence that not only at the top but also at the grass roots level the character of the party changed considerably after the workers' rebellion. Now that the party nomenclature had consolidated their position at the top, they also wanted to make sure that a second 'June 17th' would not and could not happen again. The first time, many party members had not acted forcefully enough to prevent the rebellion from happening or to help crush it, but had preferred to stay behind.

A second reason may have been that for the forthcoming capitalist reforms scheduled for the early sixties, a new party set-up was needed to ensure the support of the grass roots.

---

[141] Ehrhardt Neubert, *Geschichte der Opposition in der DDR, 1949–1989*, Bonn, 1997, p. 88; history of the GDR opposition.
[142] Hermann Weber, *Grundriss der Geschichte der DDR, 1945–1990*, Hamburg, 1991, p. 57; an outline of the history of the GDR.
[143] Ibid., p. 57.
[144] Mike Dennis, ibid., p. 81.
[145] In: Der Spiegel, no. 19, May 9, 1994, p. 91.

8. First Steps Towards the New Economic System

At the 21st Meeting of the Central Committee of the SED on November 12, 1954, Ulbricht gave a speech on 'Issues of political economy.' Now he said the time had come to "spare no effort to improve the management of the national economy and to get rid of shortcomings in planning and managing production."[146]

He went on to say that ministries and enterprises should conduct a, what he called, "resolute struggle for profitability in production."[147]

He also stressed that "the present situation of 27% of nationalized enterprises making losses had to be redressed. The non-fulfillment of profit plans by a great number of factories was tantamount to seriously damaging our great project of rebuilding the country."[148]

In other words, Ulbricht admitted that 73% of East German enterprises were profitable; so the overall picture of the economy was not that bad after all, at least as far as profitability was concerned. Why did he suddenly hit out at the low profitability of certain enterprises, even though the overall situation was pretty good due to central planning, which was still functioning at the time?

Let's first deal with the problem from a principled point of view. What is the Marxist view concerning profitability and a planned economy? Stalin was the chief architect of the well-functioning planned economy which made the Soviet Union a modern state, with a stable and growing economy, able to overcome even the horrendous trials and tribulations of the Nazi aggression against the USSR in the early forties. Here, he speaks about profitability:

> If you look at profitability not from the point of view of individual enterprises, and if you do not judge it over a period of one year or so, but from a the point of view of the whole economy and judge it over a period of, let's say, 10 to 15 years ... then the temporary unstable profitability of some enterprises or production units does not compare unfavorably with the higher form of a secured and steady profitability which is guaranteed by the law of planned development of the national economy, thus protecting us from periodic economic crises that ruin the economy and the society and cause huge material damage, and also providing us with a continuous growth of the national economy.[149]

---

[146] Archiv der Gegenwart, year 1954, ibid., p. 7,548, November 22, 1954.

[147] Ibid.

[148] Ibid.

[149] J. W. Stalin, *Ökonomische Probleme des Sozialismus in der UdSSR*, Offenbach, 1997, pp. 389 f, economic problems of socialism in the USSR.

Stalin wanted to tell his party comrades that as long as the law of a planned economy is adhered to and as long as the central planning bodies abide by this law, the long-term profitability of the entire economy is guaranteed.

From this principled point of view there was no need for Ulbricht and his team to press for individual enterprise profitability. Why then did he lament the low profitability of some individual enterprises? Philip Neumann:

> Walter Ulbricht in his speech also laments the 'rigidity and immobility of the planning system.' The centralized economy had been 'distorted to become bureaucratic centralism.' The enterprises were 'overloaded with too many numbers'...[150]

So in reality, Ulbricht was not concerned about the profitability of certain enterprises as such, but the centrally planned economy itself, using the low profit rates of certain enterprises as a pretext justifying his reform effort, a pretext for undermining the centrally planned economy.

Philipp Neumann also says that even before 1954, measures had been taken by the SED leaders to sabotage central planning in the GDR:

> This planning system was gradually undermined. In early 1951 the nationalized enterprises [VEB = Volkseigene Betriebe in German — author] became independent entities from a legal point of view. The most important ones were removed from the 'Association of Nationalized Enterprises' and these were also restructured according to territorial and technical categories. In 1952, the associations were dissolved and industrial ministries established which served as supervisory bodies for the companies. Simultaneously, the position of the enterprises was strengthened by introducing a contractual system, cost accounting, and a statute for the VEBs.[151]

In other words, the reform effort had been under way even before the crucial 21st Meeting was convened. The GDR enterprises had already become independent legal entities and had obtained the right to draw up their own plans.[152]

Between 1948 and 1950, a central body was responsible for the whole economy: the "German Economic Commission" (Wirtschafts-kommission), which had also drawn up the first two-year plan for the

---

[150] Philipp Neumann, *Zurück zum Profit*, Berlin, 1977, p. 42, citing Ulbricht's speech at the 21st Meeting of the Central Committee of the SED on November 12, 1954; back to the profit.

[151] Ibid., p. 39.

[152] Jörg Roesler, *Die Herausbildung der sozialistischen Planwirtschaft in der DDR*, Berlin, 1978, p. 98; the emergence of a socialist planned economy in the GDR.

GDR economy. But in 1952, separate industrial ministries were created: a ministry for the chemical industry, one for the steel industry, etc., thus compartmentalizing the economy, and, starting from March 20, 1952, the GDR enterprises were also given the right to manage their own funds for the first time.[153]

So the 21st Meeting did not have to start from scratch, but it took an important additional step in further undermining the centrally planned economy, leading to even greater problems for the GDR than before: the number of indices handed down to the individual enterprises was reduced, more general indicators were introduced and the profit, even though it did not become the key component of the plan at this early stage, was now given a greater role to play:

> It was made an important economic category...Parts of the wages and salaries of the workforce were now dependent on the profit made by the companies.[154]

Since then, the largest part of a company's profit no longer had to be transferred to the state, and this caused budgetary problems. Philipp Neumann again:

> To guarantee the operational independence of the enterprises, the financial funds were also restructured. A decree on how to use the profit was issued, stating that the entire profit did not have to be transferred to the state budget anymore, but only 20% of it [as some sort of tax]; the rest could be used for the self-financing and operational funds. Thus the profit became a powerful economic lever for the enterprises on which also parts of the income of the workforce were made dependent.[155]

In addition to that, a so-called director's fund was created to hand out premiums to the workforce and the directorate. The fund was financed by the company's profits. A new bonus system came into being:

> As from 1955 the director's fund was completely financed out of the profit fund. At the same time, a new bonus system for leading personnel and also for the technical intelligentsia was created, raising bonus payments...[156]

The leading personnel profited most from the new system, getting higher bonuses than the workers and employees at the bottom.

---

[153] Ibid., p. 63.
[154] Ibid., p. 46.
[155] Philipp Neumann, *Zurück zum Profit*, p. 46
[156] Ibid., p. 47.

The 21st Meeting of the CC of the SED introduced three new elements to the centrally planned economy, originally modeled on the Soviet economy introduced under Lenin and Stalin in the early twenties:

1. Decentralization. Individual enterprises obtained greater autonomy and, what is more, the center in Berlin was split into various entities called industrial ministries;

2. Enforcement of enterprise profitability. The company profit was given a greater role;

3. Introduction of a new bonus system which worked in favor of the company directorate. Bonuses were linked to the fulfillment of the profit plan, no longer to the production plan.

However: The role of the profit was still limited, as the planning for the utilization of the profit did not occur in the enterprises themselves but was done in the various industrial ministries at the top echelon in East Berlin.

These measures which deepened and further sabotaged the centrally planned economy were not taken at a Party Congress but at a Party Conference. Ordinary party members were kept out of the decision-making process and were more or less in the dark.

Philipp Neumann says,

> To sum up, one could call this reform a precursor of NESPL [the later large-scale reform introduced at the 6th Party Congress in early 1963 — author], because all the elements of NESPL are already here. Eight years later they will be fully elaborated and transformed into a system.[157]

This was not a system yet but a set of preparatory measures for what was yet to come: the restoration of capitalism in the GDR.

This major step required much preparation. Without this step-by-step approach many ordinary SED members would have been up in arms or might have turned their backs on the 'socialist' party.

9. The Events Preceding the Building of the Berlin Wall

In the years leading up to the construction of the separation wall between East and West Berlin on August 13, 1961, the SED party leaders, in tandem with the Khrushchev leadership in Moscow, took further steps to sabotage and wreck the socialist planning system.

Economic planning lost the prime role it had played in the late forties and even in 1950. Why? Because...

---

[157] Ibid., p. 48.

1. The annual plans were often passed with considerable delay. For example: the one-year-plan for 1957 passed by the GDR People's Chamber [the East German parliament — author], was only adopted on April the same year, causing a delay of almost five months.[158] The one-year-plan for 1961 was passed on March 25, 1961 with a delay of almost four months;

2. The long-term plans were also delayed: the second five-year-plan which should have been up and running in early 1954, following the first five-year-plan ending in 1954, was adopted only in 1958;

3. This second five-year-plan was then prematurely terminated in 1959 and replaced by a seven-year-plan modeled on Khrushchev's 7-year-plan in the Soviet Union. According to this overly ambitious and unrealistic plan, valid until 1965, the East German economy was scheduled to reach West German economic and financial standards by late 1961. That project was canceled at the Party Congress in January 1963;

4. Those party officials who had misgivings about undermining central economic planning and who voiced their concerns openly, among them Professor Fred Oelßner, were simply expelled from the Central Committee to make way for more 'flexible' and reform-minded candidates.

The official reason for Oelßner's dismissal is that "Comrade Oelßner was in favor of maintaining over-centralization."[159]

Next, the range of commodity circulation in the GDR economy was drastically extended by selling the Machine Tractor Stations to the Agricultural Producers' Cooperatives [LPG, Landwirtschaftliche Produktionsgenossenschaften] in 1959. Here is Politburo member Eric Mueckenberger:

> We are in favor of transferring the technology of the MTS to the LPG and we want the tractor drivers to become members of the collectives.[160]

Khrushchev sold the MTS to the Soviet agricultural cooperatives in 1958. First Secretary Walter Ulbricht, the initiator of the new measure, followed in Khrushchev's footsteps:

> The Worker and Peasant State is handing over the technology [of the MTS — author] to the Agricultural Producers' Cooperatives to take responsibility for them.[161]

---

[158] Archiv der Gegenwart, year 1957, ibid., p. 10,803.

[159] Ibid., p. 11,694.

[160] Erich Mueckenberger, *Der Weg unserer Landwirtschaft*, in: Einheit, 14th year, April 1959, no. 4, p. 506; the path for our agriculture.

[161] Walter Ulbricht on collectivization, in: *Der deutsche Kommunismus. Dokumente*, edited by Hermann Weber, Cologne/Berlin, 1963, p. 625; German communism, documents.

"Transferring to the LPG" meant selling to the LPG. Thus the members of the cooperative farms became owners of the machine tractor stations, and the tractor drivers now were employees of the farms and no longer employees of the state. This followed the model of the Moscow Central Committee: in February 1958, the Plenum of the CC of the CPSU adopted a resolution to sell the Soviet MTS to the kolkhozes, making them owners of the technology.[162]

In 1952, when Stalin was still in charge in Moscow, he severely criticized some people in his party who had planned to do just that. They were two company directors, Sanina and Wensher, two followers of Nikita Khrushchev. Stalin told them this:

> What does it mean if one...demands selling the MTS to the farming cooperatives? It means to cause great losses for the cooperatives and to ruin them, to endanger the mechanization of agriculture and to slow down the speed of production of the collective farms. Comrades Sanina and Wensher with their proposal to sell the MTS to the cooperatives are taking a step back and are trying to turn back the wheels of history.[163]

Why did Stalin consider such a step a reactionary move which would inflict great damage to the cooperatives as well as to socialism as a whole?

First of all, the kolkhozes could not afford the most modern technology, however the Soviet state could. Secondly: by making such a "step back in history" the farming cooperatives would become proprietors of means of production, leading to an even greater rift between collective property and national property. This would not mean getting closer to communism but departing from it, taking a step back toward capitalism. It would entail an expansion of the range of commodity circulation because...

> huge amounts of means of production in agriculture would then enter the realm of commodity circulation.[164]

The leaders of the SED did not follow Stalin's advice but modeled their decision on what Khrushchev had done in the post-Stalin USSR in 1958. Stalin was no longer considered to be "a classic" (Ulbricht in 1956) and soon all his works disappeared from GDR bookstores and were even banned. Nobody was to read his landmark book on *Economic Problems of Socialism in the USSR*.

---

[162] Boris Meissner, *Russland unter Chruschtschow*, Munich, 1960, p. 86; Russia under Khrushchev.

[163] J. W. Stalin, *Ökonomische Probleme des Sozialismus in der UdSSR*, Berlin, 1953, pp. 91f.; economic problems of socialism in the USSR.

[164] Ibid., p. 92.

By taking such a step back to capitalism, Ulbricht and his followers, now in full control of the party apparatus, also intended to create favorable conditions for the forthcoming big reform effort, the Neues ökonomisches System der Planung und Leitung — New Economic System of Planning and Leadership.

10. The Building of the Berlin Wall on August 13, 1961

Finally, another precondition had to be met to make the scheduled economic reform project a success: the growing emigration of dissatisfied GDR citizens towards the West had to be stopped by all means. Only behind a wall of protection could the ambitious project of restoring capitalism in the GDR succeed without having to pay the price of surrendering power to the West German state. To do nothing and to sit idly by would have led to the inevitable collapse of the East German state and its economy, which was already in dire straits. The SED leaders would be thrown out, as was the case in the years 1989–1990.

In the mid-fifties the wave of emigration to West Germany had continued uninterruptedly:

1955	252,870
1956	279,189
1957	261,622[165]

In 1960, this trend became even more pronounced. Young people in particular saw no future for themselves in Ulbricht's GDR: between 1954 and 1960 almost 100,000 people below the age of 25 emigrated to the Federal Republic of Germany.[166]

The figures broken down into occupational groups were as follows:

Physicians	3,110
Teachers	15,885
Engineers and technicians	15,536
Police and military 11,941	
Peasants 41,300[167]	

---

[165] Archiv der Gegenwart, year 1958, ibid., 11,667.
[166] Ibid.,year 1961, p. 15,159.
[167] Ibid.

Even many members of the youth organization of the SED, the Free German Youth, turned their backs on the GDR. If the saying is true that 'he who has the youth also has the future,' the Ulbricht regime certainly did not have a future as long as there was an open border in Berlin. Something drastic had to be done to prevent a further exodus and brain drain.

> Only a fortnight before the Berlin Wall was built, Ulbricht, in an interview to the London Evening Standard, made the following statement: Mark Wilson (interviewer): Are there any kinds of threats on your part, Mr. Ulbricht, to close the border?
>
> Ulbricht: There is no such threat. You see, it depends on the Western powers, not on us...
>
> Mark Wilson: So there is no question whatsoever that the border might be closed? Is it fair to say that you have no intention of closing the border?
>
> Ulbricht: That's correct.[168]

Even at a press conference on June 15, 1961, two months before the wall was erected, Ulbricht said that "nobody has any intention to build a wall."[169]

In an essay written for a book on Ulbricht, edited by Egon Krenz, the last General Secretary of the SED before the collapse of the GDR, Viktor G. Kulikov, Commander-in-Chief of the Soviet Forces in Germany between 1969 and 1971, said that...

> the measures taken on August 13, 1961 were the result of a decision taken by the Political Advisory Board of the member states of the Warsaw Treaty.[170]

If that is true, then Ulbricht must have known that such a decision had been taken by the alliance. But he denied it just two weeks before. He must have known of such a decision well in advance, if it existed at all. So he lied to the public in order not to cause a panic reaction. One of Ulbricht's staunchest supporters at the time and his eventual successor, Eric Honecker, was the man in charge of building the wall. It cut through close-knit communities and neighborhoods. There were border guards who defected to West Berlin in full uniform while the wall was being built — their last chance to leave the country. Honecker was assisted

---

[168] Ibid., p. 15,714.

[169] Egon Krenz, ed., *Walter Ulbricht*, p. 331, Berlin, 2016.

[170] Wiktor Kulikow, *Die DDR war souverän, aber nicht auf militärpolitischem Gebiet*, Berlin, 2016, in: Walter Ulbricht, edited by Egon Krenz; the GDR was a sovereign state, but not militarily and politically.

by his comrade Willi Seifert, a former chief overseer at the Buchenwald concentration camp who had been involved in war crimes against Russian camp inmates.[171]

How did Ulbricht himself describe the problem of mass emigration? In Archiv der Gegenwart, a reliable source, he is quoted as saying that the emigration of citizens of the GDR to West Germany was:

> a result of the Cold War, of human trafficking, of psychological warfare and sabotage against the GDR.[172]

He was right in that there had been many attempts by the West German Adenauer regime to worsen the economic situation in East Germany by taking unilateral measures against the country. And West Berlin was indeed a nest of spies; that cannot be denied. In 1960, for example, the FRG unilaterally revoked the treaty on German–German trade.

But it can also not be denied that the most important imperialist power, the United States (the Kennedy administration at the time), did not oppose the closing of the border, apart from making rhetorical noises of protest. Quite the opposite.

Some weeks before the closure, President Kennedy and General Secretary Khrushchev had met in Vienna. Kennedy must have been told of what was going to happen, but to all intents and purposes made no objections. The United States was still interested in having two German states to be able to justify its military presence in Central Europe.

The main reason for building the wall was economic. The mass exodus had to be stopped to stabilize the economic and political situation in the GDR. This is also confirmed by a high-ranking GDR official who admitted just that in an interview he gave German economists in 1993:

> The building of the Wall was preceded by an increasing wave of emigration by doctors and highly qualified parts of the population. West Germany was in a big upswing economically, and there was no prospect at all of withstanding the pressure. Something had to be done about it, something was looming. Either everything stayed the same, and the GDR would bleed white, or something would happen to avoid just that...The building of the Wall didn't come as a surprise.[173]

---

[171] Prague Ministry of Justice, *Prozess gegen die Leitung des staatsfeindlichen Verschwörungszentrums mit Rudolf Slánsky an der Spitze*, Prague, 1953, p. 337. Josef Frank's testimony before the court; trial against Rudolf Slánsky and others.

[172] Archiv der Gegenwart, ibid., p. 15,714.

[173] Interview with Professor Dr. Claus Kroemke, Berlin, October 18, 1993, in: Theo Pirker et al, ibid., pp. 37f.

Once it was being built, the project was officially called an "Anti-fascist Protection Wall" to suggest that the East German government had successfully preempted a fascist aggression against the GDR. The phrase became the standard justification for the closure of the border and even entered GDR textbooks.

This was a mere pretext to justify the building of the separation wall in hindsight and to suggest that the GDR possessed a genuine "anti-fascist state." The real reason was different: peace was needed in the GDR to reconstruct the economic system without risking the collapse of the economy and the demise of the SED nomenclature.

It was also not the first time that the SED leaders had wanted to close the border to West Berlin: as early as 1953, when thousands of people were emigrating to the West, the SED leadership also tried to close the border by stationing border guards at the dividing line between East and West Berlin, but they did not get Moscow's go-ahead. At that time, Khrushchev had not yet come to power. The Soviet leadership under Malenkov and Beria prevented it from happening, telling them that such a measure was counterproductive and would damage the reputation of the Soviet policy for Germany:

> To carry out such measures in Berlin with a population of several million people would cause disruption of the present city life, it would disorganize the city's economy and negatively affect the interests of the population not just in the western part of the city but also in the east; it would lead to embitterment and dissatisfaction among the Berliners against the government of the GDR and the Soviet armed forces in Germany, which would be exploited by the Western powers against the interests of the GDR and the USSR.[174]

And indeed, profound embitterment and dissatisfaction was caused by the Berlin Wall, and the reputation of communism was gravely impaired. Now the Western propagandists and their media could claim with some justification that communism was much the same as German fascism, that it was true totalitarianism, and that the poor people in the GDR now got their 'concentration camp'.

---

[174] Telegram of the Soviet government, dated March 18, 1953, containing orders no. 8/1517 and 8/1543, see: http://digitalarchive.wilsoncenter.org, russ. source: AVP RF, fond 06, opis 12, papka 18, port 283, Archive of the Russian Federation.

11. "De-Stalinization"

After the Berlin Wall had been erected, the SED leaders could feel safe enough to set to work on restructuring the own economy.

But someone was still in the way: Joseph Stalin, who had successfully built a viable socialist economy in his own country, a process reaching over more than 30 years, transforming the backward country of Russia into a modern socialist superpower called the USSR.

The anti-Stalin propaganda campaign started soon after the separation wall had been finished in late 1961. A news item in the official party paper *Neues Deutschland* dated November 14 read as follows:

> After studying the documents of the 22nd Party Congress of the Communist Party of the Soviet Union, the city council of Berlin, in view of the violations of the revolutionary legality in the period of Stalin's personality cult and the grave consequences resulting from this, during its session of November 13, 1961 has taken the following decisions:
>
> 1. The section of the hitherto called 'Stalin Allee' from Alexander Platz to the Frankfurter Tor will be renamed in 'Karl-Marx-Allee';
>
> 2. The section from the Frankfurter Tor in eastern direction will get the name of 'Frankfurter Allee' [instead of Stalin Allee — author];
>
> 3. The Stalin monument will be removed;
>
> 4. The metro station 'Stalin Allee' will be renamed 'S-Bahnhof Frankfurter Allee'...
>
> 5. The VEB Elektrowerke J. W. Stalin will drop Stalin's name. In future, the enterprise will bear the name of 'VEB-Elektroapparate Berlin-Treptow'
>
> The regional administration of Frankfurt–Oder, at their 18th Meeting on Monday approved of various motions to merge the towns of Stalin-Stadt and Fürstenberg/Oder to become the district-town of Eisenhüttenstadt together with Eisenhüttenkombinat Ost.[175]

At the 22nd Congress of the Soviet Communist Party, Nikita Khrushchev denounced Stalin again as he had done five years earlier in February of 1956, using all sorts of swearwords against him. Obviously, he expected his close friend Ulbricht to follow suit.

Another move in the same direction had been made one month later:

---

[175] Archiv der Gegenwart, year 1961, pp. 16,118ff.

In December the diplomatic relations with the only socialist state left in Europe where Stalin was still in high esteem, Enver Hoxha's Albania, were ended. Johannes Koenig, the GDR Deputy Foreign Minister, submitted the following note to his Albanian counterpart, Mr. Gaqo Paze, on December 18:

> The Government of the GDR has decided to recall the ambassador of the GDR in the people's Republic of Albania and to reduce the diplomatic staff of the embassy of the GDR. At the same time, the Government of the GDR asks the Government of the People's Republic of Albania to recall its ambassador in the GDR and to reduce the diplomatic corps of the embassy.[176]

Enver Hoxha's Albania stood for a principled Leninist line, and this was clearly not to the liking of the GDR leadership.

12. A Former Nazi — Ulbricht's First Choice for the "Economic Reform"

On January 12, 1963, according to ADN, the official East German news agency, a Central Committee meeting of the SED recommended that the GDR Council of Ministers appoint "Dr. Erich Apel Chairman of the State Planning Commission and Deputy Chairman of the Council of Ministers."[177]

The former high-ranking Nazi official Apel was Ulbricht's first choice to replace Karl Mewis as chairman of the planning body. Mewis, a former anti-fascist resistance fighter, was dismissed from his post. He was also removed from his position as "minister and was no longer member of the Council of Ministers."[178]

Mewis belonged to those during the Nazi era who, in his Swedish exile, over years had tried hard to assist his communist comrades who had stayed behind in Germany, to rebuild the Communist Party of Germany.[179] He also participated in the Spanish Civil War on the side of the Spanish Republic and against the Franco fascists.

By this move, a former Nazi war criminal, who had been on the leading staff of Buchenwald-Dora concentration camp in the Harz Mountains during the war and had also been involved in developing Hitler's "wonder weapon V2" in the last months of the war in the town of Peenemuende,

---

[176] Ibid., p. 16,246.
[177] Ibid., p. 17,605.
[178] Ibid.
[179] Karl Mewis, *Im Auftrag der Partei*, Berlin, 1972; on Party orders. The book, the memoirs of an anti-fascist resistance fighter, was banned in the GDR in the mid-seventies.

on Ulbricht's initiative became one of the most influential politicians in the GDR. This influence was needed to plan, direct and carry out the economic reform.

Apel joined the SED only in 1957. He had never been a communist. Only one year later he was appointed chief of the Economic Commission by Ulbricht, a newly created authority to put him in charge of economic matters at the top of the Party[180]. From then on he was the superior in economic matters of even those sitting on the Central Committee and could overrule any decisions taken by the CC. Be became Ulbricht's strong man in the party and also his planning chief. In 1965 he was suddenly found dead in his office. The official version: Eric Apel had killed himself.

Another of Ulbricht's favorites was Karl-Heinz Bartsch who was brought into the SED politburo at the Sixth Congress of the SED in January 1963 as an expert in agricultural matters. This was the congress that adopted the resolution on restructuring the East German economy. In April 1941 he became a member of the infamous Nazi terror organization Waffen SS who committed countless war crimes in the occupied territories, especially in Russia. In 1939, he was decorated by the Nazis and given the Danzig Cross. In the GDR Bartsch was also decorated and received the Patriotic Order of Merit in bronze.[181] But someone must have known about his past, and only two months after his appointment he had to go again.[182] Unlike other high-ranking SED officials who often also had a Nazi past he had kept his fascist connections in the dark. He was not deposed due to his Nazi past, but only because he had not given the pertinent information to the GDR Secret Service Stasi. This explains why he was not punished but only demoted and then became director of an agricultural institute and also CEO of a GDR enterprise.

The main players who were commissioned by Ulbricht to draw up the plans were: Walter Halbritter, Dr. Wolfgang Berger, Herbert Wolf, Otto Reinhold and Prof. Dr. Helmut Koziolek.[183] All these people later received the GDR National Prize for their achievements. Eric Apel was the man who was to put theses plans into practice together with Guenter Mittag, the SED Secretary for the Economy.

---

[180] André Steiner, *Die DDR-Wirtschaftsreform der sechziger Jahre*, Berlin, 1999, p. 27; the GDR economic reform of the sixties.

[181] Olaf Kappelt, *Braunbuch DDR*, Berlin, 1981, p. 145

[182] Margarete Mueller, *Er wollte Praktiker im Politbüro*, in: Egon Krenz, ed., in: *Walter Ulbricht*, ibid., p. 313; he wanted practical-minded people in the politburo.

[183] In: Theo Pirker et al, *Der Plan als Befehl und Fiktion*, ibid., p. 255.

13. Final Preparations

In preparation of the Sixth Party Congress (January 15–21, 1963), which was to adopt the plans for the economic reform, the party leadership appointed work teams ahead of the event. Originally, these teams were not charged with drafting the reform plans, but were pushed more and more in that direction.[184]

Basically, there were two schools of thought to draft the reform plans: the first advocated only partial reforms of the administrative and economic system, a "small solution" or a "moderate approach" as it were; the second, however, wanted to go much farther. Those belonging to this team were in favor of "the big solution" — a radical overhaul of the system. This second approach was represented by Ulbricht himself, Eric Apel, Walter Halbritter, Herbert Wolf or Helmut Koziolek who opted for a radical restructuring of all sectors of the GDR economy and the existing planning system.

They were encouraged by a similar reform process going on in Khrushchev's Soviet Union. There a broad-based discussion on economic reforms was already in full swing, and those economists taking part in these discussions clearly prioritized the 'big thing' put forward by Kharkov professor Evsey G. Liberman.

According to Liberman, the profit motive was to become the most important lever for economic activity and therefore for the fulfillment of the economic plans. As profits could only be realized through the market, the enterprises had to carefully watch the markets, both demand and purchasing power that enabled customers to buy things. The social needs of the majority of the population were no longer the number one criterion.

Soon Liberman became very popular in the USSR and his article Plan, Profit, Premium was widely read and new editions were brought out several times. It was also published in the GDR, for example in Presse *der Sowjetunion, Wirtschaft* and *Deutsche Finanzwirtschaft.* Stalin's landmark book on Economic Problems of Socialism in the Soviet Union was banned from publishing. There he had warned of such experiments which would turn the clock of history back to capitalism.

After dismissing Leuschner, Mewis and other "moderates" who remained skeptical, the attitude of the SED leadership had become clear: they were going for a radical reform and would not be satisfied with

---

[184] Jörg Roesler, *Zwischen Plan und Markt. Die Wirtschaftsreform in der DDR zwischen 1963 und 1970*, Berlin, 1990, p. 23; between plan and market. The economic reform in the GDR between 1963 and 1970.

half measures. Therefore, those economists who were in support of the radical line were nominated by Ulbricht to chair the various work teams.

At the 17th Meeting of the CC in preparation of the forthcoming Party Congress, Ulbricht did not mince his words: he frequently quoted Liberman in his address, saying, "Our economists and planners should follow this discussion closely" [the Soviet discussion — author].[185]

On December 11, 1962, the SED politburo held its meeting. The main point on the agenda of course was the "Economic Reform" to be adopted at the forthcoming party congress. Only one task-force under the chairmanship of Willi Stoph, who had been admitted to the politburo after the June events of 1953, was created. All its members were hard-line advocates of the "big solution," and it was this team that became responsible for presenting the main draft resolution to the Sixth Party Congress in January of 1963. It was titled..

> The Main Features of the Economic System of Planning and Leadership in Industry.[186]

The resolution was soon made into an official document and the GDR Council of Ministers rushed to adopt it shortly before the Christmas break.[187]

When Ulbricht gave his speech at the 6th Party Congress in January 1963 on "New Questions Concerning the Economic System of Planning and Leadership in the National Economy" the "big solution" had prevailed and partial reforms here and there were no longer options. He went even further than his Soviet counterpart: Khrushchev in his address to the November Plenum of the CC of the CPSU only championed "partial reforms." Seemingly, his party was not ready yet for the big bang, but Ulbricht's SED was — also due to the drastic membership reshuffle made in 1953.

---

[185] Ibid.
[186] Ibid., p. 25.
[187] Ibid., p. 26.

PART TWO: THE "NEW ECONOMIC SYSTEM OF PLANNING AND LEADERSHIP" (NÖSPL)

1. Disregard for the Law of Central Planning

Principles of central planning

One of the main features of a genuine socialist society rests in the central planning of the economy in order to achieve steady and continuous development of production, in keeping with the basic economic law of socialism. What exactly is this basic law?

> Guaranteeing the best possible satisfaction of the steadily growing material and cultural needs of the entire society — that's the goal of socialist production. Continuous growth and permanent improvement of socialist production on the basis of the most advanced technology — that is the means to reach this goal.[188]

To achieve this goal in socialism, the whole national economy must be developed in a planned way and on the basis of absolutely binding economic plans. All sectors of the economy must move ahead proportionately to make sure that the national economy develops in sync, smoothly and in harmony. Planning the economy is a science that recognizes the objective laws for building socialism. He who ignores these laws wrecks the construction of socialism and makes way for

---

[188] J. W. Stalin, *Ökonomische Probleme des Sozialismus in der Sowjetunion*, ibid., p. 79.

other laws: the laws for building capitalism, which are also objective in character, among them the law of supply and demand.

In his conversations with Soviet economists in the early fifties, Stalin was asked this question:

> What is the content of the law of a planned and proportionate development of the economy?
>
> [Stalin's answer:] It requires that all the elements of the economy... develop in harmony with one another.[189]

The economic plans have to mirror this law, have to take it into account or else decisions will be arbitrary and the plans will fall apart after a certain amount of time. Anarchy will be the outcome.

These production plans are no guessing games, either, no nonbinding, theoretical or general prognoses or empty declarations of intent. Stalin said in his report to the 15th Party Congress in 1927:

> Our plans are not prognoses, not plans for a guessing game, but binding plans, they contain plan directives which are obligatory for the leading bodies, determining the direction of our future economic development for the whole country.[190]

So plans are binding for each and every enterprise and their directors, they constitute laws and to fulfill them is the patriotic duty of any economic leader.

Certain preconditions must be met in order to be able to plan a national economy:

> To be able to work methodically, we need a different, a socialist and not a capitalist industrial system, we need at least a nationalized credit system, nationalized land, a socialist coalition with the village, the power of the working class in the country, etc.[191]

The main tasks of planning a national economy, according to Stalin, are threefold:

1. The main task of planning is to ensure the independence of a socialist economy from capitalist encirclement. This is absolutely the most important task. It's a sort of battle with world capitalism.

2. The second task of the planned economy consists of consolidating the ownership of all the socialist economic system and shutting out all the forces giving rise to capitalism. Rykov and Trotsky, in their time, proposed the closing of unprofitable advanced enterprises, the Putilov factory and others.

---

[189] Ibid.
[190] J. W. Stalin, *Werke*, Band 10, Berlin, 1953, pp. 283f; Stalin works.
[191] Ibid., p. 283.

This would have meant the 'closing' of socialism; capital would have flown towards flour milling and the production of toys because that is what brings profits.

3. The third task is not to allow disproportions. As the economy is so enormous, branches still have their place in it. Therefore it is necessary to have large reserves — not just any funds but funds of labor force.[192]

Individual branches of the economy are not to be developed according to their profitability but according to the best interest of the whole economy:

> If we were to develop branches of the economy according to their profitability, we would only have been able to develop flour milling, the production of toys...and textiles, but we would not have had a heavy industry. Heavy industry requires great investment and is unprofitable at first.[193]

To sum up, socialist planning deals with the entire national economy and intends to coordinate its development systematically. Systematic planning is only possible if all sectors of the industry and all the land are nationalized and abide by detailed and binding directives, controlled by a workers' state, not by the bourgeoisie.

To systematically raise a national economy to a higher level, the profit motive must be kept in check: heavy industry, the basis of all the other branches, must be given priority over other branches, even though it will not be profitable at first and needs to be subsidized from state funds. Unprofitable enterprises which are important for a national economy as a whole must be given subsidies to keep them afloat. Only this way can the industrial basis of a socialist country be developed, which is also fundamental for creating a healthy light industry, and also for the mechanization of agriculture. All this also protects the independence of a given socialist country that is surrounded by capitalist countries that intend to destroy socialism. Investments in the defense industry are also needed on a large scale.

The Soviet Union under Stalin followed these principles successfully and was even able to defeat European fascism led by Nazi Germany, which was supported by nearly all the capitalist nations, including the United States.

The basic laws of building socialism must be observed, or else!

What happens if the production plans of a country that wants to build socialism do not abide by the basic economic laws of socialism? Stalin:

---

[192] Ethan Pollock, ibid.,p. 19-20
[193] Ibid., p. 19.

The laws of science cannot be created, destroyed, abolished, changed or transformed....Laws must be taken into account. If you break a law, you'll suffer.[194]

In other words, if the leading planners of a national economy ignore the fundamental laws of a planned economy, this law will fight back, seeking "retribution," so to speak.

What will that look like?

- Economic crises, supply shortages, imbalances in the economy, price inflation, indebtedness, unemployment (at first unseen, then highly visible, etc.).

What will be the result?

- Growing dissatisfaction, growing disillusionment with the "socialist" authorities, growing rift between the leadership and the ordinary people, losing trust and turning away from them, growing passivity and fatalism, concentration on private life.

How will the authorities of such a "socialist" government react?

- They will curb public expression and criticism and resort to censorship of dissent, leading to more dissatisfaction and frustration as well as to more estrangement;

- They will look for short-term and risky solutions, such as taking out loans on the international money market, with the IMF or the World Bank or with other Western creditors, at high interest rates and with strings attached which, in turn, will further undermine central planning, since a high proportion of state funds (from exports, for example) will then have to be utilized for paying back the loans and less money will be available for the improvement of the national economy, for social welfare, housing, schooling, health care, etc. In the final analysis, such a state might go bankrupt and collapse, paving the way for a hostile takeover — a takeover by foreign corporations and the state machine they control, which will then be called "the counterrevolution." These leaders will then point their fingers at the "bad" capitalists who organized a "counterrevolution," making the public forget that they themselves caused it.

Central planning is an absolute must if one wants to develop a socialist economy, and a socialist society, at that:

---

[194] Ibid., p. 49.

Therefore we can and must have a planned economy. The planned economy is not our wish: it is unavoidable or else everything will collapse.[195]

And this is exactly what happened to the German Democratic Republic and their economy.

So if one is looking for the counterrevolution that engineered the defeat of socialism in the GDR, which to this day many German supporters of the former SED regimes are doing, it is right here before their own noses: in the neglect and disregard for the law of a planned economy.

The three main tasks of NÖSPL and the socialist facade

The official pronouncements stated that "The goal is to make a better use of the economic laws of socialism and to increase the efficiency of planning and leadership of the national economy."[196]

How would they achieve this goal of "making better use of the economic laws of socialism"?

Ulbricht in 1964:

> So the point is to achieve a certain degree of self-regulation by making good use of the economic laws of socialism and by putting the New Economic System of Planning and Leadership into practice.[197]

"More self-regulation," meaning more freedom for enterprise directors to do what they like? Turning away from central planning?

What does he mean by "economic laws of socialism"?

For the chief protagonist of the new system these laws are synonymous with the law of value or the law of profit, ruling capitalist economies, which are now given the status of "economic laws of socialism." These laws should not be hampered but, on the contrary, be set free and given prominence. Former concentration camp leader, Eric Apel, Ulbricht's favorite for putting the new system into practice, put it this way:

> One of the main tasks is to integrate a system of economic levers into the whole system of planning and leadership and make it the most important component of it.[198]

What does he mean by "economic levers"? Above all, profit:

---

[195] Ibid., p. 18.

[196] Gesetzesblatt der DDR (law gazette of the GDR), part II, no. 64, date of issue: July 18, 1963, in: Philipp Neumann, *Zurück zum Profit*, Berlin, 1977, p. 97.

[197] Walter Ulbricht, *Antworten auf aktuelle politische und ökonomische Fragen*, Berlin, 1964, pp. 23F; Ulbricht answering current political and economic questions.

[198] Erich Apel, *Neue Fragen der Planung*, Berlin, 1963, p. 9; new questions of planning.

For the enterprises the profit, for example, will become the most important measure of performance.[199]

And both Apel and Mittag in tandem:

Profit plays the central role in the system of economic levers.[200]

So profit was to become the most important component of the new system.

Officially, though, it was always emphasized that profit was only one of many "economic levers" for a "modern socialist economy." Is this true?

Four years after the demise of the GDR, on May 2, 1994, Helmut Koziolek, a close aide to Guenter Mittag, the Secretary for the Economy and one of Apel's closest collaborators, became a lot more explicit as to the real intentions of the planners. He said:

NES contained three main deliberations: first to make the profit the heart of the economic system...Second...decentralization in order to break the almighty center...and third to make property more flexible, to create socialist owner mentality...[201]

The factual ending of central planning

After the introduction of NES or NESPL, central planning was made redundant — not just in practice but also in theory. The theoretical underpinning for ending effective central planning was given by Erich Apel in 1963. Of course, the word "planning" is used all the time to make people believe that this now is "true" planning:

It is necessary to understand the correlation between the plan and the economic levers: the plan provides the framework for the functioning of economic levers and they in turn actively predetermine the tasks and the targets of the plans.[202]

So if one takes a closer look, nothing substantial is left of the plan except for a so-called framework. From now on the plans are called "prospective plans" and planning from a center is replaced by "independent planning" from below, i.e., by the enterprises themselves, or, to be more precise: by the company directors, as in ordinary capitalist countries.

In a textbook on political economy we read:

Independent planning by sub-systems [by individual enterprises — author] is not just a secondary function in the sense of breaking

---

[199] Ibid., p. 16.
[200] Erich Apel/Günter Mittag, *Planmäßige Wirtschaftsführung und ökonomische Hebel*, Berlin, 1964, p. 60; methodical economic leadership and economic levers.
[201] Theo Pirker et al, ibid., p. 257.
[202] Erich Apel, Ibid., p. 9.

down and detailing the tasks set by the state, but it is a necessary precondition of central planning.[203]

Planning from above is to be replaced by planning from below. Central planning, a core component of socialism to guarantee steady growth and a crisis-free economy, is reduced to drawing up prospective plans by providing "tasks," bearing a striking resemblance to capitalist countries where the state from time to time issues general prognoses and 'trends' on the economic development through a body of experts, also called "wise men," which then are frequently changed and modified to bring them in line with the actual economic development, driven by market forces, not by planning authorities of a state dedicated to the well-being of workers.

Wolfgang Biermann, the general director of one of the biggest East German combines, Carl Zeiss Jena, in an interview with German economists openly admitted that the reformed plan had become a mere socialist facade:

> Weinert: "I've a different question concerning planning...Is it true that directive norms were becoming less and less important for you?"
>
> Biermann: "It is true that every indicator is subject to inter-pretation..."[204]

Biermann mentions a colleague director who was supposed to produce women underwear. When he realized that jogging suits yielded a much higher profit, he simply changed over to producing track suits and remained company director although he had disobeyed the plan.[205]

If company director Biermann had a problem or was annoyed about too many directive norms coming from above, he went to the phone to talk to the Secretary of the Economy, Mr. Mittag, and soon got an appointment to sort out the problem, and he mostly got his way.[206]

Another combine chief, Christa Bertag, confirms this. She says quite frankly that after the introduction of the new economic system the central planning directives became meaningless:

> Let me put it this way: the plan was a facade, of course, which was totally unrealistic; that was obvious because the whole balance didn't work out.[207]

---

[203] *Politische Ökonomie des Sozialismus und ihre Anwendung in der DDR*, Berlin, 1969; the official textbook on politcal economy under Ulbricht, p. 345; political economy and its application

[204] Theo Pirker et al, ibid., p. 225.

[205] Ibid., p. 226.

[206] Ibid., p. 224.

[207] Ibid., p. 248.

What happens to a formerly socialist national economy if the law of a planned economy is no longer operational? Then, of course, a different law takes over: the vacuum is filled by the decisions of a company director who wants to generate the biggest possible turnover and the highest profit. Ms. Bertag again:

> We as a combine producing cosmetics, for example, had a two-digit increase in sales per year, both at home and in exports. We achieved this by investments I myself forced through.[208]

The consequences of these arbitrary investment decisions then had to be borne by the workforce: "This, of course, was hard for the people...extra shifts, etc."

The directives compiled by the GDR State Planning Committee were no longer compulsory and could be revised and "corrected" at any time. Ms. Bertag :

> These combines always fulfilled the plan because the plan was corrected.[209]

By "plan" she means the general directives and guidelines handed down from above by the state planners, either as annual or more long-term plans (7-year plans or 5-year plans).

As the indices were general in nature, they could simply be "interpreted," and if they happened to be more concrete, they could be corrected.

We have already seen how combine director Wolfgang Biermann got his plan revised. He just contacted the Secretary for the Economy, Mr. Mittag, who was one of the organizers of the new system and had nothing against correcting directives. He knew him well as all combine directors had their seat in the Central Committee of the Socialist Unity Party in East Berlin and they also knew each other well. There in the CC no ordinary workers were left anymore, no more genuine elections took place and the big shots, the industrial ministers and the combine directors of the GDR economy, had their permanent seats to make sure that they got what they wanted.[210] If Mr. Biermann needed a sum of 50 million, he got it and the Planning Committee was reprimanded.[211]

Often the plan was not taken seriously by the combine or enterprise directors. Ms. Bertag again:

---

[208] Ibid.

[209] Ibid., p. 249.

[210] Also see:Dr. Günther Wyschofsky, in: Theo Pirker, ibid., p. 210: ,You got a message that you are going to be elected'.

[211] Ibid., p. 220.

> We had 500 plan indices...For research and development alone 100. But these in their majority were not genuine figures but pseudo-figures like for example the share of women in the MMM movement [Messe der Meister von Morgen — a special fair for inventors].[212]

Wolfgang Biermann mocks the big volumes containing the planning directives: "Such a plan for a combine consisted of a classified volume of 1,200 pages, and nobody read it."[213]

Former politburo member Guenter Schabowski on the planning facade:

> At the beginning of a year the plan showed high growth rates. That was good news for the general public. In the middle of a year, however, they were made 'more precise,' in fact they were reduced...This went unnoticed by the general public. At the end of the year we had fulfilled or even over-fulfilled plans, without having achieved a substantial growth rate in comparison with the previous year...A socialist planned economy no longer existed.[214]

2. Profit as Regulator of Social Production

The new emphasis on profit

Scientific central planning had ended in the GDR after the implementation of the new economic system. We have already seen that in such a case a new regulator has to take its place. Only the profit principle could fill the vacuum. The "reformers" (in fact counter-revolutionaries) openly admitted that "The net profit occupies the central position in the system of cost accounting."[215]

The official guidelines for the new system also emphasized the predominant role of the profit for the GDR economy:

> If the economic levers are correctly applied, the profit... represents the key element of the economic performance of the VVB and the enterprises.[216]

The VVBs or Vereinigungen Volkseigener Betriebe were associations of various enterprises, which in the 1960s became combines.

---

[212] Ibid., p. 254.
[213] Ibid., p. 218.
[214] Günter Schabowski, *Das Politbüro. Ende eines Mythos*, Hamburg, 1990, pp. 115, 146; the politburo — end of a myth.
[215] *Politische Ökonomie des Sozialismus und ihre Anwendung in der DDR*, ibid., p. 793.
[216] GDR law gazette II, no. 64, July 11, 1963, in: Philipp Neumann, ibid., p. 101.

The role of profit in building socialism

But why not emphasize the role of profit in socialism? What's wrong with that? Even Stalin did that on various occasions:

> We need profit. Without profit we cannot raise reserves and accumulation, address problems of defense or satisfy social needs... Without profit it is impossible to develop our economy.[217]

Thus, at first sight, nothing seems to be wrong with it. And this is true: the law of value, and thereby profit, still plays its part in socialism, and Stalin did not deny that at all. He was likewise in favor of having profitable enterprises and strict cost accounting. However, in a truly and well-functioning socialist society there are limits to the law of value (the profit principle): This principle serves to check on the management of individual enterprises and educates their top managers to economize and not to waste valuable resources. Stalin:

> For us accounting is for statistics, for calculations, for balance. Accounting serves to control the economic leaders.[218]

The principle of maximizing profit, in socialism, no longer rules the whole economy, and individual enterprises which are not profitable for one reason or another can continue to produce if they are useful for the economy and society as such. They are not shut down if they are unprofitable, and, in that case, will receive state subsidies. Stalin again:

> For our enterprises a minimal profit is sufficient and sometimes enterprises can even work without profit at the expense of other enterprises. We ourselves distribute our means. We have very profitable, slightly profitable and completely unprofitable enterprises. In our first years, our heavy industry did not make any profits but then began to make some. In general, at first heavy industry needs capital.[219]

In a truly socialist economy, it would be impossible to build a strong and reliable heavy industry sector serving as the foundation for the well-being of the entire economy, if current profit were the principle criterion.

Where profit rules, light industry would take priority over heavy industry, especially in the first stages, since it requires less costly inputs and infrastructure build-out. But \light industry cannot serve as a basis for the whole economy!

Even in socialism, the law of value plays its part as non-state property still exists. For example: agricultural cooperatives are owned by their

---

[217] Ethan Pollock, ibid., p. 51.
[218] Ibid., p. 47.
[219] Ibid., p. 51.

members and not by the socialist state, and these members sell their goods and wares at market prices where profit rules. But if the majority of industrial property has been nationalized and central planning has become possible, the law of value then only plays a marginal role the economy. The economy as a whole is ruled by the law of planned proportional development of the national economy, whereby the profit principle is kept in check.

If one tries to resurrect profit as regulator of social production, as the GDR 'reformers' did, then it is no longer possible to have a stable and blooming socialist economy and society, or, using Stalin's words: socialism will be shut down, will inevitably collapse and will be taken over by imperialism in the long run. This is exactly what happened to the Soviet Union, to the German Democrat Republic and also to other formerly socialist countries.

What was Lenin's stance?

The GDR 'reformers' headed by Walter Ulbricht and his team of 'experts' frequently referred to Lenin who, allegedly, had also stressed the key role of profit in building socialism in the early days of the Soviet Union, in the early twenties to be more precise.

So, does Lenin belong to them and is there maybe a gap between Stalin and Lenin on this issue? Did Stalin maybe deviate from Leninism and turned to 'dogmatism' and 'sectarianism' as the leading GDR politicians and theoreticians often said?

It is true that Lenin, in the early twenties, when socialism was in its early stages in Russia, often stressed that "each and every state enterprise must cover its costs and present a profit.[220]

After the tremendous devastation caused by the World War I and the huge ravages of the Civil War in Russia, lasting four years, the economy was on its knees. It had to be restored from scratch and as soon as possible. Under these circumstances Lenin opted for a New Economic Policy, allowing a certain amount of capitalism in the economy, especially in the countryside. War Communism had come to and end. But the commanding heights, the dictatorship of the proletariat, was never given up. Socialism and capitalism were allowed to compete with one another. Shops opened again and food was available again. The alliance between the working class and the peasantry, without which socialism cannot be built, and which was about to collapse, was restored again.

---

[220] W. I. Lenin, *Die Rolle und Aufgaben der Gewerkschaften unter der Neuen Ökonomischen Politik*, in: Gesammelte Werke (selected works), vol. 33, Moscow, 1973, pp.185f; the role and the tasks of the trade unions under the New Economic Policy.

Lenin presented the enhancement of profit in state enterprises and elsewhere not as a necessary measure to build socialism or even communism but to save the country from total collapse and ruin and to give it a breathing space while making the transition. A temporary retreat had to be beaten as far as the building of socialism was concerned. Lenin:

> A free market and capitalism, both subject to state control, are now permitted and developing. On the other hand, the socialist state enterprises are being put on what is called a 'profit basis'... In view of the urgent need to make every state enterprise pay its way and show a profit, and in view of the inevitable rise in narrow departmental interests and excessive departmental zeal, this circumstance is bound to create a conflict of interests...between the masses of workers and directors of state enterprises, or the government departments in charge of them.[221]

When the economy had recovered, NEP, the New Economic Policy, was quickly ended. "For one year we were on the retreat. Now, in the name of the Party, we must say: 'Enough!' The goal we pursued with the retreat has been achieved.[222]

Lenin's NEP policy was part of his political strategy to safeguard Soviet power, to safeguard the alliance between the workers and the peasants in Soviet Russia. He considered central planning to be essential for the production — not profit. The evidence: It was Lenin who initiated the first central economic plan for the electrification of the Russian Socialist Federation, called GOELRO.

There was no rift between Lenin and Stalin in matters of political economy. Both wanted a centrally planned economy, but both favored a temporary retreat in the early twenties due to a very complicated domestic situation, demanding compromises.

Why did the GDR "reformers" champion Lenin? They could not admit openly that their real intention was the restoration of capitalism or they would have faced enormous resistance from among their own party members. So they couched their designs in socialist and Leninist phraseology and pretended to "improve," "perfect" or "modernize" socialism in the name of Leninism to legitimize their anti-Leninist project. All these terms were used in official documents.

---

[221] Lenin, ibid., pp. 184f.
[222] W. Lenin, *Ausgewählte Werke*, volume III, Berlin, 1970, p. 782; Lenin in his report to the 11th Party Congress on March 27, 1922.

3. The Realization of Profit through the Market

When exactly did profit (net profit) regain its key role in the East German economy?

> On January 1, 1964, the VVB switched over to cost accounting. This step marks the end of the preparatory stage of the Economic Reform and the beginning of its implementation.[223]

The measure was based on a directive issued by the SED politburo and called Richtlinie für das Neue Ökonomische System der Planung and Leitung der Volkswirtschaft (Guideline for the New Economic System of Planning and Leadership of the National Economy). It was not adopted by a party congress but at a special conference summoned by the Central Committee, with 950 party, state and trade union officials, economists and managers taking part.

Chief "reformer" Eric Apel closed by saying, "Now, after this conference, we shall set to work. No more ifs, ands or buts..."[224]

This way the profit principle was officially sanctioned and put into place, even though it must be said that it had taken over the economy even before this official declaration.

But how to make profit a reality, how to realize and to reap the benefits of profits? To make profit, an enterprise or combine would have to sell products as marketable commodities. Now enterprises were obliged to gear their product range to the market, to the existing purchasing power and the effective demand for the product.

Consequently, market assessment and market research became more and more important. Therefore, the official textbook compiled after the 6th Party Congress that had adopted the reform also stressed sales orientation.[225] Now the quality of products was to reach "world market standards" (Weltmarktfähigkeit). Production planners had to take this into account.

The GDR "reformers" were wise enough not to use Western terms, such as public relations, advertising, market research, after-sales service, etc., instead they used their own terminology like Marktarbeit (market work), Verkaufsaktivität (sales activity) that sounded more Marxist.

Wolfgang Biermann, General Director of VEB Carl Zeiss Jena (VEB=volkseigener Betrieb, enterprise in people's ownership), saysthat advertising and PR played a key role in his corporation:

[223] Jörg Roesler, *Zwischen Plan und Markt. Die Wirtschaftsreform in der DDR zwischen 1963 und 1970*, ibid., S. 31.
[224] Ibid.
[225] *Politische Ökonomie des Sozialismus und ihre Anwendung in der DDR*, ibid., p. 795.

We had an advertising department of our own; we printed our own prospectuses, catalogs, logos, envelopes — everything was homemade. Till the very end, I had a fair pavilion of my own in the city of Leipzig, the Zeiss-Pavilion. It cost us 50 million and was the property of our combine.[226]

But what is wrong with a demand-oriented company strategy even in socialism? Is this not the same as what Stalin once defined as the basic law of socialism: to satisfy the growing material and cultural needs of the population to a maximum? Aren't material and cultural needs identical with "effective demand"? Isn't social demand the same as effective demand, the demand in a given market?

No, it is not! William B. Bland explains:

> ...the unequal distribution of income is inherent in capitalist societies, so that this causes 'effective demand' to bear little resemblance to real social demand, to the real requirements of the consuming public — leading, for example, to the building of superfluous office blocks while working people experience a fundamental housing shortage, since the social demand for houses is overridden by the effective demand for office blocks.[227]

So "effective demand" is not the same as "social demand," expressing the needs of the people and not that of the market.

But was the distribution of income really unequal in the GDR? If not, if there was a high degree of equality of income, as is still maintained by apologists of the GDR, there must still have been a prevalence of social demand over effective demand.

Let's have a brief look at income distribution in the GDR in 1975, 12 years after the economic reform:

Gross income of top earners	GDR marks
Head physician	6,000–10,000
Natural scientist/engineer in R&D	3,000–15,000
Politburo member	5,000
Minister	ca 4,500
Army officer or general	ca 2,500–4,500
Professor	2,500–4,500
First regional secretary of the SED	3,500

---

[226] Wolfgang Biermann, in: Theo Pirker et al, ibid., p. 216.

[227] William B. Bland, *The Restoration of Capitalism in the Soviet Union*, at: http://www.oneparty.co.uk/html/book/ussrindex.html, chapter 1: The Socialist Market, no page.

Director of an industrial combine	ca. 2,000–3,500
Chairman of a regional council	ca. 2,500

(Source: Heinz Vortmann, 1985)[228]

Next, we have the gross average monthly income of fully employed workers and salaried employees in nationalized enterprises, by economic sectors, 1974.[229]

Monthly income, workers/ salaried employees in nationalized enterprises	GDR marks
Total	867
Industry	865
Construction	922
Agro	859
Transport	954
Post	801
Domestic Trade	767

Frank Goetz and Dieter Voigt, two GDR sociologists, also collected data on income differentials in their country in the late sixties and early seventies. In 1970, the lowest income, that of a messenger in an industrial enterprise, was 340 marks; the highest, that of a general director, was approximately 3,000 marks, according to their findings.

Earnings from bonuses, however, were not included. Had they been, they would have revealed even sharper income differentials, as high-income earners benefited most from the bonus system introduced as part of the economic reform.

These studies provide evidence of the fact that unequal distribution of income actually did exist in the GDR. What does this lead to? A Soviet economist explained:

> The unequal distribution of income between different sections of the population leads to the lower groups not being able to

---

[228] In: Mike Dennis, *German Democratic Republic. Politics, Economics and Society*, ibid., p. 55.
[229] Statistical Yearbook of the German Democratic Republic, 1986, Berlin, 1986, in: ibid., p. 56.

completely satisfy their elementary needs, while the higher income brackets are able to satisfy less urgent essential needs.[230]

In other words: in view of unequal income distribution, effective demand no longer reflects the real needs of a given society but the needs of those who possess high or relatively high money income. In such circumstances, market demand no longer mirrors social demand — the demand of the majority of the population.

To satisfied effective demand is not the same as to satisfy the "always growing material and cultural needs of the population," as Stalin put it when describing the basic law of a socialist society. It is synonymous with satisfying the demands of those who have the money. This leads us to the conclusion that the demand of the market has little or nothing to do with satisfying social demands. They are two different things.

"I don't produce what is needed but what yields the highest profit for me,[231] said the general director of a GDR combine manufacturing machine tools in a conversation with GDR planning chief, Gerhard Schuerer.

Thus, after the introduction of the "economic reform," the GDR enterprises acted like ordinary capitalist enterprises, trying to satisfy effective market demand but no longer social demands. They were no longer "socialist," and to call them "socialist enterprises" was mere propaganda to mislead the general public.

4. Means of Production Becoming Commodities

Profit rate = profit relative to productive assets or capital, in percent

To put the profit rate on a sound footing, the means of production or assets (for example, fixed assets like real estate, buildings, machines but also circulating assets, such as labor, work material, etc.) had to be acquired by the enterprises or combines themselves. Before the 'economic reform,' the state provided these assets free of charge.

One of the pioneers of the Soviet "economic reform," the economist L. A. Leontiev, once put it this way:

> To make use of profit as a criterion for the profitability of a given enterprise, it is necessary to solve the problem of payment for productive assets...The introduction of the principle that

---

[230] Rumiantzev, A. M., *The Management of the Soviet Economy today. Basic Principles*, in: William B. Bland, ibid., chapter 1, no page.
[231] In: André Steiner, ibid., p. 158.

productive assets have to be paid for, would be a powerful incentive for a better utilization of these assets.[232]

In September 1964, the principle that enterprises had to pay for their productive assets, for capital, that is, was approved by the CC of the CPSU. In the GDR the same principle was adopted three years later, in 1967, when a tax on capital with the mysterious name of Produktionsfondsabgabe (production fund charge) was introduced. From then on, every enterprise, or directorate of an enterprise or combine, had to pay a certain amount of money to the state — a sort of a tax or interest rate for the capital used.[233]

In Marshal Tito's Yugoslavia this instrument already had been invented by his reformers in the second half of the fifties.

At first, this charge on productive assets was calculated as a fixed percentage on the existing production funds. Originally, it was only 1%, then 4%, and finally it reached 6%.[234]

In February of 1967, the charge was made compulsory. From then on, all GDR enterprises became leaseholders of state property, and each and every company or combine had to pay a 6% rate of interest to the state, thereby changing state-owned property into private capital — a fact which was, of course, vehemently denied by the 'reformers,' arguing that "Payment for productive assets...is completely different from interest on capital."[235]

Unofficially however, it was admitted that these assets had actually become capital on which a certain amount of interest had to be paid:

> One of the most important components of the new system...is the introduction of obligatory payment for capital.[236]

Western analysts, keeping a close eye on what was going on in the GDR, soon found out that this measure had wide-ranging implications for the whole economic system. André Steiner:

> This interest on productive means...was seen by Western analysts as the number-one measure with wide-ranging implications for the whole system.[237]

---

[232] L. A. Leontiev, *The Plan and the Methods of Economic Management*, in: *Pravda*, September 7, 1964, in: William B. Bland, *The Restoration of Capitalism in the Soviet Union*, ibid., no page.

[233] Philipp Neumann, ibid., p. 164.

[234] Jörg Roesler, ibid., p. 58, citing GDR law gazette II, February 2, 1967, p. 115.

[235] Rakitzki, B., *The Bourgeois Interpretation of the Soviet Economic Reform*, in: William B. Bland, ibid.

[236] R. Krylov et al, *On the Procedure and the Conditions of Switching over to the New System*, in: ibid.

[237] André Steiner, ibid., p. 236.

The enterprises, now being able to rent the formerly nationally owned property (or state property) by paying a fixed annual rate of interest, were now also given the right to sell their productive assets, or their capital, like a commodity if it was no longer needed. Simply put, unused machines and plants were sold.[238]

Steiner notes that in one of those factories being used for experiments in the preparatory stages of the 'reform,' "four-fifths of...the installations were sold."[239]

Professor Dr. Helmut Koziolek, one of the economists on Guenter Mittag's team of "reformers," confirms:

> As far as property was concerned, it is clear that the NES people were enemies of the foggy and general term of people's property. This property was wobbly...I was an advocate of a people's property that was handled economically by the administrators of this property as property of the economic units, if you like — to push forward the idea of profits...[240]

For the professor, "people's property" should be handled as "property of the economic units" (the enterprises led by a top manager called director) leaving the term "people's property" null and void.

At that time nobody dared to admit that people's property no longer existed in the GDR, but after the collapse of the country, it could be freely admitted.

Company directors now became capitalists and were allowed to sell unused, outmoded means of production and could also purchase new productive assets even abroad.

Combine director of "VEB" Carl-Zeiss Jena, Wolfgang Biermann:

> And this combine...owned eight mixed capitalist companies, with me as the main shareholder. We had these so-called mixed companies in England, in France, in Italy, in Austria, in Brazil... which were administered by a citizen of the respective country, but his deputy was from the GDR who was sent there by me and we had 99% of the shares in our safe.[241]

Since when exactly was it possible in the former GDR to sell and buy means of production and to treat them as commodities?

---

[238] Ibid., p. 246.
[239] Ibid.
[240] Helmut Koziolek, in: Theo Pirker, et al, ibid., p. 257. Koziolek was director of the Central Institute for Socialist Economic Leadership in the GDR and member of the Central Committee of the SED.
[241] Wolfgang Biermann, in: Theo Pirker et al, ibid., p. 216.

It all started in 1959, when a decree was issued, allowing the sale of MTS, machine and tractor stations owned by the state, to the Agricultural Producers' Cooperatives, also called LPG (Landwirtschaftliche Produktionsgenossenschaften). Thus, the members of such a cooperative became owners, proprietors of means of production and were permitted to sell these means if they saw fit. From then on the people in the GDR kolkhoz enjoyed a special status in the GDR, the status of capitalist proprietors who also acted like that in practice; in fact, they had to.

We have already mentioned this. It was a measure modeled after what Khrushchev had done in the Soviet Union a year before, even though the Party Congress of the CPSU held in February of 1956 did not allow him to do that. It had guaranteed the old status of the MTS. So it was illegal, and the Ulbricht people imitated this illegal act in their own country to show allegiance to the Khrushchev regime and, at the same time, to justify similar measures if criticism was raised.

From that time on the main difference between a socialist economy and a capitalist one became blurred. Stalin, however, had very clear and outspoken views on this difference. In his conversations with reform-minded Soviet economists who were writing a new textbook on political economy, he told them this in the early fifties:

> All our enterprises are unified; for them [for the capitalists — author] a few trusts or cartels can be unified within narrow parameters, but they are not capable of organizing the entire economy...Make it simple: for us things are unified, for them things are disconnected...They have a disconnected economy, property is disconnected, but here socialist property is unified.[242]

As soon as the means of production become commodities, which can be bought and sold and also pawned, the socialist property is gone — gone for good. The GDR heads of combines and enterprises, the well-paid and powerful company directors, became capitalist managers and even capitalists who followed their own special interests; they had long since ceased to be state employees the way they were in Stalin's times. Their production units There was a disconnect from the rest of the economy, enterprises were no longer unified under one roof. And this in turn also destroyed the unified population, created dissatisfaction, chaos, splits and petty self-interest. The people who suffered most from the new situation were the ordinary people, the GDR underdogs.

By regaining the quality of capital, the relationship of exploitation between the owners of means of production, the leaders of enterprises

---

[242] Ethan Pollock, ibid., p. 19.

who are now also allowed to hire and fire workers and ordinary employees, developed into a new class of proprietors, a new class of the privileged few. The state authorities in the shape of the SED nomenclature became the midwife of a new capital relationship between the exploited working class of the GDR and its exploiters of company directors and their managerial staff.

In his interview with German economists, Wolfgang Biermann (combine chief of Carl-Zeiss Jena, an arms manufacturer with 70,000 employees), became very frank and talkative and told them about all the nice things he was allowed to do:

> Zeiss had its own police department, its own firefighters, its own customs clearance.[243]

They even had their own bank with thirteen clerks and income from their foreign exports went to their own bank in Jena; the top managers were allowed to travel to the West and spend their vacations there — something unthinkable for the ordinary GDR citizen; Zeiss employees received copious old-age pensions which were two or three times as high as the ordinary state pension; they had their own statute never questioned by the authorities, they had cars and houses. Biermann, boasting about his pay:

> I was the best-paid general director in the GDR and got 4,500 marks gross per month and on top of that a year-end bonus which amounted to 80% of my gross salary.[244]

And, of course, he had his permanent seat on the Central Committee of the 'Socialist' Unity Party. Biermann, the prototype of the new GDR manager class.

5. The New Banking and Credit System

After the 6th Party Congress in January 1963, when NESPL was adopted, profit became the main criterion for GDR company directors to manage their enterprises, and the profit rate, the amount of profit in relation to the total costs of production, became the most important indicator to judge an enterprise, its economic standing, its "good" or "bad" management, its "good" or "bad" performance or its credit rating. To make profit a reality, the old practice of state subsidies had to be scrapped or only to be permitted as an exception to the rule.

---

[243] Wolfgang Biermann in: Theo Pirker et al, ibid., p. 229.
[244] Ibid., p. 222.

Financial handouts to enterprises could no longer be given free of charge, but had to be paid for: a fixed interest rate had to be charged, turning the former state subsidies into bank-credits. It goes without saying that these loans or credits had to be repaid after a certain amount of time.

Gerd-Jan Krol wrote a book on the GDR economic reform process; he puts it this way:

> In principle, the individual enterprise has no right to receive hand-outs from the state budget anymore. Through good and careful management it must obtain the necessary means for sustaining and expanding production (investments and premium funds in the first place) as well as the taxes fixed by its superiors (mainly interest on capital and part of the profit which has to be transferred to the state) solely by itself.[245]

There were two decrees revoking the previous right of enterprises to receive state subsidies free of charge: the first one was issued in 1964 and the second three years later, in 1967.

While the first decree on investments stipulated that the enterprises and associations of nationalized industries, VVB for short, were now obliged to invest on their own account according to the maxim of self-financing or inside financing, the second one from 1967 forced the companies to take out loans for those investments which could not be financed by them alone (outside financing).

This implied that creditors were now in very strong position and were able to control the investment activities of the debtor enterprise by targeting crediting. As banks also had to follow the profit principle like all the other economic units in the country, this made them of course prioritizing favorable credit handouts to those clients being in a position to guarantee early and reliable repayment. Of course, highly profitable enterprises or combines (groups of enterprises under one administrative roof) benefited most from the new rules and regulations which inevitable led to a wider gap between these companies and those who were less profitable or not even profitable at all, creating disproportions in the economy.

These unprofitable enterprises were now forced to take out huge loans to make ends meet and to become profitable, thus becoming more and more dependent on the lenders. This was even admitted in the official GDR textbook on political economy:

---

[245] Gerd-Jan Krol, *Die Wirtschaftsreform in der DDR und ihre Ursachen*, Tübingen, 1972, p. 126; the economic reform in the GDR and its causes.

> This economic leverage has the effect that the enterprise, by taking out loans, makes itself dependent on the bank granting the loan.[246]

—So this was the desired effect.

What kind of banks were these lenders? Were they really 'socialist' banks as they were officially called? No, they were ordinary capitalist banks abiding by the profit principle. Thus formerly state-owned banks, socialist banks, were transformed into commercial banks or even full-blooded investment banks. The official wording:

> It is an objective necessity to have banks operating like commercial banks.[247]

It also became "an objective necessity" to transform the entire banking sector, to "perestroika" it in ways similar to what was done in the industrial and agricultural sectors. Joerg Roesler was a supporter of these measures:

> The banking sector underwent a considerable transformation in late 1967. The German Central Bank (Deutsche Notenbank) and the German Investment Bank (Deutsche Investitionsbank) were taken over by the Bank of Industry and Commerce of the GDR (Industrie- und Handelsbank der DDR) as a commercial bank for industry, construction, trade and communications. The bank was run on cost accounting lines, i.e., it granted credits not on the basis of state directives but with a view to improving its own profitability.[248]

Some big combines even had their own private banks, among them Carl-Zeiss. This was illegal, but nobody cared. Wolfgang Biermann in an interview with German economists:

> Our branch enabled us to negotiate favorable interest rates...The person in charge then got a bonus. It was illegal, but that was the way it was.[249]

Biermann's remark shows that the big combines (Kombinate), being fairly profitable and financially sound, benefited most from the banking reform, and these "socialist" concerns were not economically dependent on the new restructured commercial GDR banks either. They had excellent contacts to the GDR nomenclature right to the very top to arrange favorable credit terms for themselves and mostly got what they wanted.

---

[246] *Politische Ökonomie des Sozialismus und ihre Anwendung in der DDR*, ibid., p. 821.
[247] Ibid.
[248] Jörg Roesler, *Zwischen Plan und Markt*, ibid., p. 62.
[249] Wolfgang Biermann, in: Theo Pirker et al, ibid., p. 217.

So the tasks and the role of banks changed fundamentally in the wake of the 'economic reform.' Previously, they had been administrative bodies of the state which saw to it that investments without no — or very low — interest rates could be made in line with the state plan, serving those regions where the need for investments was highest. Now, they had become relatively autonomous institutions, working independently on the basis of the profit principle and were trying to reap the highest possible profit. Credit was no longer allowed free of charge in order to foster the proportionate development of the socialist economy but were negotiated with the economic units with a lot of haggling involved, and those big units being most profitable got the best conditions and those least profitable the worst.

These were now capitalist banks, but for reasons of public consumption they were still called socialist — "socialist" investment banks or "socialist" commercial banks. The veneer of socialism was still a must.

6. The Reform of Industrial Prices

The denunciation of Stalin

In the era of socialism, Stalin's Soviet Union and in the first period of the GDR in the late forties and early fifties, prices were generally fixed by the state according to social needs, even though the value of goods had to be taken into account. As long as commodity production exists, which is still the case in the first stage of communism, also called socialism, this law exerts an influence on prices which cannot be ignored at will. Stalin:

> Sometimes the question is asked: does the law of value exist in our socialist system and does it exert an influence? Yes, it exists and is influential. Where you have commodities and commodity production, the law of value is automatically at work..[250]

The law of value not only exists in the sphere of commodity circulation but also in production, but this law is no longer the regulator of social production in socialism:

> However, the law of value in our socialist production has no regulatory importance.[251]

In socialism the law of a planned economy is in charge as there is no private property of means of production and these means are by and large

---

[250] J. W. Stalin, *Ökonomische Probleme des Sozialismus in der Sowjetunion*, ibid., p. 20.
[251] Ibid.

nationalized. This is the precondition to keep the law of value limited and in check. This led to an uninterrupted economic growth in the Soviet Union without the usual cyclical crises typical of capitalist economies. Growth rates in the USSR were much higher than in capitalist countries and often exceeded more than 10% annually — much to the envy of the protagonists of capitalism in imperialist states who were faced with crises on a regular basis, leading to chaos in production, chronic unemployment, price inflation and "minus growth." The Soviet Union remained completely unaffected by the Great Depression in the years 1929–1932 for example.

In foreign trade the law of value also existed as imported goods are priced according to their value in capitalist countries. Nevertheless, prices in the Soviet Union under Stalin were kept down by subsidies to avoid price inflation on goods that were urgently needed.

The protagonists of the GDR "economic reform" called Stalin's views "dogmatic" and 'sectarian' to discredit him and to not allow a genuine public discussion on the matter. As long as Stalin lived, there was such a debate, especially in the early fifties in which he was taking an active part. There was a lively discussion in the new textbook previously mentioned. But the GDR 'reformers' did not want such an open debate. Without an public discussion, the law of value was rehabilitated and became a 'law for the building of socialism.' In textbook on political economy published in 1969 we read, "The value...is the key category of socialist commodity production."[252]

Eric Apel and Guenter Mittag, whom we have already met on several occasions, were especially outspoken on Stalin:

> In contrast to Stalin's theses, the law of value exerts its influence in all spheres of socialist production.[253]

Stalin's theses! The two authors, referring to one of Walter Ulbricht's speeches, call the law of value "a genuine economic law of socialism" which supposedly operates on the basis of socialist property relations and is "closely connected to them"[254]

Thus, the most important law of a capitalist economy, the law of value, was allegedly also a "genuine law of socialism"!

This was done to mislead the East Germans and especially the working people, who were told:

---

[252] *Politische Ökonomie des Sozialismus und ihre Anwendung*, ibid., p. 275.
[253] Erich Apel, Günter Mittag, *Planmäßige Wirtschaftsführung und ökonomische Hebel*, Berlin, 1964, p. 57; planned economic leadership and economic levers.
[254] Ibid.,p. 27.

Look what we are doing! It is only in the interest of socialism! You're going to get a better socialism and you'll benefit from it! Just wait and see!

A closer look at the law of value

In *Das Kapital* (volume 3), an analysis of capitalism which has never been surpassed, Karl Marx explained the basic law ruling a capitalist economy: the law of value:

W = k + m, or: commodity value = cost price + surplus value.[255]

The price for the manufacture of a commodity equals its manufacturing costs, plus an average profit. Marx wrote, "The production price of a commodity therefore equals its cost price plus...an average profit."[256]

In capitalism, the price of a commodity roughly equals its value.

It happens that this is not always the case, but under normal circumstances it is: the production price comes close to the value of a commodity.

So, if you reintroduce the law of value as the regulator of social production for the whole of a given economy, where so far the law of value has been kept in check through good and sound planning, then this economy is ruled by the same law by which a capitalist economy is governed. Does this makes sense for a socialist-minded person?

Paradoxically it means trying to rule socialism by capitalist laws and principles. In other words: you introduce capitalism in a formerly socialist economy ruled by the law of proportional planning of the economy. In a socialist economy there is a gap between the value of a commodity and its price. Normally, prices are much lower due to state subsidies.

New price fixing

The need to bring the price of commodities into the closest possible equivalent with their value was the reason for the reform of wholesale prices of industrial products. It was already mentioned in the new party manifesto of the SED adopted by the 6th Party Congress in January of 1963. Apel and Mittag, citing the new manifesto:

> The price formation system has to be rearranged in such a way that the socially required labor will become the basis of pricing and that state subsidies will no longer be necessary in the future.[257]
> The result: huge price increases.

---

[255] Karl Marx, *Das Kapital*, Dritter Band, Berlin, 1969, p. 34; capital, vol. 3.
[256] Ibid., p. 167.
[257] Erich Apel, Günter Mittag, ibid., p. 83, citing the new SED manifesto.

According to the schedule for the price reform, industrial prices of basic and raw materials were to rise by 70% as from 1964–1965, with semi-manufactured goods rising by 40% and manufactured goods by 4% (from 1964).[258]

Principally, prices were to be fixed where they originated: "23% by the bodies for price formation; 77% by the VVB and enterprises.[259]

The price reform was put in place in three stages to avoid chaos and social unrest. The last stage ended in January 1967.[260]

For the first stage, an official committee under the chairmanship of Finance Minister Willy Rumpf was set up, also called State Committee for Prices. Soon more than 100 working groups mushroomed to get things done.

During the first two stages the new system was valid only for manufactures. Obviously, one did not want to rush things in order to avoid sharp price increases for GDR consumers. They were well aware that sharp price increases had played an important part for the rebellion on June 17, 1953.

To avoid a watershed in this first stage, price groups were introduced: certain products, such as consumer goods, were put into a lower price category to avoid sudden price inflation and subsequent political upheavals; prices of a higher category, however, were permitted to rise freely as they were considered not so sensitive. The big combines made copious use of it.

As these "socialist groups of companies" (Walter Ulbricht's words) were monopolies without any competitors in their product range, they of course used their dominant position in the market to restrict the production of goods belonging to the lower categories and favored those of the higher ones which led to creeping price inflation.[261]

Still in the first stage, a so-called regulatory system for industrial prices was created called Industriepreisregelungsgesetz (law on regulating industrial prices) to motivate enterprises to lower their prices. This became a flop because the big combines (there were altogether 159, created in 1968–1969) used their newly won autonomy to avoid price reductions to safeguard their profits. Instead...

> they used their newly-won autonomy to manipulate the product range.[262]

---

[258] Philipp Neumann, ibid., p. 152.
[259] Ibid., p. 160.
[260] André Steiner, ibid., p. 208.
[261] Philipp Neumann, ibid., p. 161.
[262] Ibid.

So decentralization of price formation had its price:

> By decentralizing the formation of prices and by introducing
> various new types of prices, the enterprises were given room to
> maneuver to put up prices surreptitiously or openly without
> higher performance and at the expense of the society in order to
> increase their profits.[263]

Is this kind of decentralized price formation compatible with a centrally planned economy?

According to the official propaganda it was of course:

> To ensure the full functioning of the prospective plan, the
> permanent implementation of prices [by combines and enterprises
> — author]..is essential.[264]

But even before the collapse of the GDR in 1989, the long-time chief of the State Planning Committee, Gerhard Schuerer, admitted that it had become virtually impossible to control prices. In 1968, it became obvious that there was no overall picture left to check on price alterations being made, following the industrial price reform.[265]

So Schuerer had to admit that his State Planning Committee had lost any leverage over combines and other enterprises if they wanted to increase prices. The real power over price formation had been lost, but also the power to give directions in general:

> We neither had the right to give directions to general directors
> nor to do something. The general directors were led by Guenter
> Mittag politically and by the branch minister economically. The
> planning we did combine-wise in our State Planning Committee,
> but these calculations were handed down to the branch minister
> only as general guidelines.[266]

But there were industrial and other ministers left. Did they at least have some influence on general directors. Could they issue directives and tell them what to do?

Wolfgang Biermann:

> Excuse me, but the ministers were poor sods. They were just grains
> between the millstones; at the top the Politburo and the Central
> Committee were grinding, then there were the ministers and
> below the grass roots, the combines with their general directors.[267]

---

[263] Ibid., p. 184.
[264] Politische Ökonomie und ihre Anwendung in der DDR, ibid.,, p. 799.
[265] André Steiner, ibid., p. 260.
[266] Gerhard Schürer, in: Theo Pirker, ibid., p. 83.
[267] Wolfgang Biermann, in: ibid., p. 222.

But if it is true that neither the State Planning Committee nor the industrial ministers had the necessary clout to check on price formation and price developments, then the central plan which was compiled by this committee, could not have any either. The plan only contained a multitude of non-binding guidelines on prices and other things which, however, could not be enforced by law, which could be observed but did not have to. Later, in the early seventies this was slightly changed when a freeze on consumer prices was enforced. More on that, see below.

The consequences

In the late sixties the drawbacks of the new pricing system became obvious:

> Prices of a whole series of consumer goods started rising and products of lower price categories disappeared from the product range, as the profit-hungry enterprises could reach their targets much better by price increases, variations of product ranges or by excessive cost calculations.[268]

In 1970 alone, more than 200 price increases occurred in the retail sector.[269] Enormous supply shortages ensued as enterprises refused to invest in cheap products:

> Again and again reports are made according to which enterprises are canceling or reducing heir production as it is no longer profitable. In 1970, for example, toothbrushes, spark plugs and various other items were in short supply only because their production had been transferred or diminished.[270]

Similar developments occurred in neighboring Poland where roughly the same 'economic reforms' were under way with prices being "reformed" — however a lot more ruthlessly.

In December 1970, the Szczecin dockworkers went on strike. Szczecin (Stettin, in German) is a port in north-west Poland situated on the river Oder, only about 20 kilometers away from the GDR border. Massive price hikes had caused the rebellion. The workers stormed the Party headquarters of the United Polish Workers' Party, set it ablaze and started singing the International. One month later, on January 19, 1971, another wave of protests and more uprisings rocked the Polish town whose port was of key importance for the Polish economy.

The GDR establishment was shocked. To prevent similar events from happening in East Germany, and lessons from the Berlin rising of

---

[268] Philipp Neumann, ibid., p. 199.
[269] Ibid., p. 184.
[270] Ibid.

June 1953 having been learned, which had also been triggered by price increases, the Politburo soon took a decision not to allow any further price increases in the retail trade sector.[271]

But now, only by massive state subsidies could sustain the frozen retail prices. Billions had to be spent on consumer price subsidies. Naturally, these huge sums could have been spent much more sensibly if central planning had not been undermined in the first place. So these sums of money were now no longer available for other urgent needs, among them city renovations, infrastructure projects, for cleaning up the environment, etc.

But for political reasons it was considered a must to have stable retail prices. The illusion that the state of the GDR was still socialist had to be preserved by all means possible to guarantee the political stability of the country. It became the centerpiece of the new strategy adopted by the 8th Party Congress in 1971, which was baptized Unity of Economic and Social Policy. Also a new face had to be at the helm of the Party. His name: Eric Honecker who became General Secretary of the Socialist Unity Party and Ulbricht, with the consent of the Soviet leadership in Moscow (Brezhnev/Kosygin), was sent into retirement while on holiday in the Soviet Union.

7. Self-financing

In Stalin's Soviet Union the enterprises received all the necessary means from the state to finance the investments they were obliged to make under a legally binding five-year-plan. They were given free of charge all the necessary funds to finance buildings, technical equipment, and other production assets, also called "basic funds"; they were also given free of charge all the necessary means to finance raw materials, semi-manufactured goods, and other materials, also called "operational funds."

Alternatively, the Soviet state bank provided them with cheap short-term credits to be able to finance these things. The interest rate for these loans was stipulated by the state and not by the money market and was generally low.

The main part of the operational profit of an enterprise had to be transferred to the state budget. Another smaller portion could be retained in the company budget to fuel the director's special funds and to be able

---

[271] Also see: André Steiner, ibid., p. 264.

to finance material incentives in the form of bonuses as a reward for plan fulfillment.[272]

This tried and tested practice guaranteed that even completely non-profitable companies, mostly those in the investment-intensive heavy industry, were also able to expand their production.

After the war, a similar practice was introduced in the early years of the GDR, when the first two-year-plan for the years 1948–1950 had been adopted. This ended with the introduction of the "economic reform" — in the Soviet Union adopted in 1965, in the GDR even a little earlier, in 1963. Now the individual profitability of an enterprise or combine was most important. To make it happen, it was necessary that the share of profit a company was allowed to retain for itself had to be raised substantially and, vice versa, that of the state had to be diminished accordingly. To quote an example: between 1968 and 1969 the net profit transfers to the state in the industrial sector decreased by 4.4% to reach 40.6% from 45% in the previous year.[273]

Only exceptionally did the state provide funds to an enterprise free of charge: in case such an enterprise belonged to a sector of "structural importance" and was to help developing ambitious projects, such as microelectronics, which was highly cost-intensive. A single enterprise, and not even a mighty combine, was unable to afford these huge investments.

Since enterprises were now free to take out loans in great quantities, a growing proportion of company profits had to be retained for repayment purposes.

So GDR enterprises now had to make investments mainly by themselves, using their own means independent of whether they belonged to the heavy or light industrial sector. As light industry is not as cost intensive as heavy industry, enterprises of the heavy industry were clearly disadvantaged.

8. Concentration and Centralization of Capital

Once the basic law of capitalism is restored (to produce surplus value in the shape of profits), all the other capitalist laws are also released and can develop freely. One of these laws is the law of growing concentration

---

[272] Also see: S. Gurowich, *Die Leitungsprinzipien in einem sowjetischen Industrieunternehmen*, in: Neue Welt, July 1948, no. 13, p. 160; leadership principles for a Soviet industrial enterprise.

[273] See: André Steiner, ibid., p. 482, table 4.14.

of means of production (or capital) in the hands of fewer and fewer capital owners. Karl Marx:

> The specific capitalist mode of production...causes...accelerated accumulation of capital Every accumulation becomes the means of new accumulation. With increasing mass of wealth functioning as capital, accumulation increases..[274]

This trend could also be seen in the GDR where capitalism was restored after the introduction of the 'economic reform':

> The merger of nationalized enterprises to become high performance combines has proved successful. This was in line with the economic law of increased concentration of production the conditions of which have ripened over the past few years.[275]

This process of concentration of capital in fewer and fewer hands was deliberately encouraged by the SED leadership:

> Concentration of production in socialism develops systematically and according to plan.[276]

A considerable enlargement of enterprises was envisaged:

> Along with the scientific technological progress the...size of enterprises is growing.[277]

Simultaneously, centralization of capital — the merger of enterprises that is — was fostered:

> Growing concentration is accompanied by centralization of production. Centralization of production means merging enterprises to create larger economic units — above all combines. Combines provide preconditions for the utilization of the advantages of concentration, specialization, combination, and cooperation.[278]

The high level of concentration and centralization of capital achieved in 1971 for example is demonstrated by the following figures: 55% of gross industrial production was created by 305 large enterprises, equaling 2.7% of all economic units where 46.2% of all working people were employed. The 34 largest enterprises employing 13.6% of the total GDR workforce produced more than one fifth of gross industrial product.[279]

---

[274] Karl Marx, *Das Kapital*, Band I, Berlin, 1971, p. 653; Capital, vol. 1.

[275] *Protokoll des Achten Parteitags der SED*, Band 1, Berlin, 1971, p. 77.

[276] *Politische Ökonomie des Sozialismus und ihre Anwendung*, ibid., p. 615.

[277] *Politische Ökonomie des Kapitalismus und Sozialismus*, Berlin, 1982, p. 576.

[278] Ibid., p. 621.

[279] Ibid., p. 620, note 11, calculated on figures provided by *Statistisches Jahrbuch der DDR*, Berlin, 1973, p. 122; from the Statistical Yearbook of the GDR.

Only four years later, in 1975,

> 45.4% gross industrial production was created by 241 large enterprises, equaling 2.9% of all economic units where 43.3 Percent of all working people were employed. The 20 largest enterprises produced almost 10% of gross industrial production.[280]

Undoubtedly, this considerable increase in concentration and centralization of capital over a period of only four years was mainly due to the creation of a growing number of combines.

The formation of combines started in 1967 on the basis of a decision taken by the Central Committee of the SED in July 1967. Walter Ulbricht:

> Combines must be established where the objective conditions for the effectiveness of VVB as economic leaders no longer exist to place the whole complicated production process...under one unified leadership. Research institutes, suppliers, production centers, and partly also foreign trade enterprises belong to combines.[281]

In 1967, 17 combines were founded and in 1968, one fourth of the total GDR workforce was employed in 35 monopolies; in 1970, already 120 combines were up and running.[282]

Entire combines were amalgamated, starting from 1978–79. This way Robotron came into being where 70,000 people were employed.[283]

This process of concentration and centralization led to a reduced role for leaders of ordinary individual enterprises on the one hand; on the other, the standing, influence and power of a combine director grew, but it also had the effect that the central plan, now called 'prospective plan,' became even less and less important. The general director himself had a hand in drawing up the plans:

> In general, it is the leader of a combine who, on account of his permanent contacts with the industrial minister, influences the planning process and determines the targets being relevant for his enterprise.[284]

As a result of this process of concentration and centralization more and more power and influence was concentrated in the hands of economic leaders whose position within the new bourgeoisie grew considerably. Side by side with the Party leaders and the state who represented the

---

[280] Ibid., p. 577.
[281] W. Ulbricht in: Jörg Roesler, ibid., p. 67.
[282] Deutsches Institut für Wirtschaftsforschung, ed., *Handbuch DDR-Wirtschaft*, Berlin, 1984, p. 89; handbook of GDR economy.
[283] J. Bethkenhagen et al, *DDR und Osteuropa. Ein Handbuch*, Opladen, 1981, p. 75.
[284] Ibid., p. 92.

overall interests of the new GDR elites, they now found themselves at the very top of the hierarchy, representing special class interests they lobbied for.

History repeats itself if one refuses to learn from it: in 1946, a referendum was held in the province of Saxony to nationalize the big German monopolies who had supported the Nazi regime between 1933 and 1945. Then, three quarters of the electorate voted in favor of nationalization to once and for all break the power of German monopolies in line with basic decisions taken at the Potsdam Conference of the "Big Four" in Berlin in July of 1945.

Twenty years later, the monopolies were also reinvented in the GDR — in the Federal Republic their rebirth had even started in the early fifties. The only difference: now they were given a "socialist" label and called "combine."

9. The New Premium System

Under socialism in Stalin's times, premium funds were quite a common phenomenon. On the one hand they were financed by the state to "raise the quality of labor and its productivity."[285]

In this context, the funds for inventions and rationalization should be mentioned. On the other, there were the special directors' funds of enterprises being financed from operational profits to provide material incentives for the fulfillment or over-fulfillment of the state plan.

This fund, however, was not dependent on the profit of a given enterprise, but on the fulfillment of the production plan. There was no link between profits and premiums but only between plan fulfillment and premiums.

Prior to the "economic reform" in the GDR, the directors' fund consisted of two parts: one for cultural and social purposes and the other to enhance performance.[286] Only one percent was used for the performance-related fund. Although the directives on premiums were gradually changed, the means provided for performance-related premiums remained below the threshold of making premiums an independent means of stimulation, as Philipp Neumann tells us.[287]

---

[285] S. Gurovich, ibid., p. 60.
[286] Philipp Neumann, ibid., p.167, citing law gazette of the GDR, no. 31, p. 305, decree on directors' funds, March 18, 1954.
[287] Ibid.,

With the resurrection of profit as regulator of social production it became a necessity to increase the enterprise's share of profit in relation to the share to be surrendered to the state to use the retained profit share to create "material incentives." Above all, it was the leading personnel who were to greatly benefit from the new rules. Thus, the salaries of the leading managers had to be 'restructured' and to be made more performance-related, meaning more profit-oriented:

> A basic salary was fixed and, on top of that, a certain percentage point — mostly between 10 and 20 percent — was distributed being dependent on the fulfillment of plan indices.[288]

For the non-leading personnel additional incentives had to be created to enhance the profit of an enterprise which meant to compile a profit-related premium system.

The "economic reform" in the Soviet Union was the brainchild of Kharkov professor Evsey Liberman, who wrote in this context:

> The higher the profit, the larger the bonus fund...The higher the enterprise's profitability, the greater will be its share of the profits... The larger the profits, the larger the bonus fund. It is suggested to establish a single fund for all types of material incentives and to make it dependent upon profit — in percentage of productive assets.[289]

In 1962, Liberman's views were widely published in the USSR, which gave the GDR "reformers" valuable insights and a green light to do likewise — and to also make bonuses dependent on profit, as André Steiner tells us.[290]

They set the ball rolling on January 1, 1964. Again, they were clever enough to choose a step-by-step approach so as not to overdo it and create public anger. The very same year, bonuses were held back for the first time if the profit target had not been met. In 1966, the criterion of net profit growth was made the touchstone for bonus hand-outs and again two years later, in 1968, the net profit was the basis for bonus payments.[291]

Higher bonuses depended on profit growth, or no bonuses were granted at all. As a rule, they were paid out at year's end — Jahresendprämie (year-end premium). Later also special bonuses were paid if, for example,

---

[288] Erich Apel, Günter Mittag, ibid., p. 72.

[289] E. G. Liberman, *Cost Accounting and Material Encouragement of Industrial Personnel*, in: W. B. Bland, *The Restoration of Capitalism in the Soviet Union*, www.oneparty.co.uk/html/book/ussrchap16-18.html.

[290] André Steiner, ibid., p. 285.

[291] Philipp Neumann, ibid., p. 168.

the export plan was fulfilled or over-fulfilled. In the large combines it was the general director who was put in charge of bonus hand-outs.

Who benefited most from the new rules and regulations on bonus payments? Obviously, the upper echelons, the upper income brackets. The year-end bonuses were calculated as a percentage of the average monthly salary.

Someone who received a higher monthly salary automatically also received a larger year-end bonus. Furthermore, it was not some low-end worker or employee who was put in charge of measuring work performance and establishing the amount of bonuses, but the directors, the top managers, the foremen or the heads of department were.

The number four in the GDR hierarchy, highly decorated Alexander Schalck-Golodkovsky, who became were talkative after the collapse of the GDR, confirms:

> The material incentives were first of all given to the leading personnel for the fulfillment of the export plan...At the end of the year, the combine director received up to 10,000 marks in bonuses if everything was fulfilled.[292]

Most advantageous were the new regulations for the leading staff of large and highly profitable combines, involved in arms production and exports, such as VEB Carl Zeiss Jena or combines of the light industry like VEB Kosmetik-Kombinat Berlin.

It is obvious that the old socialist principle of "each according to his/her performance" was ridiculed by the new rules and trampled under foot. These were capitalist principles pure and simple.

10. The Abolition of the State Monopoly on Foreign Trade

In the former Soviet Union, up to Stalin's death in 1953, conducting foreign trade was the sole privilege and monopoly of the socialist state dominated by the Soviet workers and peasants.

What is a state monopoly on foreign trade?

States with such a monopoly on foreign trade do not allow individual companies or groups of companies to exercise trade on their own and for their own benefit. It is the exclusive right of the state. Only the state has the right and the privilege to maintain economic relations with capitalist foreign trade companies or with other socialist entities. The income from foreign trade activities go to the state not to private companies or big corporations, helping to secure sound public finances

---

[292] Alexander Schalck-Golodkowski, in: Theo Pirker et al, ibid., p. 146.

and a country's economic independence. This monopoly is a hallmark of genuine socialism.

What are the main tasks of a state monopoly on foreign trade?

First: The main task of such a monopoly is to prevent foreign capital from penetrating the socialist economy and undermining it.

Second: After the end of the World War II and with the emergence of people's democracies in Eastern Europe, the foreign trade monopoly also served economic cooperation between the USSR and these countries.

Third: This monopoly makes sure that a socialist economy is not hit by the regular recurring economic crises of capitalist foreign economies. This being the case, socialist construction can go on independent of the turmoil and the chaos going on in capitalist or imperialist countries in times of recession or depression.

Fourth: It also safeguards the political independence of a socialist country which would be compromised if such a country was economically or financially dependent on or indebted to capitalist countries or their financial institutions or to global financial institutions like the IMF or the World Bank. It saves a socialist country from being blackmailed and also preserves its defense capability.

What did the Soviet Union under Stalin do to implement this principle?

- All foreign trade operations in the USSR were exercised on the basis of state export and import plans which constituted an integral part of the central plan for the national economy.[293]

- Foreign trade with capitalist countries was conducted on the basis of short- or long-term trade agreements which only the proletarian state was entitled to reach. Even in the Soviet Occupied Zone of Germany and in the early stages of the GDR the foreign trade monopoly had been introduced to guarantee its independence from capitalist countries and to raise its defense capabilities.[294]

Did the "economic reform" in the GDR deal with the monopoly on foreign trade?

Yes, the monopoly was gradually undermined and given up over many years of reforming it. First it was eroded and then even completely abolished. But first lip service was paid to maintain it. At the same time, it

---

[293] *Politische Ökonomie*, edited by the Academy of Science of the USSR, Institute for Economy, Berlin, 1955, p. 584.

[294] Rudolf Friedrich, *Grundriss der Volkswirtschaftsplanung*, Berlin/DDR, 1957, p. 316, in: Philipp Neumann, ibid., p. 40.

was stressed that it was necessary to 'make the monopoly more effective' and to reform it. To keep up socialist appearances, the official post-reform textbook on political economy wrote that the reform made the implementation of the state's foreign trade monopoly "more effective."[295]

The reality though was quite different:

Shortly after the 6th Party Congress of January 1963 and especially after Ulbricht's landmark speech in July of 1946, a whole series of experiments were launched to undermine the monopoly with a view to transferring the former state privilege on foreign trade to individual enterprises and combines, making the monopoly practically redundant. Chief "reformer," in fact counter-revolutionary, Walter Ulbricht in his speech in July 1946 underlined the necessity to "use the stimulating factors of foreign markets for the industry."[296]

Later he added:

> It is characteristic of the test period to gradually transfer preparation, division of labor, industrial cooperation, scientific and technical relations, license giving and taking, market preparation and elaboration, now being under the chairmanship of the responsible ministries and VVB, to the main export enterprises and combines.[297]

Allegedly, it was now necessary to soften up the foreign trade monopoly to overcome "mechanical and narrow thinking...as well as dogmatism in theory and practice."[298]

During the text period state-owned enterprises, still working under the supervision of the Ministry of Foreign Trade (MAW), and large enterprises and combines, such as VEB Carl Zeiss Jena, who were already allowed to conduct their own export trade, existed side by side.

What was the purpose of these experiments?

They served to gradually entrust individual enterprises with exporting and importing and, in the long run, to completely abolish the state monopoly on foreign trade.

Ulbricht's propagandists claimed that it was necessary to provide enterprises with a higher degree of autonomy and to make them accept entrepreneurial risks:

---

[295] *Politische Ökonomie des Sozialismus und ihre Anwendung in der DDR*, ibid., p. 682.

[296] Decision by the Politburo of the SED dated July 14, 1964, also see: André Steiner, ibid., p. 164, note 8.

[297] W. Ulbricht, *Die gesellschaftliche Entwicklung in der DDR*, in: Karl-Heinz Nattland, *Der Außenhandel in der Wirtschaftsreform der DDR*, Berlin, 1972, p. 55; the social development of the GDR; foreign trade as part of the economic reform.

[298] In: André Steiner, ibid., p. 165.

> The enterprise is responsible for the sale of its products..., for marketing, market research and after-sales services as well as for supplying spare parts.[299]

Now special sales organizations could be established: in January 1967, the Deutsche Pharmazie Export und Import GMGH was founded and one year later Schiffskommerz, both being independent export-import companies. For their foreign business they were liable with their own assets. So they were allowed to trade exactly like capitalist export-import firms in Western countries.

It was perfectly legal for the newly established combines to independently conclude import-export contracts directly with their capitalist counterparts on their own behalf and on their own account. Wolfgang Biermann of Carl Zeiss Jena tells the story:

> I had a foreign trade company with around 1,000 employees for export and import purposes. We also did our own import business; we had a subsidiary in Berlin on Leipziger Straße, keeping direct contact with Western firms...We directly concluded our contracts with the respective company abroad. The state of the GDR allowed us to do just that.[300]

In 1966, an entire new sector for foreign trade was established under the supervision of the GDR secret service, the Stasi; it was called Kommerzielle Koordinierung (KoKo). This was a purely capitalist sector which acted completely independently of the GDR state. It was also permitted to conduct its own foreign trade to earn foreign currency. More on that below.

To sum up:

By introducing "economic reform," the state foreign trade monopoly, being an indispensable component of socialism, was gradually eroded in the first stage of the "reform" and later destroyed. By doing so, the capitalist-minded reformers also destroyed the key mechanism protecting a socialist economy form capitalist infiltration. This was done deliberately, thus compromising the political independence of the GDR.

11. Influx of Foreign Capital

It is a tried and true maxim that when building socialism, one must ensure that the national economy remains independent of capitalism and

---

[299] In: Karl-Heinz Nattland, ibid., p. 60, citing: GDR law gazette, part II, no. 21, February 9, 1967, decree on tasks, rights and obligations of production units in people's property.
[300] Wolfgang Biermann interview, in: Theo Pirker et al, ibid., pp. 217 and 229.

imperialism, these days called globalism. All attempts to undermine a socialist economy must be nipped in the bud and blocked by the political leaders of a socialist country. They must be extremely vigilant. Economic independence creates political independence, and vice versa: continuous, crisis-free construction of socialism is only possible under conditions of political independence.

Stalin advised Soviet economists in 1952:

> The main task of planning is to ensure the independence of the socialist economy from the capitalist encirclement. This is absolutely the most important task. It is some sort of battle with world capitalism. Planning must guarantee that metal and machines are in our hands and that we are not dependent on the capitalist economy.[301]

The 'patriot' Ulbricht, as he was hailed in the book edited by Egon Krenz in 2013, the last General Secretary of the SED, had different ideas which he openly expressed at the 7th Party Congress in April of 1967. In *Archiv der Gegenwart* he is quoted as saying this way:

> The First Secretary of the Central Committee of the SED and Chairman of the GDR's State Council, Walter Ulbricht,...stated that the GDR as a modern industrial state can only move forward if its national economy is integrated into the world markets.[302]

Soon West German firms, chiefly of the light industry, rushed to penetrate the newly discovered GDR market through the door opened wide for them by the most powerful GDR politician. They were Salamander (a shoe manufacturer), Schiesser, Triumph (lady's underwear), and Blaupunkt (consumer electronics and household appliances), seizing the opportunity with both hands to make use of the cheap but well qualified East German workforce. In the seventies, when Ulbricht was no longer there and Honecker had taken over the reins, these pioneers of capitalist penetration even succeeded in concluding lucrative cooperation agreements with the GDR mega firms — the combines.

In the eighties, the auto and vehicle industry, but also the chemical industry and many metallurgical firms based in West Germany, followed suit. The biggest European car manufacturer, Volkswagen AG, started its cooperation with the GDR in the field of mechanical engineering and soon became the biggest investor. This is confirmed by Karl Hahn, the

---

[301] Ethan Pollock, *Conversations with Stalin on issues of Political Economy*, ibid., p. 19.
[302] Archiv der Gegenwart, ibid. p. 23.075, year 1967.

former Chief Executive of Volkswagen AG, when addressing the 30th General Meeting of VW in Berlin on July 19, 1990:

> Due to long-standing cooperation with the GDR suppliers and the GDR's mechanical engineering industry and through IFA [VW's partner in the GDR — author], Volkswagen was in a position to become the biggest investor in the GDR.[303] In February 1984, Volkswagen got the green light from the SED leaders to manufacture car engines.[304] And on March 3, the two West German steel giants, Hoesch and Pein-Salzgitter, got permission to refine steel in the GDR for a period of five years.[305]

Mittag, SED General Secretary Eric Honecker's right hand in matters of the economy, later admitted that he had opened the door for these cooperation agreements. But some legal restraints still had to be overcome: the GDR Constitution put legal restraints on joint ventures with capitalist countries. In his memoirs, Mittag writes that he did not care much for these constitutional rules, and then just gave the whole thing a different label: instead of calling these contracts joint ventures, he now called them compensation agreements (Kompensationsgeschäfte). These agreements were no longer in violation of the constitution and could "legally" be concluded. Mittag:

> To back up foreign trade and the industrial ministers, I took it upon myself and allowed them [the combines — author] to reach contracts with a great number of companies from Japan, France, the Federal Republic, Belgium, Great Britain, and other Western countries which came very close to a joint venture.[306]

Although foreign companies were not allowed to become owners of capital in East Germany, they did have the right to possess their investments, with the full backing of the GDR government. Mittag again:

> Legally speaking, they weren't owners of these investments, but they had a powerful say in manufacturing and marketing their products and, at the same time, there were state guarantees given by us. Under these circumstances, Western companies were prepared to invest in the GDR. The offers we got were so numerous that we could hardly cope.[307]

Mittag did not want to hear anything about protectionism or safeguarding the independence of his country form capitalist infiltration:

---

[303] In: Günter Mittag, *Um jeden Preis*, Berlin/Weimar, 1991, p. 105; at any price.
[304] Financial Times, February 2, 1984.
[305] Ibid.
[306] Günter Mittag, ibid., pp. 105f.
[307] Ibid., p. 106.

And these compensation agreements, in which in some years billions were invested, were directed against self-sufficiency and shielding. They objectively served integration into the international division of labor.[308]

Mittag sets the word imperialism in inverted commas.[309] For the architect of the "economic reform" who did not just serve as Secretary for the Economy under General Secretary Ulbricht, but also under Honecker, there was no real imperialism and no danger that West German imperialism could one day buy up the GDR economy and take it over. He even seems to be proud of the fact that the hostile take-over which occurred a little later in the early nineties, went so smoothly ahead as if he had intended just that from the very beginning:

> If you look at it [the long-standing economic cooperation with the West — author] without prejudices, then you must come to the conclusion that the way events unfolded in 1989 and, above all, h o w it happened, that it happened so peacefully, was also due to the fact that there had been long-standing and growing economic and political ties with the Federal Republic.[310]

In his memoirs Mittag says that from the late seventies there had been a close and "confidential" relationship between the GDR reformers on the one hand and the West German business elite on the other, as if both parties were sitting in the same boat and fighting on the same side of the barricades:

> There were extensive and confidential contacts between us and influential business circles represented by Otto Wolf von Amerongen, Bertold Beitz, but also by Ernst Pieper, Carl Hahn and others.[311]

The fact that the long-term "strategic interests" of the Federal Republic prevailed in the end, was not his fault, of course:

> But these were in accordance with the objective path of history.[312]

He forgot to mention that this "objective path" was a little bit distorted by the path of economic reforms introduced in the GDR in the early sixties and that he himself had been a member of the team of trailblazers from the very start.

---

[308] Ibid.
[309] Ibid., p. 99.
[310] Ibid., p. 104., emphasis by Mittag.
[311] Ibid., p. 88.
[312] Ibid., p. 89.

12. The Sector "Commercial Coordination" (KoKo)

Origins, status and the role of the "Stasi"

The final death blow to the state monopoly on foreign trade and its reduction to an ideological front to justify the GDR's Real Existierender Sozialismus (Real Existing Socialism, as the GDR propagandists used to call it) was dealt by the creation of the sector of Kommerzielle Koordinierung (KoKo) — Commercial Coordination. This new sector of the GDR economy was founded in 1966 on the initiative of Walter Ulbricht and Alexander Schalck-Golodkovsky and operated exclusively on capitalist lines. The GDR secret service, Ministerium für Staatssicherheit, also called Stasi, was secretly put in charge of the system. Its main purpose was to earn foreign currency by conducting import-export trade and to get faster and easier access to credits and loans from abroad.

Commercial Coordination was fully independent of the State Planning Committee and the directives of the central plan. It was a solely profit-oriented economic and financial institution and soon became the second pillar of the NESPL system. The difference between NESPL and KoKo resides in the fact that the first had developed gradually on capitalist lines, whereas the latter was allowed to operate along these lines right from the start.

The sector was entrusted to the Ministry of State Security whose head was Eric Mielke, a close associate of Eric Honecker, the most powerful political figure in the GDR after Ulbricht's removal from office in 1971. There was a reason for this: otherwise, the initiators would have been immediately unmasked as counter-revolutionaries.

Ordinary members of the friendly little West German party, the German Communist Party (DKP), like myself, were never told that such a capitalist sector existed in "socialist" East Germany. We were completely kept in the dark about that, even though this was closely linked to the SED and the GDR state. KoKo financed the party's printing works, their party headquarters, their publishing house, etc., as Schalck told the German economists in his interview in 1993...Nobody needed to know.

KoKo also served the purpose of speeding up the reform process in the GDR or, to put it more honestly, the restoration of capitalism in the country. It served to integrate the GDR economy into the global imperialist network, especially to connect the highly indebted country to the international money market, and especially to West German banking consortia.

KoKo got its birth certificate on January 1, 1967, by a directive of the chairman of the GDR State Council, Willi Stoph. Alexander Schalck-Golodkovsky, an officer of the Ministry of State Security, also called Oibe (Special Operations' Officer), was appointed chief executive the very same day. Schalck-Golodkovsky in an interview with German economists in 1993:

The sector was officially founded on January 1, 1967, by a directive issued by Willi Stoph, the Chairman of the State Council and was entrusted with special powers to earn profits.[313]

Schalck was a lucky man: When he started his job in the mid-sixties he officially had only one superior above him: none other than Guenter Mittag, the then Secretary for the Economy at the CC of the SED. From the beginning, he was neither bound by any directives of the state plan for foreign trade nor by those of the official government bodies. Schalck:

The tasks for Commercial Coordination were set by the Central Committee's Secretary for the Economy [Guenter Mittag — author].[314]

So even these tasks were set by the strong man Mittag, and the formal subordination of KoKo under the supervision of the Council of Ministers, was meaningless:

Officially, KoKo was subordinate to the Council of Ministers and its chairman; in reality though, KoKo was a subsidiary of the MfS [Ministry for State Security].[315]

Schalck was in charge of a great number of companies which were answerable only to him, such as Intrac, Transinter, and Forum, doing business not just at home but also abroad. Numerous such firms were operating in Switzerland, West Germany or elsewhere. They were often led by high-ranking security officers, and after the collapse of the GDR in 1989–1990, they were safely moved to West Berlin, and after that to West Germany proper. Only their names changed a little, now with suffixes like GmbH (Limited Company) attached to abide by West German business law.

On September 12, 1972, a landmark decision was taken (already under Eric Honecker): banking regulation for KoKo accounts was ended by

---

[313] Schalck-Golodkowski in: Theo Pirker et al, ibid., p. 154.
[314] Ibid.
[315] Peter-Ferdinand Koch, *Das Schalck-Imperium lebt. Deutschland wird verkauft*, Munich, 1992, p. 22; the Schalck-Empire is still alive, Germany is sold.

decree. From now on, Schalck was solely responsible not only for keeping accounts but for supervising them. He became his own supervisory board, as it were. Deputy Prime Minister Horst Sindermann had issued the following directive:

> By virtue of this decision, the Loro accounts at the DHB [Deutsche Handelsbank, a German commercial bank] and those at the DABA [Deutsche Außenhandelsbank — German Foreign Trade Bank] are from now on exempt from banking supervision.[316]

Thus KoKo, which had already been operating for almost five years, was made totally independent of any state supervision. State regulatory authority over KoKo was completely abandoned. Schalck's domain now enjoyed greater rights and freedoms than any Western capitalist corporation or currency trader. There was just one restraint left: as Schalck was an officer of the East German State Security, he was still answerable to the boss of this sector. His name: Eric Mielke — Minister of State Security. Peter-Ferdinand Koch gave this analysis:

> KoKo employees were members of the HVA [Hauptverwaltung für Aufklärung — the GDR's foreign intelligence service — author] and the MfS. The powerful secret service sent officers on assignment to serve in the GDR's foreign trade. MfS people populated GDR owned firms in the republic, and the HVA sent highly reliable cadres abroad, where they excelled in a double function: as secret service agents and as chief executives of a limited company at the same time...[317]

Thus, Eric Mielke's state security apparatus was the sole regulatory authority left for Schalck and KoKo. But was he "regulated" at all? Koch:

> Only Mielke guaranteed that in future nobody was allowed to check on him [on Schalck — author]; an audit envisaged for the fall of 1982 had to be canceled on the orders of State Security.[318]

Thus, the GDR state security, which officially was responsible for seeing to it that the Arbeiter- und Bauernstaat (workers' and peasants' state, the official terminology for the GDR state machine) was protected from the class enemy, controlled a large sector of the GDR economy and was operating entirely according to the principle of profit maximization; they had no obligation whatsoever to abide by any directives of the central plan. Thus, the East German state security, the MfS, was a great beneficiary of the restoration of capitalism and its driving force at the

---

[316] Peter Przybylski, *Tatort Politbüro. Die Akte Honecker*, Berlin, 1991, p. 127, note 23; AZ: 111-950-89; scene of crime: the politburo, the Honecker files.
[317] Peter-Ferdinand Koch, ibid., p. 9.
[318] Ibid., p. 76.

same time. It no longer protected the GDR workers from the capitalist class enemy (if it had ever done so in the past), but now its main task was to push capitalist restoration forward and to make it irreversible.

After the collapse of the GDR, the capital accumulated by the Stasi firms, running into the millions, were transferred to the former security officers and became their private property. Intrac Trading Company, for example, had accumulated assets worth 102 million GDR marks; Zentral-Kommerz 50 million, and Intrac Immobilien (a real estate firm) 10 million.[319]

These assets were stolen from the working people of the GDR and became the private property of the former chief executives of the Stasi firms who enriched themselves shamelessly, under the watchful eye of the East German state security. The state security did not protect the people; it protected those who were robbing the people.

The backers

KoKo was a monopolist with no competition to fear. Schalck, who later became an agent of the BND, the West German foreign intelligence service (code-name Schneewittchen — Snow White) and an advocate of the NATO alliance, gave an interview:

> We made a profit of three billion in the last three years [of the GDR's existence, from 1986 through to 1989 — author]...Since we didn't have to pay any taxes, this was a net profit. This was a real profit as shown in our balance sheet which was a capitalist balance sheet.[320]

These huge earnings were realized under ideal capitalist conditions that not a single West German or any other capitalist corporation enjoys today, as Schalck's KoKo had no rivals and also enjoyed the full backing and protection of the East German state:

> I was responsible for the GDR. I've honestly admitted before that there was no competition for me, and this made this variant of a market economy quite interesting, of having powers like a capitalist enterprise, but always having the state behind me.[321]

However, there is a lot more to it than that. There was even a second guarantor, a much more powerful backer:

> Interviewer Weinert: "You had two states behind you? You've just said that the other bank was the Federal Government..."

---

[319] Ibid., p. 256, cp. diagram on the *Intrac* companies.
[320] Alexander Schalck-Golodkowski, in: Theo Pirker et al, ibid.,p. 159.
[321] Ibid., p. 159.

Schalck-Golodkovsky: "The Federal Government not so much; for me the Federal Government was not so much my bank, only partially."[322]

When Schalck succeeded in getting hold of two large credits for the GDR from a West German banking consortium in 1983 and 1984, with the help of his trusted friend Franz-Josef Strauß, the far right-wing Bavarian Minister President, worth approximately one billion Deutschmarks each, the bulk of the money was set aside to be used for restoring the GDR's creditworthiness on the international money markets; but the rest is said to have been funneled straight into the coffers of Schalck's empire which he then could use for his financial machinations.

Thus, the monopolist Commercial Coordination, under the chairmanship of a state security agent with good connections to the West German foreign intelligence service, the Bundesnachrichtendienst — BND, was backed by the state of the GDR on the one hand and by the government of West Germany on the other. A double agent could not have done a better job.

The methods

How did this earner of foreign currency with the neutral name of Commercial Coordination make its profits? Let's listen to the garrulous Schalck-Golodkovsky himself:

> In any case — our tasks were to...export our mechanical engineering products abroad, together with those general directors who were directly engaged in foreign trade.[323]

By "abroad," he meant the Western capitalist markets first and foremost. As most of the GDR combines did not have sufficient means to compete on these markets with Japanese, French, British, Italian, West German or US giant corporations, the GDR state was asked to lend a helping hand. Schalck knew what to do in such cases:

> ... a general director could not decide to pay a thirty percent bribe in foreign currency if goods had to be exported to Brazil, for instance, to be transferred to a Swiss bank account. Such powers he didn't have. So he had to contact the Ministry.[324]

Corrupting prospective customers to buy mechanical engineering products from the GDR and not any other country, also with the help and advice of KoKo and the GDR state, was an inherent part of doing

---

[322] Ibid., my emphasis.
[323] Ibid., p. 144.
[324] Ibid.

business in Eric Honecker's "socialism." Schalck's huge capitalist concern deliberately wasted part of the profit from the import-export business to find interested customers in the NSW, the non-socialist currency area, instead of investing these earnings into the real economy and updating the GDR's dilapidated infrastructure, for example, where the money was urgently needed.

Commercial Coordination was not just engaged in the export trade, though. With the earnings from exports gained in capitalist countries, imports were also financed. Although the East German economy was in great need of developing its heavy industry, mainly consumer goods were imported. Schalck-Golodkovsky explains why:

> There were shouts from all directions; one wanted jeans for the youth, the other, I don't know, bananas...It was a policy of shouting. Since Sindermann [former president of the People's Chamber — author] had kids and grandchildren, who kept badgering him to buy Levis jeans, it had to be Levis...Sindermann was the leader: "Alex — come on, get us some jeans, do purchase a million jeans for the students, will you."[325]

Production equipment was imported, too, and here the "policy of shouting" also came into play. This time, it was the general directors of the industrial ministers whose voices were heard loudest:

> Interviewer Rainer Lepsius: Now the Chemistry Minister told us one day that he was facing a serious problem, he was in urgent need of an installation for one of his enterprises. He was in dire straits, and who was the savior? Schalck! So he went to Schalck, and Schalck asked him: "What do you need? I'm gonna buy you these chemical installations. But you must pay me a profit, of course."[326]

So GDR industry not only had to finance the profits of foreign manufactures, but also those of the homegrown monopolist KoKo and on top of that those to the State Security to whom the organization belonged. The earnings were kept in a secret account. Peter Przybylski, former press officer of the GDR Public Prosecutor, explains how it worked:

> Mielke [chief of State Security, MfS, and the number two in the GDR hierarchy — author] himself had created account no. 0528 for top-secret payments. Here the mega profits of Stasi, firms which had been earned through their international business activities, were deposited...Firms like F. C. Gerlach or F. Forgber

---

[325] Ibid., p. 160.
[326] Ibid.

were part of it. They provided the MfS with high tech of all types — from directional microphones to IBM computers for the Stasi headquarters.[327]

And there were electronic batons as well which were later used against demonstrators and peace marchers.

Human trafficking

There was, however, yet another highly profitable source of income for Mielke's State Security: human trafficking. Up to 1974, the money earned from the sale of political prisoners to West Germany was deposited here. Przybylski states that the total balance of this account amounted to "between 35 to 40 million Deutschmarks per year."[328]

This dubious trade started in 1962 — one year after the erection of the Berlin Wall. The GDR government charged a minimum of 40,000 Deutschmarks for each political prisoner.[329]

In 1987, the ransom was up at 50,000 Deutschmarks per prison inmate. Prison inmates were people who had been arrested for wanting to leave the country and to go to West Germany. When Schalck ordered a survey of the so-called "B-Business" in the mid-eighties, covering the years 1964 through to 1985, the total amount of ransom money amounted to "more than 2.5 billion Deutschmarks."[330]

These payments were later justified by saying that these people who wanted to go West had received their education in the GDR free of charge so that the state of the GDR had to be reimbursed for the money paid to get them educated. But this could have been achieved the way it is done in the Islamic Republic of Iran for example: if someone wants to leave the country who has received an education there, he has to work four or five years to pay his country back the expenditure; after that he is free to leave. But practically nobody was allowed to leave the GDR other than by getting arrested and then being freed by West Germany ransom payments.

Another way to "earn" income was the arms trade. Says Przybylski:

> There was a directive by Honecker to safeguard the GDR's solvency by selling arms from stock, but also by selling newly manufactured arms to earn foreign currency.[331]

---

[327] Peter Przybylski, ibid., p. 128.
[328] Ibid., p. 129.
[329] Archiv der Gegenwart, ibid., p. 35,404.
[330] Peter Przybylski, ibid., p. 148.
[331] Ibid., p. 149, citing *Die Welt*, Berlin, April 4, 1990.

This time Imes Import-Export, a KoKo firm founded in 1982, was the beneficiary. Its main depot was in Kavelsberg near the city of Rostock in the north. The depot was guarded and run by Stasi personnel.[332]

Not just light arms but also heavy weapons were traded, among them tanks and planes. Peter-Ferdinand Koch describes the network of foreign trade firms, private KoKo companies that is, this way:

> GDR foreign traders, collaborators of KoKo, officers of the HVA and MfS, were all intertwined. First they met as professionals, then also privately. Over the years, these managers, above all those of KoKo and HVA, grew together to form a secretive society. They possessed enormous influence within the Party and state. Their main weapon was their knowledge, secret business contacts with the Federal Republic, intelligence activity — all this had to remain secret as the German–German dealings, once made public, could have humiliating and degrading consequences, especially in industrial circles... The top brass of the nationalized enterprises, the directors of foreign trade enterprises, the chairmen of the MfS and HVA departments, founded businesses and ripped off sums in the double-digit millions, and real estate properties were signed over.
>
> Never before, in East Berlin alone, were there so many GmbH's [limited companies — author] or share corporations founded at the same time. The once impoverished GDR functionaries became millionaires overnight and stayed that way even after the currency union.[333]

The weapons trade started in 1981.[334] All these well-informed people, being heavily involved in arms trading, knew perfectly well that in the late eighties the GDR was close to bankruptcy and could not be saved by any means, by any credit injection from Western banks or by the International Monetary Fund. So they acted wisely and prepared for the future ahead of time. Later, after the reunification of Germany, some of them became millionaires on the money stolen from the GDR public; many of them even joined the West German intelligence service, the Verfassungsschutz (West Germany's domestic intelligence service) to spy on West German dissidents this time. Their Stasi expertise was also needed in "democratic" West Germany.

KoKo and Wandlitz

[332] Ibid.

[333] Peter-Ferdinand Koch, ibid., pp. 25f.

[334] Frank Schumann, Heinz Wuschech, *Schalck-Golodkowski — der Mann, der die DDR rettenwollte*, Berlin, 2012, p. 184; Schalck-Golodkovsky — the man who wanted to rescue the GDR.

The "top brass" of the new East German bourgeoisie, also called "the nomenclature," who had made possible all these corrupt practices in the GDR by introducing the 'economic reform' in January of 1963, were generously rewarded by Commercial Coordination for their pioneering services. KoKo also served as a "source of prosperity for the residents of the Waldsiedlung."[335]

The Waldsiedlung (forest settlement) was located near the remote village of Wandlitz, a thirty-minute drive from the city of Berlin. Schalck's empire also served the needs of the GDR top officials, mainly politburo members and ministers, who had moved house in 1960 on the initiative of General Secretary Ulbricht. The shock of June 17th was still deeply felt when the families of leading GDR politicians had to be evacuated out of East Berlin by the Soviet military to escape the wrath of the rebellious Berliners. To be on the safe side, Ulbricht opted for building a special settlement near a Soviet barracks where they could be safe and secure and not risk facing the anger of dissatisfied East Germans anymore. This was a tranquil and leafy area, surrounded by a dense hedge and well protected by State Security. Around 280 high official were housed there in single-family houses. They also had their dachas (country homes), and large hunting areas at their disposal.

According to a directive issued by General Secretary Honecker, about six million marks per year were earmarked for the growing needs of the leading representatives of the GDR. In the late stages, from January to October 1989, the sum was raised to 7.3 million, if we can believe Peter Przybylski.[336] All this despite the GDR's imminent insolvency! The money was used to import quality consumer goods purchased in West Berlin by a special staff led by Schalck's wife Sigrid.

Egon Krenz, Honecker's successor for six weeks, writes in his memoirs:

> It is true, however, that many products of Western manufacture were specially imported. They were nowhere available against GDR currency...These double moral standards I cannot absolve myself from.[337]

His Politburo colleague, Guenter Schabowsky, agrees:

> We gave ourselves goods we refused to give to the ordinary citizens. Each day we indulged ourselves like this; we testified against socialism, morally and in other ways. This caused anger

---

[335] Peter Przybylski, ibid., p. 152.
[336] Ibid.
[337] Egon Krenz, *Wenn Mauern fallen*, Vienna, 1990, p. 80; when walls collapse.

and indignation at the grass roots of the Party, but also within the population that forced us to give up.[338]

Another special staff employed by State Security was to look after the crowd round the clock. The person put in charge was former Stasi officer Gerd Schmidt. Schmidt on his tasks there:

> We employees of the Waldsiedlung were responsible for everything with regards to the apartments, the houses of the officials and their families. It went so far that sometimes we had to build rabbit hutches and swings and other recreational facilities for the kids in their front yards. We built sandboxes for the grandchildren, etc.[339]

Even during their vacations, the servants of the GDR elites had to look after their masters and mistresses. Schmidt again:

> In 1987, 1988 and 1989, Honecker spent his holidays together with his family in Drewitz [a specially-built hunting ground for Honecker — author]. He was accompanied by all his bodyguards, the technical staff, his drivers, his security people, and his cooks.[340]

Willi Stoph, chairman of the GDR Council of Ministers — the official government — took advantage of his personal security staff by having them look after his holiday resort at Birkenheide. Schmidt:

> I remember when our staff had to harvest the numerous fruit trees there in the orchard — not exactly a typical job for security personnel.[341]

The modest and selfless communist Stoph kept a permanent staff at Birkenheide to look after his increasing cultural and material needs:

> Between 15 and 20 people were permanently employed at Birkenheide only to look after Stoph's needs and to keep him happy. Even a former head of department was sent there, a lieutenant colonel.[342]

Stoph also made use of the National People's Army, the NVA (Nationale Volksarmee). Leisure organizer Ralf Opitz in his memoirs:

> Within four and a half weeks we built a house in Wandlitz, and in doing so we were assisted by a whole battalion of the NVA.[343]

---

[338] Günter Schabowski, *Der Absturz*, Berlin, 1991, p. 104; the downfall.
[339] Gerd Schmidt in: Thomas Grimm, *Das Politbüro privat. Ulbricht, Honecker, Mielke & Co. aus der Sicht ihrer Angestellten*, Berlin, 2004, p. 22; the politburo in private, from the point of view of the employees. Also see the document in the appendix.
[340] Ibid., p. 26.
[341] Ibid., p. 37.
[342] Ralf Opitz, in ibid., p. 150.
[343] Ibid., p. 147.

So Comrade Chairman of the Council of Ministers used to live like a medieval lord in a manor there with his servants, while calling himself a communist. Only a spacious harem, also to be built by the National People's Army and some attractive courtesans were missing.

Guenter Mittag, Honecker's principal economic adviser, was and one of the chief "reformers" seeking to make socialism more "modern" and "more effective." How did he live? Schmidt mentions that once Mittag had his house refurbished from top to bottom by this team, and that he had all the new furnishings brought in from abroad:

> The material was delivered; it was not from us; he had ordered everything in the West.[344]

And who helped him to get hold of the supplies needed? You guessed it: Schalck's KoKo.

The Wandlitz servants, the maids-of-all-work, were bound to secrecy which went so far that they were even not allowed to talk to their loved-ones about their duties there. One of the employees, Waltraud Oecknick, Ulbricht's personal housekeeper, tells the story:

> Not even with our relatives were we allowed to talk about our work or about with whom we had dealt on a certain day...We were lectured on a regular basis to keep quiet and reminded of our duties not to talk and observe confidentiality. These instructions became more and more extreme over time...It was also prohibited that we talk among ourselves about the officials and their families... My only privilege was to serve the functionaries day in, day out. I had no private life.[345]

Guenter Schabowski, the Politburo member quoted above, says that it was not so much individual shortcomings which lay at the root of these corrupt practices, but that the whole system was to blame:

> Wasting words about Wandlitz would be pointless if this was only due to the failures of individuals. But the settlement was part of the system.[346]

So the system was to blame, but this system was deliberately designed in the early sixties by certain individuals to, as they told the general public again and again, "modernize socialism" and to lead it away from Stalin's "dogmatism." How can one separate the system from the individual?

Did the ordinary people of the GDR know about Wandlitz? I suppose so, but the media kept quiet about it. I regularly watched GDR TV but

---

[344] Gerd Schmidt, in ibid., p. 39.
[345] Waltraud Oecknick, in ibid., p. 220.
[346] Günter Schabowski, *Der Absturz,* Berlin, 1991, p. 104; the fall.

never ever heard them speak about it. I myself as an ordinary member of the German Communist Party at the time heard about Wandlitz for the very first time in the summer of 1983, during a private trip to the GDR, when I was told by a vicar (who was no party member) about what was going on there. Our party officials never talked about it. Same with KoKo. We were completely kept in the dark and were never told that such things existed in neighboring "socialist" East Germany. These officials had excellent contacts to leading GDR functionaries and were often invited to visit the GDR. They must have known. Maybe they had instructions to keep quiet like the employees of Wandlitz.

When hundreds of thousands demonstrated in Berlin and Leipzig against the GDR elites in October and November 1989, one of the slogans heard was: "Too many officials are much too rich; now the people are taking the carpenter's plane to level all of them equal."[347]

13. Debt Policies

The socialist principle of freedom from debt

When building socialism, it is a well-known principle that one has to make sure the state and its economy do not become indebted to outside and foreign parties. Genuine socialists honor this principle and act accordingly. In socialist Albania under Enver Hoxha, for example, freedom from foreign debt was inscribed in the country's constitution. Even though this maxim was not part of the Soviet constitution passed in 1936, in practice the Soviet state in times of Stalin was never highly indebted to capitalist countries or their banking institutions. However, the Soviet workers' state was slightly indebted to its own population:

> Government bonds in our socialist society are a way by which the state can make use of funds belonging to the population with the obligation to repay these means after a certain period of time. By signing these bonds, the working people voluntarily surrender parts of their personal income to the state for temporary usage... These transfers constituted three percent of the total revenue in 1954.[348]

The Soviet state made use of the working population's savings to satisfy the needs of the whole the society. In this sense it "borrowed" from its own people.

---

[347] Slogan heard at the mass demonstration in Leipzig on November 6, 1989.
[348] Politische Ökonomie, Lehrbuch, Berlin, 1955, p. 598; Soviet textbook on Political Economy.

But Soviet enterprises too — even in times of Stalin — were sometimes allowed to take out loans. These loans were granted by the Soviet State Bank in the form of long-term credits to assist investments by enterprises and short-term ones for circulating assets to move freely. This way, unused financial means at the state banks could be utilized for productive purposes to help develop the heavy industrial sector for instance.

On the other hand, even simple commercial credit was strictly forbidden. Thus, it was not possible for an enterprise to deliver goods to another one on credit. This would have violated the principle of state control over domestic trade. No enterprise was permitted to take out loans at foreign banking institutions, as these always make lending conditional on political or economic concessions. Fixed interest rates are not guaranteed, as the interest charged is dependent on the law of supply and demand, which rules not just ordinary markets, but also money markets.

Very often a country running a negative trade balance (the value of its imports surpassing that of exports) will have great difficulty in repaying the debt or even the interest on time. Then interest on interest (compound interest) will have to be paid as well. Imperialist financial institutions such as the International Monetary Fund or the World Bank stubbornly insist on repayment, so it is easy for a country that gets into debt to these loan sharks to find that it can never free itself from their greedy clutches. In such cases it is the working population that has to pay the bills, being forced to endure an austerity regime (cuts in pensions, longer working hours, etc.) for allowing its government to become a debtor nation to the globalist money elites.

The GDR's policy of debt accumulation

Whether a government is indebted or not to other capitalist countries or to international financial institutions ruled by global elites is indicative of its quality and provides us maybe the most important clue for our judgment of such a government or regime. A government that allows debts to pile, permitting foreign lenders to intervene in its internal affairs, can by no means be called "socialist" or even "democratic." It is a government of irresponsible and weak-minded wheeler-dealers that does not care for the future of its own population and neither does it care for building genuine socialism. Building socialism requires political and economic, but also military independence. A country that is occupied or belongs to an imperialist alliance like NATO for example cannot build socialism, and a country that is indebted to international banking consortia sooner or later has to give up building a socialist society.

Was the GDR an independent country, did its leaders steer a course of national sovereignty and financial independence or did they do just the opposite?

To answer this question, it is necessary to take a closer look at the GDR's finances. Today we have several documents in our possession showing that the GDR, especially in its last years, was a highly indebted country, and in its last year, in 1989, the GDR state was very close to insolvency which was freely admitted by leading GDR officials, among them Carl-Heinz Janson, former head of department at the Central Committee of the SED. In his reminiscences he presents the following data:[349]

Year	Debt in billion valuta Marks (West German DM)
1970	2.2
1975	11.0
1980	25.3
1985	30.0
1987	34.7

Janson had first-hand knowledge about the GDR's financial standing and had no reason to exaggerate or manipulate figures.

There is a second document proving that the GDR was even much more deeply indebted to foreign capitalist countries: it is an analysis of the economic situation of the GDR made shortly before its collapse in November 1989. The full text — my translation from German — can be found in the appendix. The document was signed by Gerhard Schuerer, the GDR planning chief. Alexander Schalck-Golodkovsky, head of Commercial Coordination, the GDR's foreign minister, Gerhard Beil, and two others assisted him to draft the top-secret document "to be destroyed on December 31, 1989." The date is October 10, 1989, just four weeks prior to the big demonstration in East Berlin, attended by roughly 500,000 people and breaking the GDR's neck.

---

[349] Carl-Heinz Janson, *Totengräber der DDR*, Düsseldorf, Vienna, New York, 1991, p. 65; the gravedigger of the GDR.

There we find the following remarks on the state of the GDR's financial situation:

> State budget liabilities towards the credit system were 12 billion marks in 1970, 43 billion in 1980 and 123 billion in 1988 due to increased spending as compared to earnings. In 1989–1990 rising state budget expenditure in relation to revenues can only be met by more borrowing in the amount of 20 billion marks, so that the overall indebtedness will rise up to 140 billion marks. Money circulation and state borrowing, also from saving deposits have risen faster than the economic performance... Instead of achieving the projected export surplus of 23.1 billion marks, we are being faced with an import surplus of 6 billion marks in 1986–1990. This was connected to a rapid increase of the debt burden, reaching 49 billion marks in late 1989, amounting to 190% as compared to 1985. This burden is roughly four times as high as the value of our exports in 1989...Under these circumstances the total debt burden would be as follows in these years: 1990: 55.5 billion; 1991: 62.0; 1992: 63.0; 1993: 62.0; 1994: 60.0; 1995: 1995.[350]

The key phrase "under these circumstances" implies that extreme export surpluses of up to 10 billion marks per year would have to be achieved in the early nineties to avoid insolvency which would have meant drastically cutting on essential imports — something politically unenforceable.

The five authors concluded that the situation was dismal and the country was on the brink of insolvency and needed drastic economic reforms similar to those which Mikhail Gorbachev carried out in the Soviet Union in the early nineties. Later in his memoirs, in an attempt to embellish the GDR, Gerhard Schuerer flatly denied that insolvency had already been reached in 1989 and that there had been "no evidence" that the GDR was already bankrupt. The bills had also been paid punctually. Schuerer observed, "first of all, the GDR, at no time in her history, had been insolvent or 'broke'.[351]

In 2012, Frank Schumann and Heinz Wuschech — the latter used to be Schalck's personal physician in the GDR — published a book on Schalck-Golodkovsky titled, *The Man Who Wanted to Rescue the GDR*. In an obvious attempt to rescue Schalck's reputation and to gloss over the

---

[350] Gerhard Schürer, Gerhard Beil, Alexander Schalck-Golodkovsky, Ernst Höfner, Arno Donda, *Analysis of the Economic Situation of the German Democratic Republic, with conclusions,* October 10, 1989, source: BArch, DY 30, J IV 2/2A/3252, at: www.bundesarchiv. de/DE/Content/Virtuelle-Ausstellung/Wege-Zur-Deutschen-Einheit/006_004-finanzen-ddr_PDF.pdf.

[351] Gerhard Schürer, *Gewagt und verloren. Eine deutsche Biografie,* Berlin, 1998, p. 197; won and lost, a German biography.

debt policy he was blamed for, the authors maintain that it was not the high level of debt that contributed to the country's collapse in the fall of 1989, but the Schuerer report itself which had caused unnecessary panic and "in the final analysis had paralyzed almost the entire political apparatus of the GDR."[352]

Further down in their book they claim, "The GDR in its final stage had liabilities to foreign countries of less than 20 billion D-marks. So in terms of today's currency it was less than 10 billion euros. She was not bankrupt or broke or insolvent."[353]

This version of "only less than 20 billion" was also repeated by Dr. Klaus Blessing in an interview with Sputniknews. Blessing was a former head of department in the Central Committee of the SED (Department of Engineering and Metallurgy). He refers to a report by the Deutsche Bundesbank, saying that the GDR's liabilities were less than 20 billion valuta marks. He adds that the Schuerer Report was faked and had only been signed by the GDR planning chief pro forma, but was written by other people. The report had not taken 30 billion valuta mark deposited with Schalck's Commercial Coordination into account. This sum "had been concealed" in the fall of 1989 to draw a "false picture" of the GDR's financial standing. The situation had not been that bad. His conclusion: the GDR had never been bankrupt. That was just a "fairy tale."[354]

Is this true?

Peter Przybylski, in his book on Honecker, also includes various documents on the amount of money that had been deposited at foreign banks by Schalck's KoKo in the late eighties. A report drafted by the GDR Finance Ministry dated February 16, 1990 says:

> 1. Financial investments at foreign banks...In late 1989, the money deposited with foreign banks amounts to 1,580.5 million valuta mark, according to the survey drafted by the inspectors.[355]

The report was handed over to the Public Prosecutor of the GDR, dealing with Schalck's dubious management of public finances after his escape to the West. Other documents made public by the same author show in great detail where exactly the money was secretly invested. Big chunks of money were brought to Vienna, Lugano and also to Copenhagen

[352] Frank Schumann, Heinz Wuschech, *Schalck-Golodkovsky — the Man who Wanted to Rescue the GDR*, p. 71, Berlin, 2012.
[353] Ibid., p. 139.
[354] Tilo Gräser, *Angebliche Pleite der DDR ist ein Märchen*, at: https://freidenker.org/?p=7647, p. 4; the alleged bust of the GDR is a fairy tale.
[355] Peter Przybylski, *Tatort Politbüro. Die Akte Honecker*, Berlin, 1991, pp. 372 and 375; crime scene politburo, the Honecker files.

in Denmark which were then hidden there. The names of the banks are also mentioned in the documents. So the assertion made by Blessing that 30 billion valuta marks (!) were put aside by KoKo for a rainy day cannot be verified. The figure is purely imaginary. It is just another attempt to embellish the GDR in hindsight.

Was the GDR free of debts under General Secretary Ulbricht?

What was the situation like under General Secretary Ulbricht in the sixties? Some high officials of the GDR have claimed that at that time the GDR was practically "debt-free." General Director Wolfgang Biermann on that issue:

> I would say that this [the growing indebtedness of the GDR to foreign lenders — author] had started in the late seventies. Ulbricht, in terms of valuta currency [in terms of DM — author], handed over to Honecker a relatively debt-free GDR. Maybe it was one or two billion Deutschmarks, but for a country like the GDR no magnitude at all. But under Honecker the debt burden increased rapidly.[356]

Is it true that up until the late seventies the GDR was more or less debt-free and that its severe debt-crisis only started under General Secretary Honecker?

Is it true that when Neues Deutschland (the official party organ of the SED) wrote in 1963 that no West German credits had been offered and accepted by the GDR government?[357]

If one takes a closer look at the GDR's financial standing at the time, this statement turns out to be a piece of the official propaganda: on May 30th, 1962, the very same paper admitted that East German requests for credits had been made in February already:

> Neues Deutschland wrote on May 30 [1962 — author] that East German requests for credits were made on February 13 for the first time, referring to the delivery of three million tons of hard coal yearly for the next ten years, worth 2.25 billion Deutschmarks, plus industrial plants at a value of 500 million Deutschmarks. Credit requests have also been made regarding foodstuffs beyond the existing trade agreement.[358]

This piece of news is confirmed by an article in Die Welt:

---

[356] Wolfgang Biermann, in: Theo Pirker et al, ibid., p. 232.

[357] From: *Archiv der Gegenwart*, p. 18.643, citing *Neues Deutschland*, issue of December 12, 1963.

[358] *Keesing's Record of World Events*, September 1962, Eastern Germany, at: http://keesings. gvpi.net/keesings/lpext.dll/KRWE/krwe-118543-119121/krw-1...

According to Die Welt, the GDR requested the delivery of fertilizers of 100,000 tons per year from 1964 through 1966. She also demanded an extension of the credit line (the "Swing") for machinery and other products from 100 to 500 million Deutschmarks as well as for so-called commodities from 100 to 200 million.[359]

Thus, even in the sixties under General Secretary Ulbricht the GDR had already received short-term credits from West Germany under the "Swing" agreement and was keen on taking out more credits for consumer goods imports.

In 1970, one year before Eric Honecker succeeded Walter Ulbricht, the GDR's debt to the West stood at 2.2 billion Deutschmarks, according to Carl-Heinz Janson, who served under Economy Secretary Mittag and was head of department in the Central Committee of the SED.[360]

Janson writes that at the 8th Party Congress in 1971 Ulbricht was sharply criticized exactly because of this:

> The balance between claims and liabilities with regard to the NSW [the non-socialist currency area — author] was 2.2 billion valuta marks. This was the legacy of the Ulbricht era, and it was considered unacceptable.[361]

And there is another thing. The GDR was also indebted to the Soviet Union in the early seventies. She exported goods worth 7.4 billion in 1971 and imported commodities worth 8.2 billion GDR marks — mainly raw materials.[362]

So it is not true that the GDR under Ulbricht was more or less debt-free. The disease had already started under him and only worsened later under the Honecker regime.

Honecker's ambitious spending programs

Although there were some critical voices at the 8th Party Congress concerning the GDR's record in matters of debt, the delegates passed a binding resolution on Honecker's new concept of Unity of Economic and Social Policy to improve the social and economic situation in the country by a program of social spending to avoid growing disenchantment in the population. However, the catch was — and this was not said out loudly — that the project could only be realized by massive credit taking.

---

[359] *Archiv der Gegenwart*, ibid., p. 19,749.
[360] Carl-Heinz Janson, ibid., p. 65.
[361] Ibid., p. 63.
[362] *Archiv der Gegenwart*, ibid., p. 30,226, citing the *Neue Züricher Zeitung*, issue of April 4, 1972.

The Congress (June 15–19, 1971) passed a resolution for the Fifth Five Year Plan covering the years 1971–1975:

> ...to increase the material and cultural living standard of the people on the basis of a high degree if socialist production development, increased effectiveness, scientific-technical progress and growth of labor productivity.[363]

Among other things, an ambitious housing program was adopted "to considerably ease the problems of people seeking accommodation."[364]

Five years later, at the 9th Party Congress, further measures under the banner heading of Main Task of Unity between Economic and Social Policy were approved. The equally ambitious packet included:

> ...measures to increase the minimum wage (the monthly minimum wage for one million employees was raised from 350 to 400 marks as of September 1, 1976); improved pensions and social welfare. For 3.5 million old-age pensioners the minimum income is increased as of December 1, 1976; support for working mothers and gradual implementation of the 40-hour week.[365]

Later, both Carl-Heinz Janson and Egon Krenz had to admit, in hindsight, that this ambitious social program did not have a sound financial backing. Krenz (Honecker's successor in late 1989) noted:

> Later the society realized that this course of Unity between Economic and Social Policy had not been secured. Thus, for years, we had lived beyond our means at the expense of our children and grandchildren.[366]

Why didn't he realize it earlier when he was still member of the Politburo and one of the highest representatives of the GDR? His colleague, Janson, who is far more honest, states that the political leaders were always well informed about the main economic data:

> In numerous meetings that I took part in and in many internal documents, which I had the opportunity to read, the negative trend was already clearly visible.[367]

Gerhard Schuerer, the planning chief, also admits in his reminiscences that the leaders of the Politburo were briefed once a month about the dismal financial situation. Even then, everybody in the top echelons must have know that the GDR was importing goods from West Germany on credit, making use of the 'Swing' credit line which was frequently raised.

---

[363] Egon Krenz, *Wenn Mauern fallen,* Vienna, 1990, p. 56.
[364] Ibid.
[365] *Archiv der Gegenwart,* ibid., p. 33,005.
[366] Egon Krenz, ibid., pp. 57f.
[367] Carl-Heinz Janson, ibid., p. 63.

On December 6, 1974, for example, the GDR was granted a new credit line valid until January 31, 1981, with a yearly volume of 850 million valuta marks.[368] Some key indicators of the national economy spoke for themselves. Janson:

> I would like to mention the growing import surplus which was bridged by credits.[369]

Bridging the negative trade balance with regard to West Germany by taking on more and more debt had been standard practice from early on, and those who passed the new social program adopted at the 8th Party Convention must have been aware of it from the start. Within only ten years (1970 through 1980) the GDR's indebtedness to the Non Socialist Currency Area rose tenfold. Janson again:

> Since then [since the early eighties — author], the GDR was on the edge of bankruptcy.[370]

In view of these enormous debts owed to Western banking consortia which were deliberately and knowingly engineered to keep up "socialist" appearances and the illusion of a social welfare state for everyone, the five year plans, the foundation of every socialist building, became null and void:

> All decisions of an economic nature were determined by this threat [the threat of insolvency — author]. Even the holy plan was unconditionally scrapped when certain settlement dates approached and the money had to be found.[371]

Supply shortages ensued which were widely exploited in the Western mainstream media to blame "socialism" and to tell the public that "state socialism can't work":

> Everything was sold which could be sold if for one mark only ten pfennigs [German currency unit; one Deutschmark has 100 pfennigs — author] flowed back. Many will remember the temporary supply shortages in meat products because the best qualities were sold to the West to earn a quick buck. In those times, basic chemical materials and intermediate products were rolling across the border in tightly sealed goods trains.[372]

---

[368] Compare: *Archiv der Gegenwart*, ibid., p. 33,715, December 11, 1974.
[369] Carl-Heinz Janson, ibid.
[370] Ibid., p. 66.
[371] Ibid.
[372] Ibid.

To be able to pay the interest on all this credit, the GDR, even in 1981, had to use 30% of its exports to the West.[373] Since the GDR paid for its imports by using long-term credits (70% according to the figures provided by the insider Janson[374]), the burden of interest payments grew uninterruptedly — year by year. Janson:

> In the period of 1971–1989...58 billion valuta mark had to be paid for interest alone. This amounted to approximately 255 billion GDR marks, which roughly equaled the entire national income of 1989. Or to put it this way: during these years of the Main Task, a whole annual national income was used only for interest payments and disappeared abroad.[375]

International finance capital silently colonizes the GDR

Thus, in East Germany a process of colonization was taking place, just like in so many other countries of the world. In the early seventies, a whole series of developing countries, especially in Africa, turned to the World Bank or the International Monetary Fund, or to both, for urgent credits to "develop their economies." The sad outcome: an increasing impoverishment of these countries, many of which originally had a socialist and anti-imperialist orientation. But this policy of international high finance, their policy of exploitation and naked expropriation of commonly owned wealth could not have taken place if there had not been privileged "socialist" elites who, at least in the short run, benefited from these measures and were ready to participate in the game to stay in power a little longer. The only European country with a socialist orientation that did not have such corrupt and selfish elites and that did not fall and did not want to fall into the money trap was Enver Hoxha's Albania — a small, but highly resilient European country of less than three million inhabitants on the Adriatic Sea.

The consequences: all these countries, and first and foremost their working population, were plundered by the Big Money Mafia, by High Finance, by the globalist elites, and the promising socialist beginnings people had fought for and shed their blood for in endless liberation wars in the fifties and sixties were reversed and destroyed.

Since socialism cannot be constructed without giving priority to investments in heavy industry, the growing indebtedness of the GDR rendered the building of socialism impossible. If you are faced with

---

[373] Herwig E. Haase, *Das Wirtschaftssystem der DDR*, Berlin, 1983; p. 104, table 4, the economic system of the GDR.

[374] Carl-Heinz Janson, ibid., p. 67

[375] Carl-Heinz Janson, ibid., p. 68.

a mountain of debt, where can you take the money from to build a country's infrastructure or to modernize agriculture, how can you raise productivity and efficiency if the means are gone?

Stalin, who was defamed as a criminal in GDR literature and whose works were banned from the bookstores, explained how to build socialism on a rock-solid foundation and not on sand:

> Such basic theses of Marx' theory of reproduction, such as the principle of dividing social production up into the manufacture of means of production and that of consumer goods; the principle of giving priority to the growth of production of means of production; the theory of the relationship between section I and II, ... the theory of accumulation as sole source of expanded production — all these principles of Marx' theory of reproduction are theses not only being valid for the capitalist formation, but also for a socialist society, and which are indispensable for the planning of a national economy.[376]

Here Stalin is criticizing a chief follower of his later successor, Nikita Khrushchev, the economist Yaroshenko, who supported him in the field of political economy. The GDR economists followed in Khrushchev' steps when directing the East German national economy and sinking it into oblivion. This criticism could also be regarded as his belated criticism of the GDR economists, who even today, in case they are still alive, have understood nothing as far as their grave mistakes are concerned which led to the downfall of the GDR.

If one ignores the basic laws for building socialism, which Stalin is talking about, one has to face the inconvenient facts afterwards. Then the laws being ignored will take their revenge and cause chaos behind the backs of those arrogantly pushing them aside.

The last chairman of the State Planning Committee of the GDR, Gerhard Schuerer, whom we have met on several occasions, admitted that the debt-ridden GDR was no longer a sovereign state:

> To put it bluntly, we had to sell parts of our sovereignty or else the Federal Republic would not have been prepared to grant us any more credits any longer.[377]

Not to abide by basic principles of socialism, partly developed by Karl Marx in the 19th century, will automatically lead to a loss of sovereignty, and a state or a national economy that has lost this most valuable asset then finds itself unable to build a solid base for a well- functioning socialist society.

---

[376] J. W. Stalin, *Ökonomische Probleme des Sozialismus in der UdSSR*, ibid., pp.81f.
[377] Gerhard Schürer, in: Theo Pirker et al, ibid., p 113.

14. A New Capitalist Class

What are classes?

The GDR elites deliberately plunged their country deep into debt, thus taking part in an international scheme to plunder the East German national economy and to steal the fruits of the East German working population. They took part in the well-known game of the globalist elites, ruining other countries and their people through money lending and extortion. When the game was over in late 1989, some of the top brass fled the country and were not even ashamed to ask the West German foreign intelligence service, the BND, to provide safe havens for them. Schalck-Golodkovsky is one case; the German secret service brought him out of West Berlin to hide him in a far-away mountain hut near the Austrian border to escape the wrath of his fellow countrymen. Schalck had fled the GDR in the middle of the night on December 4, 1989, and crossed into West Berlin to escape an arrest warrant issued by the GDR state prosecutor.

One could take the view that the so-called GDR nomenclature — the term was first used by Michael S. Voslensky in his book Nomenclature. The Ruling Class of the Soviet Union — only was an elite of some slightly privileged state and party officials or maybe a "caste of power-hungry party cadres" (Dieter Voigt) and that they did not constitute a "new capitalist class" at all. These people did not own private property of means of production, thus having no economic roots to qualify as members of a new ruling class. This "upper stratum" of the GDR society obviously was not in a position to reap profits by acquiring surplus value and surplus labor, to own huge amounts of shares or sumptuous villas, or to speculate at the stock exchange (there was none!), to engage in money laundering or to deposit their riches in safe international havens like the Channel islands. So it seems that all they were able to do under the circumstances was to fight for high positions and some minor privileges.

Or was this "caste" of functionaries and company directors indeed a new capitalist class, such that they would deserve the name of a "new bourgeoisie."

How did Lenin in his time define the term "class"? In his essay "A Great Beginning" gave the following definition:

> Classes are large groups of people, differing from one another by the place they occupy in a historically determined system of social production, by their relationship to the means of production ..., by their role in the organization of labor and, consequently, by the

size of the share of social wealth which they have at their disposal and the mode of acquiring it.[378]

The question is this: Did the GDR upper strata of roughly less than two percent of the overall population (party and state nomenclature, functionaries, directors of enterprises and combines, directors of agricultural producers' cooperatives, high-ranking officers, officers of State Security ("Stasi") actually develop into a "new capitalist class" or "new bourgeoisie"?

Was there still any "people's property"?

Of course, the official documents and the propaganda vehemently denied there was any "people's property" left. Maybe they were right after all, and we should also not forget that the overwhelming majority of historians and analysts dealing with GDR historiography stick to this hypothesis.

The answer to this mystery depends on whether or not the means of production in the GDR, after the reform process was over, were still "the people's property." If they were no longer the people's property as a result of NESPL, the economic reform in the GDR, then we have good reason to believe that the germs of a new capitalist class actually burgeoned in East Germany in the early sixties. If, however, the means of production had remained the people's, then there would be no grounds to think that such a "new bourgeoisie" had come into being.

The official line in the GDR after the reform process had been accomplished in the late sixties and early seventies was the following:

> The means of production are not the property of the enterprises, but the property of everybody...Nobody has been excluded from the proprietorship of the means of production. At the same time, no member of the socialist society has the right to enjoy special privileges from the people's property.[379]

Therefore, exploiting classes had ceased to exist in the GDR:

> As is the case in socialism, the exploitation of man by man has been eliminated and exploitation no longer exists to enable exploiters to appropriate the surplus product created by surplus labor; the antagonistic contradiction between necessary and surplus labor has been abolished.[380]

---

[378] V. I. Lenin, *A Great Beginning*, in: Collected Works, vol. 29, Moscow, 1965, in: W. B. Bland, *Marxism and Class: some definitions*, http://www.oneparty.co.uk/compass/compass/com12802.html.

[379] *Politische Ökonomie des Kapitalismus und Sozialismus*, ibid., p. 430.

[380] Ibid., p. 529.

So did "the people's property" still exist in the GDR? My line of argument is the following:

1. With the introduction of a charge on the enterprises' productive funds of around 6% (from 1967 that is), the management of enterprises and combines obtained the right to treat productive assets like capital which, against payment of an annual interest, could be rented out and thus, in actual fact, became the property of the enterprise in question. Now the directors of enterprises had the legal right to sell those productive assets they wanted to get rid of or to buy new ones, as has been shown in great detail above (also see the chapter Means of Production Becoming Commodities. By introducing this landmark step away from socialism, people's property, formerly being administered by the state, was in fact transferred to the directors of enterprises and their managerial staff.

This became part of the official doctrine enshrined in GDR textbooks on political economy where we read:

> Completely new assets..., the delivery of complete plants... are included in the exchange of goods.[381]

Ulbricht himself, the champion of NES, had demanded to fully develop socialist commodity circulation.[382] This included also means of production. Not to include them and to let them remain state property, as Stalin did, was called "dogmatism."

2. Following the "economic reform" of 1963, the means of production became commodities and could be bought and sold like ordinary commodities on a market. The first step in this direction was taken by selling the Machine Tractor Stations (agricultural means of production) to the agricultural cooperatives, thus gaining proprietorship of vast amounts of productive assets. This already had been done in 1959.

The new capitalists: "capital personified"

If enterprises and combines became proprietors of production facilities, did the ordinary workers and employees of these enterprises not also become owners of the means of production, making them "socialist" owners?

After the demise of the GDR, enterprise directors freely admitted that they were the ones who made all the decisions — decisions on investments, decisions on contracts, on imports, exports, on selling and buying means of production, hiring and firing, etc. The ordinary employees, who were bereft of any efficient and independent trade union

---

[381] *Politische Ökonomie des Sozialismus und ihre Anwendung in der DDR*, ibid., p. 271.
[382] Ibid., p. 260.

representation, were left out of the equation. These bosses acted like Western capitalist managers and considered themselves proprietors of enterprise assets. Wolfgang Biermann of Carl-Zeiss Jena spilled the beans:

> Finally, I had a fair pavilion of my own in Leipzig, the Zeiss-Halle. We built it for 50 million; it was the property of our combine.[383]

It was Mr. Biermann who made the decisions on hiring and firing, not the ordinary worker represented by his FDGB union:

> For leading positions I only took on people with a university degree and ten years' practice...[384]

Hans-Herbert Götz, another interviewer, quoted Biermann as saying:

> When I asked him if someone who was not a member of the SED belonged to his managerial staff, he answered coolly, "No, and I would not even think of employing someone if he was not a member of the SED."[385]

Former General Director Biermann did not care much for plan indices. "The truth is that you can always interpret a plan index."[386]

They told their employees to work extra shifts if they considered it necessary. Christa Bertag, General Director of VEB Kosmetik-Kombinat Berlin:

> We told our people: Hey, listen guys! You'll have to put in some more work and also work this Sunday because...[387]

Due to their economic power, they also had a lot of clout beyond their domain like capitalist board directors have:

> In the city of Jena certainly nothing of importance was decided without prior consent of or even against the will of Wolfgang Biermann, and in Karl-Marx-Stadt nothing essential was decided if Rudi Werner, the director of the large engineering combine "Fritz Heckert," would not agree.[388]

These people were excellent lobbyists and had political connections to top political circles just like their West German counterparts. Biermann again:

---

[383] Wolfgang Biermann in: Theo Pirker et al, ibid., p. 216.

[384] Ibid., p. 215.

[385] Wolfgang Biermann in: *Manager zwischen Marx und Macht. Generaldirectoren in der DDR,* Freiburg/Breisgau, 1988, p. 29; managers between Marx and might, general directors.

[386] Ibid., p. 225

[387] Christa Bertag in: Theo Pirker et al, ibid., p. 245.

[388] Hans-Herbert Götz, ibid., p. 16.

I only needed to pick up the receiver and ask for Mittag, and soon I was given an appointment.[389]

They spoke the vernacular of Western capitalists. Götz:

Wolfgang Biermann's business language...is not much different from that of Western managers.[390]

So there can be no doubt that GDR company directors were the ones in the driving seat and not the ordinary worker and salary earner. They did not even have an effective trade union representative and were not allowed to go on strike either. They did not become co-proprietors because they simply had no say in company matters and were subject to the decisions taken from high above. They were the "socialist" underdogs, even more so in case they were not a member of the ruling party, the Socialist Unity Party.

But was there really no difference between, say, a West German top manager of Krupp-Thyssen Steel and his GDR colleague?

There were indeed some differences which cannot be denied: the GDR top manager was directly appointed by the Central Committee of the SED and not by the largest shareholders of a company (there were no shareholders); if his combine was in the red, he or she could be dismissed by the political leadership and be replaced by someone more efficient or should I say "more ruthless"?

All these features are not common practice in ordinary capitalist countries. But these are minor differences because the main point here is that the GDR enterprise director or his deputy acted like "personified capital" (Marx) who possessed means of production, who could trade them and who could also take on workers and dismiss them again. They then informed the FDGB union chiefs of his decision which he usually got. The dismissed did however not join the dole queues in the GDR (as there was little or no unemployment), but they were then transferred to other enterprises — possibly at a lower pay and rank. And unlike former Soviet directors in times of Stalin, they were no longer mere state employees, but largely independent economic decision-makers like "personified capital" are.

So we have to assume that there was indeed a new capitalist class in the GDR, a new bourgeoisie, consisting of enterprise directors and their leading managerial staff. The same holds true for the directors of agricultural cooperatives. After the great reset, the economic reform in

---

[389] Wolfgang Biermann in: Theo Pirker et al, ibid., p. 224.
[390] Hans-Herbert Götz, ibid., p. 28.

the sixties, the GDR was no longer socialist and had become a class-ridden society, a capitalist country of a new type.

The members of the new GDR bourgeoisie

What was the size of the new GDR ruling class, the "new bourgeoisie"? The members of the new capitalist class were not just the company directors, but also those who were directly or indirectly involved in important decision-making on behalf of this class and who acted closely together with the leading staff of industrial, commercial or big agricultural producers' cooperatives and were an integral part in the ruling hierarchy. And not to forget the nomenclature of the SED, the members of the Politburo, those of the Central Committee, the provincial and district party officials belonged to it.

We can therefore add the following groups to the new ruling class:

> High-ranking SED and state officials, the leaders of military units, generals of the state security apparatus, people working as diplomats, scientific, medical, pedagogical personnel in leading positions, those occupying leading positions in cultural and juridical institutions.[391]

The above-mentioned M. S. Volensky describes the new capitalist class in the Soviet Union like this:

> The "managers" are the nomenclature; the most important thing for the nomenclature is power; the nomenclature becomes hereditary; the "socialist property" becomes their collective property; the reap the surplus value only for themselves...[392]

The new composition of the GDR bourgeoisie

But Dieter Voigt's valuable definition ignores the landmark changes brought about by the introduction of the NESPL system. This new system of planning and leadership transferred the formerly collective property of the means of production, administered by the GDR state nomenclature, to the directors of enterprises and their staff who could now handle it more or less freely and, of course, to their own advantage. The actual right of disposal over the most important means of production in the heavy and light industry was handed down to the directors of combines and their staff. The economic units were made relatively independent entities, drafting their own plans and negotiating favorable terms and

---

[391] Dieter Voigt et al, *Sozialstruktur der DDR*, Darmstadt, 1987, p. 165; social structure of the GDR.
[392] Michael S. Voslensky, *Nomenklatura. Die herrschende Klasse in der Sowjetunion*, Vienna, Munich, Zurich, 1980, p. 165.

conditions with the center in Berlin (the State Planning Commission and the industrial ministers) if they considered this necessary. The original plan indices were then altered to fit their own plans. This indicates a remarkable shift in power from the top to the bottom. The power was decentralized.

The ruling elite in Berlin, however, was still controlling the directors and their staff and reserved the right of dismissal. It engineered and controlled state politics. The transitional stage of state capitalism that existed prior to NES had now come to an end. This stage (as regards the Soviet Union) was once described by the Albanian economists Pano and Kapetani this way:

> State property in the Soviet Union is a form of capitalist private property with a high degree of concentration of production and capital. The revisionist bourgeoisie is the real owner of state enterprises and, with the help of the state it exploits the working class and the masses of working people of the country. By this exploitation it strengthens its economic position and thereby also its political predominance.[393]

Enver Hoxha, the former Albanian leader, describing the Soviet State prior to the Soviet "economic reform" of 1965–1966:

> Today's Soviet state is a collective capitalist who administers the means of production on behalf and in the interest of the new Soviet bourgeoisie. The socialist common property has been transformed into a new type of state capitalism.[394]

Hoxha's analysis is also applicable to the GDR. Here, too, the state was the collective capitalist who controlled the means of production — not on behalf of the workers and peasants, but on behalf of the new bourgeoisie. After the "economic reform" in the sixties, the collective property was given in trusteeship to the directors of enterprises and combines and their "socialist" managers, excluding the working people from ownership and any decision-making.

The ruling class was thus strengthened from below by creating a new layer of the privileged few at grassroots level. So the old ruling class, the Berlin nomenclature, was propped up by a new component of "personified capital." This process was systematically and intentionally

---

[393] Aristol Pano and Kico Kapetani, *Der kapitalistische Charakter der Produktionsbeziehungen in der Sowjetunion*, at: http://www.revolutionarydemocracy.org/albind/socalb2htm, in: *Socialist Albania*, journal of the Indian-Albanian Friendship Society, no. 14, July 1980; the capitalist character of production relations.

[394] Enver Hoxha, *Bericht an den 6. Parteitag der Partei der Arbeit Albaniens*, Roter Morgen, no. 15, December 6, 1971; report to the 6th Party Congress of the Party of Labor of Albania.

engineered by the "reformers" to inject new blood to their class rule and to put it on a broader and more solid foundation.

15. The GDR Working Class — An Exploited Class

Officially, neither exploiters nor exploited existed in the GDR:

> In socialism the means of production are the property of all working people and serve to satisfy the growing material and cultural needs of the people. The labor force has ceased to be a commodity. The new relations of property exclude any exploitation of man by man.[395]

We have seen, however, that the means of production in the GDR had never been the property of the working people, but were in collective ownership of the East German state and, following the "reforms," they even became the factual property of the directors of enterprises who were given the right to buy and sell them like ordinary commodities on a market place.

The ordinary working man had no such rights. The Federation of Free German Trade Unions (FDGB) was merely a mouthpiece of the SED politburo people whose long-time leader, Mr. Harry Tisch, was also a long-standing, veteran politburo member. After the collapse of the GDR, this was readily admitted by enterprise directors like Christa Bertag:

> No, no the FDGB didn't play any role whatsoever [in her cosmetics combine — author]. I'm very frank about this. I didn't have any problems with the FDGB people.[396]

This trade union was a union of the establishment and saw to it that the workers and the other employed towed the party line, behaved "responsibly," did not protest and did not go on strike either. Tisch, who was also interviewed after the demise of the GDR, told the same interviewers that "the Federal Board of the FDGB and our heads of department belonged to the nomenclature.[397]

And the "Communist" nomenclature had no interest in representing the working class either. On the contrary: they were deeply afraid of it. Tisch saw to it that there were practically no conflicts between the FDGB and the Central Committee of the SED in Berlin. Tisch, when asked if there had ever been conflicts between the two:

---

[395] *Politische Ökonomie des Kapitalismus und Sozialismus*, ibid., p. 426.
[396] Christa Bertag in: Theo Pirker et al, ibid., p. 244.
[397] Harry Tisch in ibid., p. 139.

Rainer Lepsius: "Do you remember a conflict between the FDGB and the Central Committee?" Harry Tisch: "During the fifteen years I was trade union chairman it did not happen."[398]

And Tisch also admits that there were practically no conflicts — apart from two minor events — between the management and his trade union.[399] Apparently, Tisch made sure that such a thing did not occur.

The ordinary employee of a GDR enterprise had no effective representation at work and was also not allowed to go on strike. The GDR constitution passed in the seventies had outlawed strikes. They were not permitted to found independent unions, either, or to take spontaneous action to get a fair share. Therefore, they were not able to realize the full value of their labor force at the labor market. Rosa Luxemburg, the co-founder of the Communist Party of Germany:

> The trade union plays an indispensable and organizational role in the modern wage system. Only trade union representation enables the human labor as a commodity to be sold at its full value.[400]

To sum up, the GDR working class was an exploited class, possessing only its labor to be sold on the labor market. In the absence of an efficient trade union representation, the GDR worker was not able to receive the full value of his or her labor force. It was the deep-seated fear of the working class on the part of the SED leadership that made them adopt pro-working class legislation in the early seventies to appease the exploited working class, also because the Polish workers, in the early seventies, had shown convincingly how to act efficiently in the absence of genuine trade unions. They founded their own independent union.

16. The Consciousness of the GDR Working Class

The fact that the East German working class was an exploited class was reflected in its consciousness. Let's have a look at the key element of the working class: the industrial construction workers.

In the mid-sixties, when the Ulbricht reforms were in full swing, Dieter Voigt, an East German sociologist, conducted a comprehensive empirical study on the state of consciousness of building workers (1966). It was based on a total of more than 900 interviews he had done at GDR construction sites.

[398] Ibid.
[399] Ibid., p. 140.
[400] Rosa Luxemburg, *Einführung in die Nationalökonomie*, Berlin, 1925, p. 276, in: Fred Oelßner, *Rosa Luxemburg — eine kritische biografische Skizze*, Berlin, 1951, p. 61; introduction into the national economy.

It revealed, among other things, that a core element of the East German working class did not identify with the ruling "socialist" SED party (see Table 1 below), had almost no idea about the economic significance of their enterprise (Table 2), thought they were badly informed by the media and the party (Table 3) and judged the wage system unfair (Table 4).[401]

Here are his findings.

I = skilled workers(% of total)
II = unskilled (% of total)
Total number people interviewed: 911

Table 1. "Do you think that the FDGB and the SED do anything for you at the construction site?"

Answers	I	II	total
No	73.3	75.6	74.1
Yes	6.8	6.6	6.7
No answer:	9.4	7.9	8.9

Table 2. "Can you tell us something about the economic significance of your enterprise?"

Answers	I	II	Total
Nothing	43.8	59.2	49.0
A little	29.7	28.6	29.3
Yes, I can	22.6	4.3	16.5
No answer	3.9	7.9	5.2

Table 3. "Would you like to be better informed?"

Answers	I	II	Total
Yes	86.2	56.3	76.2
Don't know	7.7	28.0	14.5
No	6.1	15.7	9.3

---

[401] Dieter Voigt, *Montagearbeiter in der DDR*, Darmstadt/Neuwied, 1973, p. 110; construction workers in the GDR.

Table 4. "Do you think that the present type of wage is just?"

Answers	I	II	Total
No	62.3	61.5	62.0
Yes	4.1	6.6	5.0
No answer	6.1	5.6	5.9
More or less	26.2	22.4	24.9

With astonishing frankness one quarter of the construction workers welcomed a colleague not being a member of the official trade union FDGB, and 75% said that they did not know the name of the SED party secretary at the site who was responsible for them.[402]

What happened to the GDR sociologist after he concluded his study? He was arrested, but he succeeded in smuggling his manuscript abroad. He had no chance to evaluate his results in the GDR. Only in 1969, when he was finally allowed to leave the country, was he able to finish his book and to publish it in West Germany.

Why did the authorities arrest someone whose only "crime" had been to conduct a scientific study?

He was arrested because the study clearly showed that the ordinary East German worker neither identified with the country's leadership and the official trade union nor believed that the system he was living under was just and fair and represented his interests. This, of course, ran counter to the official line propagated in the media.

What was the official line?

> There is a growing recognition that an identity exists between the interests of the individual and the interests of society.[403]

This was said in 1965 at the height of the "economic reform."

Mr. Voigt's findings clearly contradicted the official version that the GDR workers identified with the system. Scientific and fact-based data on the consciousness of the East German workers did not suit the rulers at all. These data gave evidence to the fact that the attitude of the ordinary GDR worker in reality had not changed much from the time when hundreds of thousands of working people rose up against the SED leaders on June 17, 1953. Then it also was the core of the working class, the Berlin construction workers, who had protested against a 10% rise in

---

[402] Ibid.

[403] Horst Müller, *Der Mensch arbeitet nicht fürs Geld allein*, in: *Arbeit und Arbeitsrecht*, Berlin, 1965, no. 17, p. 390, in: Dieter Voigt, *Montagearbeiter in der DDR*, ibid., p. 87; man does not only work for his money.

work norms as well as against rising consumer prices and had made an efficient attempt to get rid of the SED leaders. They had also demanded free and fair elections. Then only the Soviet military saved Ulbricht and his entourage from having to step down. The fear of the working class was still uppermost in the minds of the SED party bosses which might have motivated them to have Voigt arrested and to silence him.

17. The GDR State — An Instrument of the New Ruling Class

Marxism holds that the state is a machinery of power through which a certain social class dominates and controls the rest of the population. The state is an instrument of class rule, it is not a neutral institution, hovering above the populace and treating everybody fair and equal. To be able to perform its class rule, a social class relies on this apparatus, on the "executive," the police force, the security services, the standing army, etc.

The GDR "reformers" maintained and repeated again and again that the state of the GDR was a machinery of power through which the working class and its allies, the peasantry and the petty bourgeoisie, could exercise their political dominance:

> The rule of German imperialism and militarism has been eliminated with all its roots; the working class, side by side with the toiling peasants and other working sections of the population, conquered political power and, for the first time on German soil, erected the dictatorship of the proletariat.[404]

Thus, allegedly, the East German state was the state of the GDR proletariat through which it was able to exercise its class rule, closely allied with its other social partners.

Let us for a moment assume that the authors of the official textbook during the era Ulbricht, who claim that the GDR continued to be a "dictatorship of the proletariat," were right, then it must be allowed to ask the following questions:

1. Why would the overwhelming majority of the working population of the GDR have been interested in restoring the profit principle as a regulator of social production in the sixties? Did they profit from it or maybe some other people?

2. How could the GDR working people, who allegedly held the reins of power, be interested in abolishing the centrally planned economy from which it benefited most? (stable prices, social welfare, continuous and

---

[404] *Politische Ökonomie des Sozialismus und ihre Anwendung in der DDR*, ibid., p. 84.

How Socialist East Germany's Elite Turned Capitalist

uninterrupted economic growth, etc.)? Why would they be interested in causing supply shortages or disruptions in production which were the result of sabotaging central planning?

3. Why would the allegedly powerful working class of the GDR have been interested in giving the enterprises, which they themselves had tirelessly rebuilt after the war under very complicated circumstances, a status of autonomy, thus sabotaging and wrecking central planning and ignoring the interests of the overall economy?

4. Why were the working people in the GDR interested in abolishing the state's monopoly on foreign trade which safeguards the independence of a country from outside interference, which also safeguards their own interests?

5. Why was the East German working class, if it was the "ruling class," interested in creating the sector "Commercial Coordination" from which the GDR spy agency "Stasi" (chiefly spying on its own citizens) and the nomenclature in Berlin profited in particular by being provided with Western luxury goods?

6. Why did the East German working class, if it was in power, allow a tiny minority of state leaders to make exclusive use of huge areas of hunting grounds where they could follow their hunting passion? Note: In the GDR there were 22 state hunting grounds reserved for the nomenclature and also their guests, covering an area of five percent of the overall expanse of the country?[405] Why would the GDR workers be interested in depriving themselves from huge areas of commonly owned forests and lakes?

7. Why should the GDR working class and their allies have been interested in driving the country into debt by taking out huge loans in Western countries, causing workers and employees to become slaves for foreign banking consortia? Why would the working class be interested in enslaving themselves?

All these things were not in their interest, but solely in the interest of the GDR's new bourgeoisie that had usurped state power from the very start of the existence of the GDR — even in times of the SBZ, the Soviet Occupied Zone, even before the foundation of the second German state. THEY had an interest in all the enumerated phenomena and they benefited most from them.

---

[405] Hannes Bahrmann, Christoph Links, *Finale. Das letzte Jahr der DDR*, Berlin, 2019, p. 62; the last year of the GDR.

158

It follows from here that the state of the GDR was a machinery of power of the new capitalist class and the old nomenclature who was in full control of state affairs. At no point in time had this class allowed free and fair elections. If they had done it, they would have been removed from power by a plebiscite immediately.

Part Three: The End Of The Ulbricht Era

1. The plot to get rid of Walter Ulbricht

On January 28, 1971, the 15th Session of the Central Committee of the Socialist Unity Party took place in East Berlin. Its main task was to prepare the 8th Congress of the Party scheduled to take place on June 14–19.

Nobody contradicted Walter Ulbricht, the incumbent General Secretary, when he proposed the agenda for the forthcoming convention. Once again he had the intention "of running for the post of General Secretary for the next four years.[406]

Quite relieved, he departed for a five-week stay at the Barvicha health resort near Moscow. When he came back on March 18 to take up his official duties, he found that he was no longer in power. What had happened?

One week before the 15th Session a majority of the Politburo of the Central Committee of the SED, thirteen of its members, among them Eric Honecker, had written a letter to Leonid Brezhnev, the then Soviet leader in order to "give his consent for Ulbricht's dismissal."[407]

Even half a year earlier, in July of 1970, Honecker had reached a secret understanding with Brezhnev to oust his long-standing comrade and

---

[406] Norbert Podewin, *Walter Ulbricht. Eine neue Biografie*, Berlin, 1995, p. 443; a new biography.
[407] Ibid., p.445.

mentor as chief of the SED. Brezhnev, talking to Honecker on July 28 this year, said:

> To be quite frank, he won't succeed in sidelining us in his policy and act stupidly against you or other members of the politburo. We've troops stationed at your place...For quite some time, we've held the view that you should lead the Party. The issue is settled. Let him work for two or three more years...as president. Now it's time to settle the issue.[408]

Ulbricht was faced with a fait accompli. He had no choice but to give in and face the facts. He had lost the support and the trust of the Soviet leadership he had enjoyed for so many long years, but especially in times of Khrushchev whom he admired.

Officially, he resigned "due to old age and delicate health.[409]

When Honecker was later asked about the incident, he said that it had been Ulbricht's own proposal.[410]

When Brezhnev had given green light, those politburo members who had second thoughts and had originally refused to sign the petition against Ulbricht, also consented. Thus unity was restored in the Party leadership.

2. The reasons for Ulbricht's removal: The economic crisis in the GDR in 1970

Even Guenter Mittag, the long-standing Secretary for the Economy under Ulbricht and Honecker, later admitted that a grave economic crisis had emerged in the early seventies. Mittag in his reminiscences:

> But very soon disillusionment set in when reality had found access to the ideal world of visions for the future. Disruptions in production, supply shortages and dissatisfaction became frequent phenomena.[411]

A great number of enterprises, now being allowed to follow the profit principle, changed their product range and productions plans and preferred investing in the manufacture of those consumer or other goods being more profitable. Investments in consumer goods that were not so

---

[408] Ibid., pp. 425 f, Podewin quoting the minutes of the conversation between Leonid I. Brezhnev and Eric Honecker, July 28, 1970, in: SAPMO, state archive of parties and organizations, BA, SED, ZK, IV2/2A/3196.

[409] In: Reinhold Andert, Wolfgang Herzberg, *Der Sturz. Erich Honecker im Kreuzverhör*, Berlin and Weimar, 1990, p. 273: The fall. Eric Honecker cross-examined.

[410] Ibid.

[411] Günter Mittag, *Um jeden Preis*, ibid., p. 191.

cheap anymore had now become attractive for the management, causing price increases:

> In 1970, in the consumer goods sector alone, more than 200 unscheduled price increases were registered.[412]

At the time, the GDR media published reports about various enterprises which had refused to supply products of lower price ranges or only supplied them in insufficient numbers. The result: supply shortages and disruptions.

André Steiner in his books about the "economic reform" confirms:

> The population...complained about the lack of warm underwear, children's wear, track suits, winter shoes, batteries, flat irons, furniture, chemical articles, toothbrushes, or spark plugs...Due to unfavorable profit rates, enterprises reduced or halted their production in low-priced product ranges.[413]

Retail trade prices rose by 20% on average every year.[414]

Investments, too, became more expensive due to industrial prices having been freed on a step-by-step basis:

> In ESS [the second stage of the "economic reform" process, also called "Economic System of Socialism" — author] prices became more flexible, the main criterion being the modernity of the product.[415]

The outcome — stagnant investment activity:

> In 1971, the economic situation became so acute that for the first time in the history of the GDR investments had to be scaled down by 1.5% in the official plans.[416] Guenter Mittag, the former powerful Secretary of the Economy and one of the masterminds of the "economic reform," called it "breakdowns in production."[417] These breakdowns reflected declining investments in means of production as these are a lot more expensive and cost effective than those in the light industry.

Originally it was intended that 20–22% of the annual national income should be invested for productive accumulation, according to former

---

[412] W. Hößler, *Preisdisziplin gehört zur politischen Verantwortung von Industrie und Handel*, in: *Die Wirtschaft*, Nr. 15, 1971, aus: Philipp Neumann, ibid., p. 184; price discipline belongs to the political responsibility of trade and industry.

[413] André Steiner, ibid., p. 515.

[414] Statistisches Jahrbuch 1976, pp. 249, 306, in: ibid, p. 515; statistical yearbook quoted.

[415] Jörg Roesler, *Das neue ökonomische System — Dekorations- oder Paradigmenwechsel?*, Hefte zur DDR-Geschichte, no. 3, p. 14; the new economic system — window dressing or paradigm change?

[416] Philipp Neumann, ibid., p. 199.

[417] Günter Mittag, ibid., p. 191.

head of the Central Committee's Department for the Economy, Mr. Carl-Heinz Janson, since a lower rate of investment would have endangered economic development. But his own figures show that from 1971 this rate was constantly on the decline:[418]

Year	Percentage
1971	19.4
1975	17.1
1980	16.5
1985	12.0
1986	11.8
1987	11.4
1988	10.5
1989	7.4

This downward trend in the accumulation rate led to more wear and tear on infrastructure and equipment, and also to a higher depreciation rate. However, most of the GDR enterprises and also some of the combines did not possess the financial means to replace the old machinery and then took the easy road and turned to Schalck-Golodkovsky's KoKo for help. He then tried to find firms abroad who were prepared to export plants to the ailing East German economy. As a result, the Moscow leaders became more and more suspicious. Ulbricht — at that time still General Secretary of the SED, admitted this much:

> Moscow, too, sometimes asks us this question: "What kind of deals are you doing with the French, the West Germans, or the Japanese," and everybody wants to know how we are doing it. That's fairly simple: we run up debt with the capitalists."[419]

When Eric Honecker, Ulbricht's successor in 1971, meets with Leonid I. Brezhnev on July 28, 1970 to talk to him about his resignation, the latter is well briefed about the dismal economic situation in the GDR. The deeply worried Brezhnev commented, "Believe me, Eric — the situation in your country is deeply worrying!"[420]

---

[418] Carl-Heinz Janson, ibid., p. 70.
[419] André Steiner, ibid., p. 522, citing Ulbricht's talks with the Deputy Prime Minister Tikhonov on June 25, 1970.
[420] In: Peter Przybylski, *Tatort, Akte Honecker*, ibid., p. 280, document 15.

3. The "Prague Spring"

What was the General Secretary of the Communist Party of the Soviet Union so worried about? Was he worried about the process of the restoration of capitalism in the GDR initiated under Ulbricht's chairmanship?

This does not make any sense. Brezhnev himself and his Minister President Aleksei Kosygin had introduced similar "economic reforms" in 1965. The two most influential Soviet leaders after Khrushchev's ousting in October 1964 had championed more or less the same reform process as their East German comrades did, who had started the project only two years earlier.

Brezhnev therefore could not have been worried about the reintroduction of the profit principle into the formerly socialist economy, but about something quite different:

He was deeply afraid that the GDR under the Khrushchevite Ulbricht could distance itself from the Soviet Union and get too chummy with Western imperialism. Contacts between the GDR rulers and the Bonn leaders, which started in Erfurt and Kassel in 1970 between West German Chancellor Willy Brandt and GDR Minister President Willi Stoph were cut short, as Moscow feared the possible foundation of a German-German confederation.

On top of that, in Alexander Dubcek's Czechoslovakia where a similar economic reform process following Evsey Liberman's principles had gone under way, anti-Soviet sentiment was running high. When the reform-minded Czechoslovak leaders brought the ending of the alliance with the Soviet Union into play and started talking about neutrality, Soviet tanks came in crushing the experiment in August 1968, also called "Prague Spring," assisted by other army contingents of Warsaw Pact countries, but not by East Germany. The Brezhnev Doctrine was created.

Ulbricht himself harbored great sympathies for the "reform communist" Dubcek. Norbert Podewin:

> After his return from Prague in February 1968 he expressed his deep satisfaction over the fact that with the installation of Alexander Dubcek as First Secretary of the Communist Party of Czechoslovakia, the dogmatists in the leadership of the party had lost a lot of ground. He himself had suggested to Dubcek to purge another five dogmatists from the Presidium of the Central

Committee of the CPCh and to replace them with younger politicians who were closely linked to the Academia.[421]

By supporting Honecker against Ulbricht, Brezhnev and the Soviet leadership wanted to block any attempt of rapprochement between the GDR and the Federal Republic. Brezhnev:

> Let's be honest: Erfurt and Kassel was a flop, nothing good came out of it. Brandt has different intentions regarding the GDR than we have.[422] When Walter Ulbricht hinted at the 15th Session of the CC that he intended to remain in office for four more years to come, "the Group of Thirteen" applied the emergency brakes and filed their petition to General Secretary Brezhnev, asking for help and reminding him of his previous promise to dismiss Ulbricht from the key post in the country.

Guenter Mittag, Ulbricht's Secretary for the Economy, and the number two in the country, even though his closest ally in the sixties, also signed the petition to preserve his influence on further developments in the GDR. Later, in the mid-seventies, he got his position back and again became the Number Two under Eric Honecker who had no clue about economics.

4. The Polish rebellion

There was still another reason why many former Ulbricht loyalists thought it appropriate to distance themselves from their former master: the events in Poland close to the GDR border which have already been mentioned.

Let's take a closer look at what happened in December 1970 in "socialist" Poland.

Under party leader Vladyslav Gomulka massive price increases occurred leading to a workers' rebellion in the northern part of the country. The protest movement forced Gomulka to resign to be replaced by Edvard Gierek who then tried to appease the movement by introducing a price freeze on urgently needed commodities. Gierek, the new party leader, one day went to Szczecin (Stettin) on the river Oder, close to the GDR border, where the port workers were on strike and made an attempt to get them back to work. Among the protesters were also communists of a different caliber who tried to get a word in. At a protest rally this speech was heard:

---

[421] Norbert Podewin, ibid., p. 396, quoting Wilfriede Otto's essay in *Neues Deutschland*, September 29–30, 1992.

[422] Peter Przybylskik, *Tatort, Akte Honecker*, ibid., p. 284.

There is much talk here among the workers that our society is divided in classes again. There is one group of people who already enjoy their socialism so that they don't know what to do with it, and they seem to believe that they are better than others. And they have this type of socialism because they have a lot of things to waste. We had a comrade called Skrzydlovsky here. After only eleven months he was paid more than 170,000 zloty — not his basic salary, but with all kinds of big and small bonuses combined. Comrades! I think we must end this practice of small and big bonuses and pay only for real work...It has become a bad habit that some even get several bonuses and the worker is his slave. The director is the landlord here. Is that what they call "cooperation"?[423]

Quite obviously, the GDR party bosses were afraid of the "Polish disease" spilling over into East Germany should Ulbricht remain in power for another four years. Ulbricht was ready to increase prices like his Polish counterpart Gomulka which could have caused massive problems for the stability of the GDR regime as well. A new and fresh "socialist" face was needed for the GDR to not allow similar "diseases" to happen there. So the scene was set for a new policy, another "New Course," and more appealing to the disgruntled East Germans than the old policy. There was also the danger that the GDR workers might see through the pseudo-socialist facade as the Polish speaker did. The "New Course" was baptized "Main Task of Unity between Economic and Social Policy." The Honecker era was about to get under way.

5. Honecker's "Main Task"

Honecker's price freeze and spending programs

Shortly after the end of the Polish workers' rebellion in January 1971 and even before the new Party Congress got under way, first steps were taken in Berlin to appease the East German working class:

> According to Neues Deutschland, the Council of Ministers of the GDR, on the basis of
>
> a common proposal of the CC of the SED, the Council of Ministers and the Federal Board of the FDGB, on January 29, took a decision to lower certain prices...and to raise social security and lower pensions.[424]

---

[423] Excerpts from a speech of a Polish worker at a protest rally at a Polish shipyard, in: Philipp Neuman, ibid., p. 201.

[424] Archiv der Gegenwart, ibid., p. 28,772.

Additionally, social insurance payments for people with a monthly income below 600 marks were raised.[425]

Three months later, on April 27–28 (1971), the CC of the SED meets for its 5th Session to adopt further measures, among them a rise in pensions for 3.4 million citizens, for practically all GDR pensioners; lower rents for newly built apartments and also more benefits for working mothers.

On June 15–19, the Eighth Congress of the SED convenes in East Berlin. The new five-year plan for 1971–1975 included wage raises of 21–23% in real terms.[426]

Furthermore, a new housing program was brought forward.

After the Congress even further social measures are taken: on November 9, the Politburo and the Council of Ministers proclaim a freeze on consumer goods prices, on the prices of catering services and repairs within the framework of the new five-year plan.[427]

Five years later, on May 18–22, the Ninth Congress of the SED adopts another generous social spending program:

> -the monthly minimum wage for about one million full-time employees is raised from 350 to 400 marks by October 1st; -the minimum pensions for 3.5 million old-age pensioners are increased from December 1; -maternity leave is extended from 18 to 26 weeks without reduction in payments; the 40-hour-week is scheduled to be introduced by May 1, 1977 on a step-by-step basis.[428]

The consequences

As we have seen, the GDR economy was in a rather bad shape in the early seventies, following the completion of the "economic reform." The capital accumulation rate was in decline, the trade balance negative, imports were surpassing exports by a big margin and, as Mittag himself admitted, there were growing disruptions in production and supply shortages.

However, the spending program required a lot of money the ailing economy could no longer provide on its own. So the money had to be found elsewhere to keep the promises made to the East Germans. Where to find it? The answer: on the international money markets. At that time

---

[425] Ibid., p. 28,773.

[426] Keesing's Record of World Events, @Keesings.gvpi.net/keesings/Ipext.dll/KRWE/krwe-00689/krwe-99689/krwe-100484/krwe-10..., p. 2.

[427] Hermann Weber, *Grundriss der Geschichte der DDR, 1945–1990*, Hamburg, 1991, p. 316; outline of the history of the GDR.

[428] Archiv der Gegenwart, ibid., pp. 35,009f.

it was not difficult to find the money, as there was plenty available. According to Mr. Janson, "Many were prepared to help the GDR."[429]

But anyone who is not completely out of his mind knows that raising money on the international financial markets is a very risky and problematic issue in the long run. There are always strings attached to the granting of credit and interest rates may rise substantially during the credit period, according to the capitalist law of supply and demand.

In 1983, the GDR was already so highly indebted to foreign lenders that the Politburo asked KoKo chief Schalck-Golodkovsky to contact Bavarian Prime Minister Franz-Josef Strauß to arrange a huge loan amounting to one billion Deutschmarks (West German currency) to breathe new life into the GDR economy. The Bayerische Landesbank was the chief donor. One year later, in 1984, another loan also worth almost one billion was raised in the Federal Republic — this time provided by a consortium of 24 banks under the leadership of Deutsche Bank.

Schalck was sent to Bavaria to get things done and later Strauß visited the GDR.

Thus, in 1985, GDR indebtedness stood at 30 billion valuta mark.[430] In 1970 it "only" amounted to 2.2 billion, according to Janson's data.

To pay the interest on the debt burden, a whole annual national income had to be spent on debt servicing alone. CC department head Carl-Heinz Janson who belonged to Guenter Mittag's team sums up the consequences this way:

> The outcome of this policy is visible in the infrastructure, in the deplorable structural state of many buildings, in environmental pollution which can be seen with the naked eye.[431]

On the one hand it was now urgently necessary to export as much as possible for cash even if the exports were not profitable at all, and on the other the country imported goods on the basis of long-term crediting. This could only be sustained at the expense of capital accumulation, creating growing gaps in product ranges and leading to illegal price increases even with goods of basic necessities which, officially, were exempt from price hikes. In agriculture old machinery could not be fully substituted by new one. Janson continues:

> In 1987, 65% of all plants and installations were worn out.[432]

---

[429] Carl-Heinz Janson, ibid., p. 64.
[430] Ibid., p. 65, see Janson's statistics there.
[431] Ibid., p. 68.
[432] Ibid., p. 72.

And the infrastructure suffered as well: railroad ties were no longer stable enough; almost every second railway line was affected by serious damage.[433]

In early 1978, a group of "Democratic Communists," working in the underground, in its manifesto summed up the economic situation in the GDR this way:

> Wage, price, and structural problems have not been solved. The quality of production is declining…, losses are growing, indebtedness to foreign lenders in East and West is increasing. The people of the GDR are living beyond their means, and payments on interest and debt servicing are eating up investments…[434]

These, among other things, were the results of excessive social spending by the GDR government and the resulting indebtedness and financial dependence on foreign lending institutions.

What were the consequences of the freeze on consumer goods prices?

If price controls, on consumer goods for example, are not released in an economy where profit (or the law of value) has been fully restored as the regulator of social production and where enterprises are allowed to produce more or less independently from a center, then it is up to the state (or the government) to subsidize the enterprises and to pay them compensation for the losses in profit incurred.

Or else: this government (or state) makes a U-turn and is prepared to return to a principled Marxist line and reintroduces effective central planning form a center, thus binding the economic units together again and making them follow strict directives under a scientific and detailed plan which is legally binding for all economic units, thus also restoring the monopoly on foreign trade in the hands of the state.

This would have meant to undo the entirety of economic reforms and to return to the basics of a centrally planned economy which, under Lenin and Stalin, proved to be highly efficient and successful.

Was the Honecker government prepared to do that, thus solving the root problem, or was it not and preferred to keep the economic reform in place (maybe allowing for some minor alterations) which had caused all these difficulties and had steered the GDR economy into such a mess?

The vast majority of analysts dealing with the history of the GDR are of the opinion that NESPL was halted by the new Honecker regime and that the new government undid most of Ulbricht's "promising" reforms. But is that really true?

---

[433] Ibid., p. 78.
[434] Archiv der Gegenwart, ibid., p. 36,806.

The Honecker government was indeed prepared to pay huge subsidies to enterprises to compensate for the loss in profits. Biermann himself noted, "Every year, 75 billion from the national income was spent for price subsidies.[435] He also stated that the GDR economy only exported goods worth 15 billion to Western countries (the so-called Non-Socialist Currency Area) — only one fifth of the amount.

Janson confirms:

> To guarantee relatively stable retail prices, state budget subsidies had to be sharply increased. Their share of produced national income grew from 7.8% in 1971 to 22.8 in 1987.[436]

The result: the value of the GDR mark declined more and more.

The choice made had been debt management policy, plus subsidies, and no return to "dogmatic" and "Stalinist" central planning.

Was Guenter Mittag, together with former concentration camp leader Eric Apel, the mastermind of NESPL, dismissed and replaced by a true Marxist in Eric Honecker's environment, if there were still such people left?

No — after a short break, when he had a "minor job" in the Council of Ministers, where be became Deputy Chairman, he was soon back again and reinstated as Secretary for the Economy (his former post under Ulbricht) by Mr. Honecker personally, so that the period during which he had to make do without Mittag only lasted three years.[437] Honecker put complete trust in him.[438]

Other "reformers," or should we better call them "capitalist roaders," also kept their positions in the SED apparatus, even without such a downturn in their career. Here are some names:

Helmut Koziolek, director of the Central Institute for Socialist Management at the CC of the SED, was not even removed temporarily, but kept his post all the way long; Claus Kroemke, Mittag's personal assistant since 1962, also remained in place; Walter Halbritter, appointed by Ulbricht himself, one of the chief planners and Deputy Chairman of the State Planning Commission (up to 1965), kept his position as Chairman of the Office for Prices until 1989. He belonged to the few who had voted against the ousting of Ulbricht after the plot in 1971.

The list is incomplete.

---

[435] Wolfgang Biermann in: Theo Pirker et al, ibid., p. 225.
[436] Carl-Heinz Janson, ibid.,p. 81.
[437] Ibid., pp. 232f.
[438] Ibid., p. 233.

There was no change of staff at the top of the SED apparatus nor at the top of the GDR state, apart from Ulbricht's removal.

The above-mentioned Marxist U-turn would have required a completely different type of personnel in leading positions, a radical shake-up and reshuffle, but those people were no longer there; they were gone for good! They had been thoroughly purged from the Party even in the early fifties. Rudolf Herrnstadt, the former editor-in-chief of *Neues Deutschland* or the veteran Spanish freedom fighter Wilhelm Zaisser, ex Minister of the Interior of the GDR before Eric Mielke took over, were purged after the events of June 17, 1953. Nikita Khrushchev and the Soviet generals stationed in East Berlin had helped Ulbricht to do just that.

NESPL was to stay in place and only minor changes and corrections were made to adapt the system to the new realities, but the system as such was not abolished. Guenter Mittag himself confirms:

> Honecker was the man who deprived Ulbricht of power and made necessary corrections in the policy of the SED.[439]

What sort of corrections? Mittag:

> In the highly sensitive area of price policy a virtual blockade was installed.[440]

In another field things were not to be taken to the extremes for political and ideological considerations and a more careful approach was favored by Honecker and his team. Koziolek:

> NESPL also envisaged the possibility to let unprofitable enterprises go bankrupt...It was not possible to include bankruptcy of enterprises in our system.[441]

To preserve the "socialist facade," the GDR "reformers" preferred not to dismiss workers and to send them into unemployment. Enterprises had to be subsidized to get them out of the red. Mass dismissals for economic reasons were not an option for Honecker. But he had no intention to distance himself from the reform project and to undo all the various measures introduced in connection with the new economic system which, even under Ulbricht, he himself had vehemently supported and applauded. Even in early fifties, when Ulbricht had lost his majority in the politburo after the events of June 17, 1953, he was one of the few loyalists who did not vote for Ulbricht's ousting.

In his speech at the 8th Party Congress in 1971 he had this to say:

---

[439] Günter Mittag, *Um jeden Preis*, ibid., p. 190.
[440] Ibid., p. 195.
[441] Helmut Koziolek in: Theo Pirker et al, ibid., p. 268.

An important yardstick for the work performed in the nationally owned enterprises in industry, construction, agriculture, transport, communications, and trade is the profit. It is the most important source for our socialist state to cover its expenses and, at the same time, to finance extended reproduction and to increase bonus funds and cultural and social services for the working people.[442]

Like his predecessor Ulbricht, he stressed that each and every enterprise and combine ought to strive for the realization of a maximum of profit:

Cost accounting must be raised to such a level that enterprises can make maximum profits and increase their funds if their products and performances are to meet the requirements of the national economy regarding quantity, assortment, quality, and costs.[443]

For Honecker the economic categories of capitalism were also valid for his "socialism":

Considerable importance must be attached to balancing and to an even more effective implementation of categories such as profit, wage, costs, industrial prices, credit, and interest.[444]

The "dogmatist" Stalin denied this categorically. In his last work on political economy he wrote:

It is obvious that Marx was using terms [categories] which suited capitalist conditions perfectly well [categories like profit, credit, interest, etc. — author]. But it is more than strange to operate with these terms now...[445]

According to Honecker and his entourage, to which also and especially Mittag belonged, the enterprises in the GDR were to remain basically independent economic units that were obliged to finance themselves out of their own funds — from the profits they were able to make. They had to finance their investments out of their own funds, too, or by credit taking. The status of credit and interest remained untouchable which, in practice, meant that the banks continued to control the enterprises and not the proletarian state as is the custom in genuinely socialist countries.

Only the price policy was to remain a government prerogative.

He also emphasized the importance of creating more GDR monopolists, also called combines, thus fully supporting Mittag's concept

---

[442] Protokoll der 8. Parteitags der SED, Berlin, 1971, p. 29; minutes of the 8th Party Convention of the Socialist Unity Party of Germany.
[443] Ibid., p. 30.
[444] Ibid., p. 77.
[445] J. W. Stalin, Ökonomische Probleme des Sozialismus in der UdSSR, ibid., p. 19.

of establishing "socialist" monopolies nationwide. Honecker also said that these combines should be able to operate even more independently than before:

> The responsibility of our enterprises, combines, and VVB [associations of enterprises — author] must be further enhanced on the basis of the state plan to enable them to solve technological and economic problems.[446]

In other words, those analysts who maintain that Ulbricht's successor Honecker and his team halted or even reversed the "economic reform" are wrong. Honecker assisted by Ulbricht's chief economist, Guenter Mittag, merely introduced some "corrections": a freeze on prices, credit-financed spending programs, often financed by the Federal Republic of Germany, to appease popular discontent, to save NESPL and to stay in power at the same time.

To safeguard the political stability of the pseudo-socialist regime, huge amounts of money were pumped into the economy, were used to subsidize prices, fares, or rents. This was a constant drain on the country's resources and the state budget, leading to a decline in spending on infrastructure projects, on capital accumulation and rendering the economy more and more dependent on foreign investors and international financial institutions. Thereby the GDR was weaned away from the Soviet Union and driven and pushed into international capitalism. The country became a colony of the globalists who now controlled the GDR's finances and plundered the working class which had to pay the bills in the final analysis. But the people of the GDR rose up against the corrupt system and their protagonists and won in the end, but having to pay a heavy price as well: now becoming a colony of the Federal Republic and its corporations. And we all know that this Federal Republic is a close ally of the US imperialism and not completely independent either. The conclusion: the Eastern part of Germany became also a semi-colony of the US and NATO.

---

[446] Protokoll des 8. Parteitags der SED, ibid.,p. 338.

Summary And Conclusions

1. Shortly after the end of World War II, and even before, a wide variety of anti-fascists, socialists, communists and other democratic forces, of whom many had been inmates of Nazi concentration camps and penitentiaries, were trying hard to create a broad-based anti-fascist front to take the reconstruction of the destroyed country into their own hands and to build a new democratic and united Germany. Nobody was to be excluded who was honestly interested in overcoming German fascism and nobody wanted a divided Germany. It was the fight for a new beginning.

2. These forces were also assisted by Joseph Stalin, the Soviet leader, who advocated the establishment of a broad anti-fascist front which was to adopt a common anti-fascist platform.

3. This broad-based movement, which became very strong soon after the collapse of the Nazi regime and the liberation of the concentration camps, was rapidly developing in nearly all major German cities and also and especially in the capital Berlin. Here anti-fascists of the first hour were trying to rebuild essential services, when they were told by the Ulbricht group to stop their work. This group, consisting of two parts, had been assembled by Georgi Dimitrov, the former head of the Communist International in Moscow and was then sent into Berlin shortly after the capitulation of the Nazi regime.

4. When the Ulbricht group had returned (early in May 1945), it soon began to liquidate the anti-fascist grass-roots movement in Berlin, but also in Hamburg through like-minded people. Those German communists

who had led a very risky struggle against the Nazi tyranny and had started setting up their own independent organizations, were forced to shut them down again in Berlin. They were denounced as "sectarian" and "Nazi fronts" and said to be "infiltrated by Nazis." Later Ulbricht also dissolved the "Association of the Victims of Nazi Persecution" (VVN), the main anti-fascist organization of anti-Nazi resistance fighters and founded his own "anti-fascist" organization, the "Committee of Anti-fascist Resistance Fighters" (1953).

5. After having forbidden these groups, the Ulbricht people then staffed the highest positions in the Berlin administration and also in trade and industry with reactionary politicians and in some cases even with former active Nazis (Ferdinand Sauerbruch).

Ulbricht can neither be considered a genuine anti-fascist nor a "Stalinist," since he ignored Stalin's advice to find common ground with anti-fascist forces and to create a bloc with them.

6. When Ulbricht and his close friend Wilhelm Pieck realized that the majority of German communists were not supporting their line, they turned to certain Soviet generals in Berlin/Karlshorst for help and asked them to bring a number of prisoners-of-war back to Germany from Russia prematurely who were kept in there due to their war crimes. Among them were former members of the Nazi party. Pieck, who headed the German Communist Party in Berlin, called them "devoted anti-fascists" or "friends of the communists" who were "urgently needed" in Berlin. So Wilhelm Pieck, who later became President of the GDR, cannot be considered an anti-fascist either. Both Ulbricht and Pieck were tools of reactionary forces masked as "communists."

7. In April 1946 the Socialist Unity Party (SED) was founded in Berlin. It was a merger between the Ulbricht-Pieck group that had usurped the leadership of the former Communist Party of Germany at a special conference way back in 1935, and the East German wing of the Social Democratic Party (SPD). Otto Grotewohl, the chief politician of the East German Social Democrats, became one of the leaders of the newly established party and later Minister President of the GDR.

8. Only three months later, a correspondent of the Soviet Occupied Forces in Germany or SMAD for short, sent a report to the Central Committee of the Communist Party of the Soviet Union in Moscow, outlining growing discontent among a great number of disgruntled communist activists with the way the new party was being run. Many

of these activists who had been active resistance fighters during the Nazi era inside Germany were given only minor posts in the SED and were excluded from leadership positions, thus losing any influence on the running of the party. In some instances they called the new SED leaders "traitors."

9. Only two years after the war it had become obvious that the administrative machinery in East Germany had not undergone thorough democratization even though this was claimed by the SED leaders. A high-ranking official of the SMAD summed up his criticism in a speech, pointing to a whole number of shortcomings.

10. However, there were other SMAD officials and generals who supported the Ulbricht group and their entourage, among them General Tulpanov who was later dismissed from his post by the Moscow center and replaced by a more trustworthy official. There were two lines in the SMAD: one was still loyal to Stalin and his policy on Germany (create a united, neutral and democratic Germany!) and the other, represented by the leading SMAD military, secretly boycotted Stalin's line (Zhukov, Sokolovsky) and favored a divided Germany like the Americans and their allies. The Ulbricht-Pieck group of false communists who dominated the newly founded Communist Party of Germany and after that the Socialist Unity Party supported those SMAD generals who stood in opposition to Stalin and the leadership of the CPSU, among them Marshal Georgi Zhukov, who had arbitrarily appointed himself chairman of the SMAD by issuing Order Number One in June 1945. Later he was withdrawn from Germany when plenty of war booty from Berlin villas was found in his dacha near Moscow.

11. To the Ulbricht loyalists also belonged Eric Mielke, later to become chief of the GDR's infamous secret service "Stasi." He had returned from France where he had been an asset of the American secret service Office for Strategic Services (OSS), the forerunner of the CIA. The code name given to him was Leistner. Later he became the third most powerful politician of the GDR. The proven fact that he was a spy of the American imperialists in Nazi occupied France had been known to the SED leadership, when he was appointed head of State Security in November 1957. It did not disqualify him getting the job.

12. After the foundation of the Federal Republic of Germany in September 1949, only weeks later, on October 7, 1949, the German Democratic Republic was established. Prior to the foundation, Pieck, Ulbricht, Grotewohl, and Oelßner — four politburo members of the SED

— had been in Moscow, but were shunned by Stalin. But they had talks with other members of the Soviet politburo instead, among them Nikita Khrushchev. Stalin had serious misgivings about the early foundation of the two German states, as this thwarted his efforts to create a united democratic Germany.

13. To undercut Stalin's policy on Germany, the SED leaders arbitrarily changed the agenda of the Second Party Conference in July 1952 to begin with the "accelerated construction of socialism." Originally, the conference was meant to support the official Soviet policy of creating a united, neutral and peaceful Germany and to make proposals to specify this policy. Pieck had been in Moscow for discussions with Stalin on the issue. However, the decisions taken at the conference contradicted this line and declared the "building of socialism" its main purpose. After the conference, a growing number of people, among them many small peasant farmers, fearing collectivization, fled the country, leaving their farms behind.

14. It was the First Secretary of the SED, Walter Ulbricht, who, despite the tense situation in the GDR and the mass exodus towards the West, pushed for a 10% increase in work norms by which the working class was hardest hit. Shortly before the ensuing uprising of June 17, the main leaders of the SED had been summoned to Moscow to discuss a document presented by the Soviet leaders to ease tensions among the population and to stem the flow of migrants to West Germany. It contained the main points for a "New Course" and was grudgingly approved by the SED politburo. The 10% increase in work norms remained in place however, provoking the rebellion of June 17, which rapidly spread in the entire GDR. It could only be smashed with the help of the Soviet Army stationed in Berlin/Karlshorst. Shortly after the event, Nikita Khrushchev, assisted by the deposed Marshal Zhukov, had Stalin's most trusted lieutenant, Lavrenty Beria arrested, put on trial and executed.

15. Backed by the new pro-capitalist putsch regime in Moscow, Ulbricht won the power struggle against his adversaries Wilhelm Zaisser and Rudolf Herrnstadt who had suggested that he should step down as First Secretary. Both were expelled — first from the politburo, then from the CC and after that from the party as well. Herrnstadt was not allowed to enter Berlin anymore.

16. Following these events, the social structure of the SED remarkably changed: former members of the Hitler youth and the Nazi party NSDAP were readily accepted as members to make the party a more reliable

instrument in case new uprisings should occur, but also for carrying out the envisaged capitalist reforms by which nearly all socialist beginnings were liquidated on a step-by-step basis.

17. In February 1956, the 20th Congress of the Communist Party of the Soviet Union took place in Moscow where Khrushchev gave his notorious "secret speech" to defame Stalin and what he called his "personality cult." But it was Khrushchev himself who had nurtured this cult during Stalin's lifetime and put it to the extremes, mainly to justify his purges in Moscow and the Ukraine. Ulbricht and his followers, among them also Eric Honecker, the then leader of the youth organization of the SED, the Free German Youth, welcomed the outcome of the Congress. Now the formerly "wise" Stalin, "our great teacher," had ceased to be a Marxist-Leninist "classic." His books were banned from the bookstores. Nobody should know how to build a genuine and solid socialist economy.

18. At the 22nd Congress of the CPSU Khrushchev stepped us his defamation of Stalin and called him a "tyrant." Ulbricht and his closest followers soon followed in his footsteps: the Stalin monument was torn down in Berlin and all streets, squares, and enterprises named after Stalin were given new names. They called it "de-Stalinization." Shortly afterwards, in December 1961, diplomatic relations with socialist Albania that did not allow "de-Stalinization" were broken off.

19. In the late fifties, the SED leaders adopted a series of measures similar to those taken by Khrushchev in the USSR, among them the sale of the Machine Tractor Stations to the agricultural cooperative, thus extending the range of commodity circulation — a major preparatory step in the direction of restoring capitalism.

20. Even before, Ulbricht had started gathering around him a team of young economists who were tasked with drafting the first plans for a GDR specific New Economic System, also called NESPL (New Economic System of Planning and Leadership). Eric Apel, a former Nazi war criminal, who, at one time occupied a leading position in the concentration camp of Buchenwald-Dora in the Harz mountains and in the village of Peenemuende where he had belonged to a team testing Hitler's V2 rocket, was put in charge together with Guenter Mittag and other reform-minded economists to draft the plans for the project.

Apel had been a member of the SED only since 1957 and soon became the rising star in the party thanks to Ulbricht's patronizing. Later, he became chairman of the State Planning Commission to implement the project from above. The new system was adopted at the 6th Party Congress in January 1963. In July 1963, the guidelines for the new system were made public. The population was made to believe that the plans were designed to make socialism "more efficient," "more modern" and that the old system had put too much emphasis on "quantitative production" instead of "qualitative manufacturing." Only this way labor productivity could be increased.

21. By introducing NESPL (later called ESS for Economic System of Socialism) the law of value (the profit principle) was comprehensively restored throughout the GDR economy as regulator of social production. Also other capitalist categories, among them credit, price, cost, interest, value, supply and demand, etc. were reintroduced as what the reformers called "economic levers." Falsely named "economic laws of socialism," but in fact laws of capitalism, were to be made use of to camouflage the comprehensive restoration of capitalist principles under cover of socialist rhetoric.

22. By creating the sector "Commercial Coordination"(KoKo) under the auspices of the security apparatus ("Stasi") to keep it hidden from the public, to earn urgently needed foreign currency and to get better access to foreign credits, a whole new capitalist branch was created and the state monopoly of foreign trade dismantled which guarantees the independence of a socialist country.

23. Schalck-Golodkovsky, the head of KoKo, even traded the cultural heritage of the GDR, and political prisoners were sold to West Germany to earn extra foreign currency to finance imports from Western countries. So KoKo was also involved in human trafficking. Bribe money was set aside to win lucrative contracts abroad. For his "excellent services" Schalck received a whole series of medals and decorations, among them the Order of Karl Marx.

24. After that efficient central planning from a center to coordinate all sectors of the economy and to keep the economic units united under one roof, was reduced to a socialist facade. The plans were often adopted late and without any binding directives for enterprises and combines. Following the introduction of the autonomy of the economic units, especially of the newly established combines (almost 160 in number) in 1967, combine directors were given the right to change plan indices at will.

25. The reform with the greatest systemic relevance was the introduction of a tax on enterprise capital. This reflected the fact that the means of production had already become commodities and could be bought and sold like consumer goods. Companies had to pay an annual interest rate of 6% on average to the state which had ceased to be the proprietor of the means of production, marking the end of people's property. The company directors became the new proprietors who could hire and fire personnel. Workers did not become unemployed though, but could be sent away to take up new employment elsewhere. For leading positions in enterprises SED membership was a must.

26. The reintroduction of capitalist categories, especially the profit principle, soon led to severe disproportions in the economy, disrupted the production process and caused supply shortages, leading to growing dissatisfaction among the population.

27. The "economic reform" of 1963–1970 also caused changes in the social structure of the GDR: a new capitalist class of combine directors, enterprise directors, heads of department, etc. Emerged acting as "personified capital," thus joining the GDR nomenclature at the top of the hierarchy. On the other hand, the working class was once again deprived of the means of production and had no say in company matters. They had no right to go on strike and to organize in independent trade unions. The East German working class became an exploited class again.

28. This was reflected in the consciousness of a key element of the working class: the construction workers. An East German sociologist who had conducted a study into the consciousness of ordinary GDR workers and employees found that many were of the opinion that the SED did not represent their own interests and also took the view that the wage system was unjust. When the SED regime was swept away by a powerful civil-rights movement (called "counterrevolution" by the top brass), the workers remained passive and abstained from defending the SED regime, showing that they did neither identify with the state nor with the reformed economy.

29. In 1971, Ulbricht was ousted by Honecker in a bloodless coup assisted by the Soviet leaders. The fundamentals of the "economic reform" were left untouched under the Honecker regime, but certain "corrections" were made to nip rebellions like those in neighboring Poland in the bud. The working-class rebellion of June 17th, 1953 had not been forgotten.

30. Under the new General Secretary a new policy called "Main Task of Unity between Economic and Social Policy" was installed to appease the dissatisfied masses. A whole series of social measures was taken and, at the same time, retail prices frozen. To finance the freeze on prices huge amounts of money were needed, clearly being beyond the means of the GDR economy. The money was found on the international money markets.

31. A return to Marxist principles of building socialism was no longer possible because no genuine Marxists were left in the politburo due to Ulbricht's various purges of the party headquarters in the fifties. Corruption and abuse of power was the order of the day, testified by the corrupt lifestyle of the top 280 party officials residing in the settlement of Wandlitz near Berlin.

32. The policy change had a positive and a negative aspect for the new regime: for the short term, the domestic political situation in the GDR was relatively stable again, prolonging the lifespan of the regime for more than fifteen years. On the other hand, however, it became increasingly dependent on foreign donors and imperialism, especially on the Federal Republic of Germany.

33. But in the early eighties the FRG and international imperialism were still interested in stabilizing the GDR by means of a generous credit policy. Two huge credits worth almost two billion Deutschmarks were granted in 1983 and 1984 — the second loan with political strings attached. An early financial collapse of the GDR might have triggered a Soviet military intervention like in Czechoslovakia in 1968 (Brezhnev Doctrine of limited sovereignty of Warsaw Pact countries) which would have thwarted West German plans to take over the GDR economy and to liquidate the GDR state.

34. When Mikhail Gorbachev came to power in the Soviet Union in 1985, these fears vanished in the West, as he had indicated not to use force against the GDR to prevent a takeover by West Germany from happening. Due to excessive credit-taking in West Germany and elsewhere in the West, the GDR had become susceptible to blackmail on account of its economic and financial dependency and, on top of that, could no longer count on Soviet military assistance as was the case in 1953.

35. In 1989 the vast majority of the population was fed up with supply shortages, lack of freedom of movement, the decade-long spoon-feeding

by the SED, the permanent spying on people's opinions and intentions, their political convictions, and the state of the GDR, being on the brink of insolvency, was swept away by a powerful mass movement.

36. The GDR had reached such a high degree of capitalist restoration that, in 1990, it was relatively easy for West German imperialism to swallow up the whole of the GDR economy and to restructure it according to its wishes. The Treuhandanstalt, the authority in charge of privatizing the companies of the GDR, ironically set up by the last "socialist" government under the chairmanship of Hans Modrow on March 1, 1990, was then used by the West Germans to swallow up the entire wealth of the GDR economy and to hand it over to the highest bidders. The "socialists," in their limitless opportunism, had laid the ball up for Big West German Money.

37. The pseudo-socialist political system of the GDR, however, was a great obstacle for such a hostile takeover and had to be demolished. It had to be substituted by a bourgeois pseudo-democratic system which serves the interests of imperialism best. The replacement took place after the elections of March 18, 1990, won by the Christian Democrats. The former SED, now renamed SED-PDS (shortly afterwards just PDS), only received around 16% of the votes. The newly elected GDR regime willingly consented to reunification, meaning "Anschluss" (joining imperialist West Germany). Broad sections of the GDR population were not prepared to fight for a separate independent East Germany, though there were hopeful signs in the early stages of the peaceful revolution. The demise of the GDR had therefore become inevitable similar to that of other East European states and similar to the USSR itself, which also had been "reformed" over years and decades under Khrushchev, Brezhnev and Gorbachev according to the same ideas of "market socialism."

38. The counterrevolution does its work mainly from the inside of a specific socialist country, assisted by outside interference. The main reason for the collapse of the GDR was the "economic reform" process, leading to the restoration of a market economy, or otherwise also called capitalism.

39. Those who deplore the "defeat" of socialism in the GDR should ask themselves how this defeat came about and what exactly had caused it. The people around Ulbricht and Honecker were the chief culprits of this process of restoration and should therefore be blamed for that instead of whitewashing their crimes and rehabilitating them.

APPENDIX I. CHRONOLOGY OF THE GDR'S FINAL TWENTY YEARS

Events from the 8th Congress of the Socialist Unity Party in 1971 up to German reunification on October 3, 1990

Main source: Archiv der Gegenwart, Deutschland 1949 bis 1999, Berlin, 2004.

1971

June 15–19

8th Congress of the SED taking place in East Berlin. The delegates adopt Honecker's "Main Task of Unity between Economic and Social Policy." Various social measures are put forward, among them an ambitious housing program. The delegates and the general public are told that the financing is secured. The new Five-Year Plan for 1971–1975 is adopted.

Nov. 19

The Politburo of the Socialist Unity Party (SED) and the Council of Ministers of the GDR (the GDR government) announce a price freeze on consumer goods, repairs, and catering services for the duration of the new Five-Year Plan.

Nov. 26

The Constituent Assembly of the GDR's People's Chamber (Volkskammer) elects Eric Honecker Chairman of the National Council of Defense.

Dec. 17

Contacts between the leaders of the GDR and those of the Federal Republic of Germany are continued: the GDR's chief negotiator Michael Kohl and West Germany's Egon Bahr sign an agreement to regulate German-German transit traffic, taking effect on June 3, 1972.

1972

Jan. 16

Honecker, for the first time, calls West Germany "a foreign country."

May 26

A treaty on traffic is signed between the two German states, ushering in a thaw in relations.

June 15

Negotiations between the two states on a "Basic Agreement" (Grundlagenvertrag) started.

Nov. 7

The "Basic Agreement" to regulate relations between the GDR and the FRG is approved of by the Politburo of the SED.

1973

Feb. 9

Great Britain and France establish diplomatic relations with the GDR. In January, 13 states had already entered into diplomatic relations with East Germany, including Italy and Spain.

May 14

The Central Committee of the SED adopts further measures on social spending, coming into effect in July.

Sept. 18

The GDR and the FRG becoming members of the United Nations.

Oct. 2

The Central Committee adopts a new housing program for the years 1976–90

1974

Jan. 1

The GDR becomes a member of the International Labor Organization.

In April

In the GDR and the FRG "Permanent Representations" are opened, thereby establishing quasi diplomatic relations between the two German states.

Sept. 4

The GDR and the USA establish diplomatic relations.

Sept. 27

The 13th Session of the People's Chamber adopts the "Law on the Amendment and Completion of the Constitution of the GDR" where the term "German nation" is omitted.

Nov. 12–15

Josip Broz Tito, the Yugoslav head of state, is visiting the GDR.

Dec. 1

The US embassy opens in East Berlin.

1975

The GDR's foreign debt reaches 11 billion valuta mark, five times as much as in 1970 (2.2 billion).

June 11–15

The Chairman of the GDR Council of Ministers (GDR government), Horst Sindermann, on an official state visit in Yugoslavia.

July 30

Helsinki Summit — Conference on Security and Cooperation. The GDR is also present. Honecker signs the "Final Act of Helsinki" (Schlussakte von Helsinki). The GDR pledges to guarantee human rights. Helmut Schmidt, the West German chancellor, and Honecker meet on this occasion.

Aug. 1

The GDR and Canada enter into diplomatic relations.

Oct. 7

The day of the GDR's foundation is celebrated as a national holiday. Brezhnev and Honecker sign a "Treaty of Friendship, Cooperation and Mutual Assistance."

Late in November

In New York, a conversation takes place between GDR State Secretary Gerhard Beil and the president of Chase Manhattan bank, David Rockefeller. Rockefeller had visited the GDR prior to the talks.

Dec. 16

Joerg Mettke, the accredited journalist of Der Spiegel in the GDR, is expelled from the GDR, after having reported on "forced adoptions" in East Germany.

Dec. 19

The GDR and the FRG signing an agreement on the Marienborn-Berlin Autobahn as well as on other routes to and from Berlin.

1976

May 18–22

The 9th Congress of the SED adopts a new program and statute for the party. First Secretary Honecker is promoted to become "General Secretary." The convention adopts a new series of social measures, among them the increase of the minimum wage from 350 to 400 GDR marks.

May 30

The two German states sign an agreement in the field of telecommunications and postal services, coming into effect on July 1.

June 24

The People's Chamber decides to elect assemblies for a period of five instead of two years.

June 29–30

The International Conference of Communist and Labor Parties taking place in East Berlin. The Albanian leadership is not invited.

Oct. 17

Election to the People's Chamber and provincial assemblies with 99.86% votes for the candidates on the "united lists."

Oct. 28

The 3rd Session of the CC of the SED elects Guenter Mittag successor of Werner Krolikowski as Central Committee's Secretary for the Economy. After a period of three years, Mittag is back in his old position — the one he had occupied under Honecker's predecessor Ulbricht.

Honecker and Mittag now occupy the key posts in the GDR state and party hierarchy. Mittag can now continue with his reform effort.

Nov. 26

Prof. Robert Havemann who spent time in prison together with Honecker in the penitentiary of Brandenburg-Goerden during the Nazi era is put under house arrest. The arrest is only lifted on May 9, 1979. Havemann had voiced sharp criticism of the methods of the GDR regime.

1977

Jan. 12–15

Honecker on an official state visit to Yugoslavia. Tito is decorated with the Order of Karl Marx.

Feb. 4–6

Honecker is received by Nikolai Ceausescu, the Romanian party chief and head of state.

Feb. 17

In an interview with Saarbrücker Zeitung Honecker confirms that approximately 10,000 citizens have applied for emigration.

Aug. 23

The dissident Rudolf Bahro is arrested. Later he is sentenced to eight years in prison. He had his book Die Alternative published in West Germany.

Sept. 26

Honecker in defense of the Intershops — special stores for privileged people who own foreign currency.

1978

June 30

Rehabilitation of former General Secretary Ulbricht on the occasion of his 85th birthday. He is again called a "leader of the working-class movement."

Nov. 16

Treaty signed between the FRG and the GDR on the construction of the autobahn Berlin-Hamburg and the Teltow Canal in Berlin is reopened.

1979

Mar. 1

According to a bulletin of the West German Economics Ministry deliveries from the GDR in the field of mechanical engineering and electronics are declining. The GDR's trade deficit has risen to 688 million clearing units only in the past year and the country is increasingly running out of foreign currency.

Mar. 13

Mittag meets with West German Economics Minister Otto Graf Lambsdorff at the traditional Leipzig fair.

April 25

Preliminary proceedings are instigated against Prof. Robert Havemann, the East German dissident, who is now accused of "violation of the Law on Foreign Currencies."

April 20

Local elections in the GDR: 99.83% for the candidates of the "united list."

June 28

Facing growing protests and dissatisfaction, the GDR's People's Chamber adopts the3rd Amendment to the Penal Code, coming into effect on August 1, with higher penalties for political offenses. Any substantial and fundamental criticism of the state or the leading party can now be punished with up to ten years in jail.

Oct. 6

In his speech on the occasion of the 30th Anniversary of the GDR Honecker says that "never before in German history has there been a state in which the people could breeze so freely." (Archiv der Gegenwart, p. 38,540).

Leonid Brezhnev, the Soviet leader, who has come to East Berlin to take part in the celebrations, is decorated with the order "Hero of the GDR" and also with the Karl Marx Order. Honecker calls Brezhnev "successor of Lenin."

Oct. 11

The GDR releases 21,928 people from prisons under an amnesty, among them the dissident Rudolf Bahro. He goes to West Germany and joins the Green Party.

1980

The GDR foreign debt now stands at 25.3 billion valuta mark, up from 11.0 billion in 1975.

Jan. 1

The GDR becomes a non-permanent member of the UN Security Council.

June 15

The GDR and Augusto Pinochet's fascist Chile agree on opening trade offices in East Berlin.

Sept. 19–22

Strikes of the West Berlin staff of the GDR railways (Reichsbahn).

Oct. 13

The minimum obligatory exchange for trips to the GDR is raised to 25 GDR marks, substantially reducing visits to the country.

1981

Mar. 25–31

Honecker on a state visit to Japan.

April 11–16

10th Congress of the SED. Honecker reelected as General Secretary.

The new Five-Year Plan for 1981–85 is passed. It is a mere "program" for the economy without binding plan indices for the enterprises. The plan is only adopted by the People's Chamber on December 3, 1981.

The price freeze on agricultural products is partially lifted. The Congress states that a total of 157 combines has been founded over recent years. No more are envisaged.

Dec. 15

Chancellor Helmut Schmidt and his Economics Minister Graf Lambsdorff are visiting the GDR.

On the same day the GDR welcomes the state of emergency in neighboring Poland imposed by the Polish government.

1982

The Soviet Union reduces its oil supplies for the GDR by 12%; deliveries are cut from 19 million tons to 17 m. The Soviet leadership now demands world market prices for its deliveries. The GDR, more than ever before, is forced to increase its exports to earn enough foreign currency for oil imports.

Feb. 13

More than 5,000 people gather in Dresden to take part in a "peace forum."

Mar. 17

Graf Lambsdorff of West Germany is negotiating with Mittag on an extension of the "swing" credit line, granted by the FRG. In return, the minister wants the compulsory exchange rate for visitors of the GDR to be reduced.

Early in July

The GDR grants the Soviet Union the right to deploy nuclear short-range missiles in the country in response to Nato's deployment of nuclear medium-range Cruise Missiles and Pershing II in the FRG.

Nov. 14

Honecker meets with Carl Carstens, the West German federal president on the occasion of the funeral celebrations for Leonid Brezhnev in Moscow.

1983

April 18

Guenter Mittag in Bonn holding talks on the economic relations between the two states with leading representatives of CDU, FDP, SPD, and with a delegation of the West German industry.

July 1

The Süddeutsche Zeitung reports that a credit agreement worth one billion Deutschmarks has been signed at Bayerische Landesbank in favor of the GDR. The credit bears 6.55% interest, the period is five years. The Federal Government acts as a guarantor for the credit. The GDR's financial standing is thus restored for the time being. Now the country has again access to the Euro money market.

July 3

The independent GDR peace movement organizes a "workshop for peace" in East Berlin with approximately 3,000 participants.

July 24–27

Franz-Josef Strauß, the Bavarian Prime Minister, is on a "private visit" to the GDR and is also welcomed by Eric Honecker.

Sept. 1

Pacifist pickets are dissolved by the GDR police in East Berlin.

Sept. 5

Former Chancellor Schmidt is received by Honecker in Berlin.

Nov. 15

A new postal agreement between the two German states is signed.

1984

Feb. 2

Volkswagen and the GDR are negotiating on engine manufacturing in East Germany.

Feb. 13

Honecker meets Helmut Kohl in Moscow on the occasion of Yuri Andropov's funeral. Andropov was Brezhnev's successor in late 1982.

April 6

Mittag is meeting Kohl and Strauß in Bonn, the capital of West Germany.

June 27

55 GDR citizens are trying to force their exit from the country by intruding into the West German representation (=embassy) in East Berlin. Later, they are allowed to leave the GDR.

July 8

In an interview with the Italian newspaper Il Messagero, Honecker acknowledges that Western firms, among them some from Italy, may be allowed to invest their capital in the GDR.

July 24

Honecker calls the GDR a "stable cornerstone of socialism."

July 25

The Federal Government of Germany approves of a new large credit for the GDR, granted this time by a consortium under the auspices of Deutsche Bank, worth almost a billion Deutschmarks, with the West German government acting as a guarantor. The GDR commits itself to dismantle the minefields at its border to the FRG, to grant a greater number of exist permits and to lower the minimum compulsory exchange for old-age pensioners.

Nov. 30

As promised, the GDR government has dismantled the mines at its border to the FRG and is allowing more exit permits.

1985

This year, the net foreign debt of the GDR rises to a total of 30 billion Deutschmarks.

Jan. 9–12

The last GDR citizens who tried to find refuge at the Prague embassy of the FRG return home after having been assured immunity from prosecution.

April 23–24

For the first time, Honecker is visiting a Nato country: Italy. He is also received by Pope John Paul II.

May 4–5

Honecker meets with the new General Secretary of the CPSU, Mikhail Gorbachev, in Moscow.

Sept. 1

Honecker and Strauß meeting in Leipzig.

Oct. 2–4

Honecker visits the Yugoslav leaders. Only a week later he is in Greece.

1986

April 9–10

Mittag is received in Bonn and Hanover for talks with major West German representatives, among them Federal President Richard von Weizäcker, Chancellor Kohl, Federal Ministers Bangemann and Schäuble as well as provincial leaders Strauß and Rau.

April 17–21

11th Congress of the SED. Soviet leader Mikhail Gorbachev is also present. In his opening speech Honecker stresses the "successful development of the GDR in contrast to that of the Federal Republic." He points out that in the GDR there is "growing prosperity, social justice, full democracy, and genuine freedom."

The delegates pass another ambitious program of "accelerated development of key technologies," meaning micro-technology, which can only be financed by more credit taking in the West.

Sept. 15

Members of "Greenpeace" demonstrate in front of the GDR's Ministry for the Environment against the pollution of the river Werra. Only after a few minutes, the protest is ended by the police.

Oct. 18–20

Honecker in North Korea, meeting with Kim Il Sung, the North Korean leader. He also visits the Republic of China and the Mongolian People's Republic as well.

1987

This year the GDR's net foreign debt reaches 34.7 billion valuta mark, according the data provided by Carl-Heinz Janson of the CC of the SED. These figures are presented to the Politburo once a month (cp. Gerhard Schuerer, chairman of the Planning Committee in Theo Pirker et al, ibid., p. 78).

Jan. 12–14

Yasuhiro Nakasone, the Japanese Prime Minister, on a state visit to the GDR.

Feb. 13

Minister President Vogel of the Rhineland Palatinate meets Honecker in East Berlin.

Mar. 11–12

Oscar Lafontaine, Minister President of the Saarland, visits the GDR.

Mar. 27

Wolfgang Schäuble, Chief of the Federal Chancellery in Bonn, meets Honecker.

April 1–2

Mittag meets with Chancellor Kohl again, also with Economics Minister Martin Bangemann and Jochen Vogel, the opposition leader and also with Strauß, the Bavarian Prime Minister.

June 3–5

Honecker on an official state visit to the Netherlands.

June 15

Honecker meeting Perez de Cuellar, the UN General Secretary, in East Berlin.

Late in June

GDR security forces block access to the border of West Berlin for 3,000 rock fans. Clashes with the police in front of the Soviet embassy.

Oct. 13–15

Honecker in Belgium

Oct. 28–29

Honecker visits Romania.

Nov. 7–11

Honecker in West Germany on an official state visit. Soviet leader Gorbachev gave green light for the visit. His predecessor Chernenko still had denied him to visit the FRG. Honecker meets with Kohl, President Weizäcker and other high-ranking representatives of West Germany. Various agreements signed.

Dec. 10

Ten members of an East Berlin peace group arrested, but later they are released.

1988

39,832 migrants leave the GDR this year to settle in West Germany.

Jan. 7–8

Honecker in France.

Jan. 17

100 members of the GDR peace movement arrested on the fringes of the traditional Luxemburg-Liebknecht-Lenin demonstration in East Berlin. They were carrying banners displaying Rosa Luxemburg's famous motto: "Freedom is always the freedom of the dissenter."

May 27

Chancellor Kohl in East Berlin on an unofficial visit.

August 15

The GDR establishes diplomatic relations with the European Community.

Oct. 3–5

Honecker in Spain.

Nov. 20

11 members of the group "Church for Justice and Peace" are arrested. Four of them are later given prison sentences of between 12 and 22 months. Four days later seven more are arrested.

1989

Jan. 15

At least 80 people are arrested when demonstrating in Leipzig on the occasion of the 70th anniversary of the murder of Rosa Luxemburg and Karl Liebknecht, the founders of the Communist Party of Germany. They were carrying banners in favor of freedom of the press, free speech and freedom of assembly.

Feb. 6

GDR border guards shoot 20-year-old Chris Gueffroy when trying to cross the border to West Berlin.

April 27

Lower Saxon Prime Minister Albrecht is received by Honecker.

May 7

At local elections in the GDR 98.85% have allegedly voted for the "unity lists." Opposition circles are speaking of election fraud. Politburo member Krenz, later to become Honecker's successor, says: "This is a clear referendum of the people for a strong socialism and secure peace."

June 7

120 people arrested when attempting to hand over a petition against vote rigging at the recent local elections to the State Council of the GDR.

June 27–28

Honecker in Moscow, meeting Gorbachev. He emphasizes his "full trust of the population of the GDR into the policy of the party" and also underlines the support of the GDR for Gorbachev's policy of Perestroika. By initiating the process of Perestroika or restructuring, the USSR has started a "very difficult, complicated, but necessary process being of great significance for the consolidation of peace all over the world."

July 4

Honecker tells Rudolf Seiters, the head of Helmut Kohl's chancellery, that the "order to shoot for GDR border guards has been abolished."

July 21

GDR media admitting supply shortages.

Aug. 13

28th anniversary of the building of the Berlin Wall. Neues Deutschland, the official organ of the SED, but also the rest of the GDR media, are defending the border: "The Wall will not be torn down!"

Aug. 14

Speaking in Erfurt to workers, Honecker rejects any criticism of the economic and social system: "The old slogan of the German workers' movement that socialism can neither be stopped by oxen nor donkeys is confirmed by the great initiative of the working people in the GDR."

Sept. 2

3,500 GDR citizens, wishing to emigrate, have fled to Hungary.

Sept. 10–11

The Hungarian government is prepared to let these people emigrate to the West. Till the end of the month, more than 25,000 migrants take this route to get to West Germany. The Hungarian government will later be rewarded for the step by the FRG with a large credit of half a billion.

Sept. 11

After a "prayer for peace" in the city of Leipzig, mass arrests are made. 11 participants will later be sentenced to up to six months in jail; a further 104 are sentenced to pay fines.

Sept. 19

Neues Forum becomes the first opposition group to apply for recognition as a legal association. One day later, the application is rejected, as the group is allegedly "hostile to the state."

Sept. 30

The 5,500 people who have fled the GDR and sought refuge in the West German embassy in Prague, are allowed to emigrate; likewise the 800 at the FRG embassy in Warsaw.

Oct. 2

20,000 people demonstrating in Leipzig for reforms in the GDR. Several arrests made.

Oct. 4

The opposition groups Neues Forum and Demokratie jetzt! demanding elections under the supervision of the UN.

Oct. 5

In the cities of Magdeburg and Dresden mass demonstrations are violently disbanded. The police use electric batons against demonstrators and in East Berlin special courts are set up to speed up judgments.

Oct. 6–7

The GDR leaders celebrate the 40th anniversary of the foundation of the GDR. Mikhail Gorbachev has come to Berlin to take part. The same day, more than 1,000 "hooligans" (the official language) are arrested in various cities.

The Social Democratic Party (SDP) is founded in Schwante near Potsdam.

Oct. 9

In Leipzig 70,000 people demonstrate for a democratic renaissance of the country. In view of the enormous size of the demonstration, the police show restraint. Dresden's mayor, Mr. Berghofer, welcomes a delegation of demonstrators in his office.

Oct. 17

Honecker's own Politburo asks him to step down. Unanimous vote.

Oct. 18

At the 9th Session of the CC of the SED, Eric Honecker is released from his duties "at his own wish." His close friend, Guenter Mittag, also loses his seat in the Politburo and his post as Secretary for the Economy. Joachim Herrmann is likewise expelled. Egon Krenz becomes new General Secretary of the SED and also Chairman of the State Council and of the National Defense Council. He is now the most powerful man in the GDR. The move is designed to appease the protesters.

In several cities hundreds of thousands take to the streets for free and fair elections and against the new "concentration of power."

Oct. 30

In Leipzip alone, 300,000 people demonstrate for free elections and freedom of movement, the biggest demonstration in the history of the city. The following day there are more demonstrations.

November, whole month

Between 1.5 and 2.5 million demonstrators in November alone (Yana Milev, Das Treuhandtrauma, Berlin, 2020, p. 71).

Nov. 4

More than 500,000 people demonstrating in East Berlin, demanding free elections, freedom of opinion, the end of the SED's political monopoly, the stepping down of the government, and the official recognition of all opposition groups. Also in other cities of the GDR large demonstrations are held.

Nov. 6

Hundreds of thousands demonstrate in Leipzig again.

Nov. 7

The GDR government under Willi Stoph resigns.

Nov. 8

The old Politburo steps down and a new one is voted in. Egon Krenz, one of the most loyal followers of Ulbricht and Honecker, gives a speech blaming Honecker and Mittag for the crisis in the GDR. Now he is in favor of "reforming the political system" and proposes a new electoral law, "guaranteeing free, general, democratic, and secret elections under comprehensive public scrutiny." On May 7, he had still praised the last local elections as fair and as being "a referendum of the people for a strong socialism."

Nov. 9

Politburo member Guenter Schabowski, in an improvised press conference, announces the opening of the Berlin Wall. The borders to West Germany and West Berlin are reopened.

Nov. 10

The CC of the SED adopts an "action program," providing, among other things, for free, general, and secret elections.

The new head of state, Hans Modrow, Willi Stoph's successor, presents his cabinet to the public, consisting of 28 ministers! In his inaugural speech he says that there will be no more state plan for the year 1990. He takes first steps in the direction of reunification with West Germany, proposing "A Union of Treaties" and disbands the security apparatus Stasi as demanded by the demonstrators. But the Stasi is replaced by an "Office for National Security."

Nov. 20

50,000 people demonstrate in Leipzig alone. For the first time, the demonstration has been authorized.

Nov. 23

Legal proceedings are instigated against Honecker by his former comrades and Mittag is expelled from the Party.

Nov. 27

For the first time demands for reunification are heard at a demonstration in Leipzig.

Nov. 28

Chancellor Kohl of West Germany presents his plan for a reunified Germany. Famous personalities of the GDR, however, want the sovereignty of the country respected.

Dec. 3

At the 12th Session of the CC of the SED the new Politburo resigns. The CC follows suit. Honecker and another 11 top officials of the SED are expelled from the Party. The former members of the Politburo, Harry Tisch, the long-standing chairman of the official trade union FDGB and Guenter Mittag are arrested and accused of "having damaged people's property and the national economy."

Dec. 6

Egon Krenz resigns as chairman of the State Council and head of the National Defense Council. The remaining members of the National Defense Council are also dismissed. Manfred Gerlach, a liberal, is nominated chairman of the State Council by the People's Chamber.

Dec. 7

The "Round Table" meets in East Berlin for the first time. 12 parties and other groups take part. The body decides to draft a new constitution and to fix a date for the next election of the People's Chamber (May 6).

Dec. 8

An extraordinary party congress of the SED takes part in Berlin: Gregor Gysi, a lawyer, is elected chairman.

Dec. 14

The new GDR government headed by Hans Modrow, the former mayor of Leipzig, decides to dissolve the new security apparatus and to establish an intelligence service, but also an "Office for the Protection of the Constitution," even though a new constitution has not been drafted yet.

The two German ministers for the economy, Luft and Bangemann, take course on reunification, proposing a common trade committee as well as an agreement on economic cooperation between the two German states.

Dec. 16–17

The SED is renamed "SED-PDS" (PDS = Party of Democratic Socialism).

Dec. 18

The "Round Table" takes up Modrow's proposal and is also now demanding "A Union of Treaties" with the Federal Republic.

Dec. 19–20

Chancellor Kohl arrives in Dresden to meet Modrow. The two politicians decide on negotiations to establish a German-German "Union of Treaties," as proposed by Modrow.

Dec. 22

The Brandenburg Gate is reopened.

1990

Jan. 3

Demonstrations against neo-fascism and anti-sovietism taking place in front of the Soviet memorial in Treptow.

Jan. 15

Thousands storm the headquarters of the former security apparatus "Stasi" and ransack it.

Jan. 21

Egon Krenz and 13 other former members of the Politburo are expelled from the SED-PDS.

Jan. 28

The elections to the People's Chamber are brought forward to Mar 18.

Jan. 29

Honecker is arrested.

Jan. 31

In January alone, 58,043 East Germans have migrated to the Federal Republic.

Feb. 1

Modrow pushes for reunification, presenting a plan called "In Favor of a United Germany and Fatherland — Concept for a Road Towards a Unified Germany."

Feb. 11–12

Chancellor Kohl visiting Gorbachev in Moscow. He tells him that a neutral Germany is not an option. Gorbachev has no objections.

Feb. 13

Prime Minister Modrow is in Bonn to talk to Chancellor Kohl on preparations for a currency union and economic union. A commission of experts is set up. All experts are from West Germany.

Feb. 21

The East German People's Chamber makes a plea in favor of a united Germany. Modrow gives a speech, proposing to enter into negotiations on German reunification immediately.

Mar. 1

The GDR Council of Ministers, headed by Hans Modrow (SED-PDS), decides on the transformation of combines into Western-style corporations and also announces the establishment of a trusteeship, an institutional trust company to transform GDR property into private joint stock companies whose shares can be bought and sold on the stock market. Later, the trusteeship is taken over by West German "experts" and the depreciated East German enterprises are sold cheaply to West German banks and oligarchs, making huge profits. Modrow later declines all responsibility. He only wanted to "save GDR people's property"(in: Ralph Hartmann, Die Liquidatoren, Berlin, 2008, p. 13).

Mar. 15

The trust company Treuhand is founded.

Mar. 18

The first free elections to the East German People's Chamber taking place. The Christian Democratic Union, massively supported with money and expertise from West Germany during the election campaign, gains more than 40% of the votes cast, becoming the leading force in the chamber. The former SED, now PDS, only gets 16.32% of the votes. The turnout is a record 93.39%.

Mar. 31

Schalck's Commercial Coordination is dissolved and replaced by the Berliner Handels-und Finanzierungsgesellschaft mbH. 300 million Deutschmarks are provided as capital stock from the trusteeship's capital, diminishing the assets by a third of a billion.

April 12

Lother de Maizière, a Christian Democrat, becomes GDR Prime Minister heading a coalition government.

April 19

De Maizière gives his inaugural speech, declaring that it is his wish to bring about reunification as soon as possible.

April 24

Chancellor Kohl and Prime Minister de Maizière agree on the introduction of an "Economic Currency and Social Union," starting from July 2, 1990.

April 27

Negotiations on a German-German State Treaty are under way.

May 5

In Bonn the Two-Plus-Four-Talks begin, with the foreign ministers of the four powers and those of the two German states taking part.

May 6

The first relatively free local elections taking place: the Conservatives (CDU) to become the strongest force, getting 34.37% of the votes. The successor party of the SED, the PDS, only gets 14.59% of the votes cast.

May 14

The 13th Congress of the FDGB, the former official trade union, passing a resolution on its dissolution.

May 18

The State Treaty on the Creation of a Currency, Economic, and Social Union between the GDR and the FRG is signed in Bonn, coming into effect on July 1 and introducing the West German Deutschmark (DM) as the GDR's new currency. Kohl: "This is a decisive step on the road towards a unified fatherland." By signing the treaty, the representatives of the GDR have given up the sovereignty of their country and have agreed to Anschluss, the GDR's joining the Nato member FRG.

June 7

De Maizière for talks in Moscow, meeting Gorbachev. The Soviet leader gives green light for reunification. Moscow, however, insists on respecting the Polish border with Germany.

June 13

The Berlin Wall is torn down, enthusiastically welcomed by thousands of Berliners from East and West Berlin.

June 21

The West German Bundestag and the East German People's Chamber passing the State Treaty and a declaration, guaranteeing Poland's western border.

July 1

The currency union comes into force. From now on, the DM is the only legal tender in the GDR.

July 14–16

Kohl in Moscow for more talks with Gorbachev. The latter agrees to NATO membership of a united Germany, removing the last obstacle for the GDR to join the imperialist bloc.

Aug. 23

A special session of the GDR's People's Chamber decides on the GDR joining the FRG under the West German Basic Law — the provisional constitution of West Germany, imposed by the USA, Britain, and France on West Germany in 1948.

Aug. 31

Wolfgang Schäuble on behalf of the FRG and Guenter Krause for the GDR sign the Unification Treaty which is adopted both by the GDR on September 9 and by the FRG on September 21.

Sept. 12

The foreign ministers of the four powers, plus the GDR Prime Minister and the Foreign Minister of the FRG, sign the Treaty on the Final Settlement Regarding Germany in Moscow, whereby the united Germany allegedly gets its "full sovereignty over its home and foreign affairs."

Oct. 3

The GDR (founded on Oct. 7, 1949) officially joins West Germany. On this day, at midnight, the GDR, having existed for almost 41 years, has ceased to exist, whereby the sphere of influence of German and US imperialism is considerably extended: the FRG not only gets 16.4% new citizens (17 million former GDR inhabitants), but also five new provinces, a relatively well-educated workforce and a lot more economic clout. The 157 East German combines are integrated into the FRG's economic power house, becoming joint stock companies.

Appendix II. Documents

(These documents translated from German by the author)

Document 1. The political legacy of Anton Saefkov

Anton Saefkov was executed by the Nazis in September 1944 in the prison of Brandenburg-Görden. Saefkov was Honecker's fellow prisoner

> "... point 4: Make sure that the broadest possible democratization is achieved; build the new Germany on the basis of people's committees. Supplement: no more Weimar Republic!...Power must be shifted to the grassroots! But that's not all...the people must rule themselves; the self-elected bodies (People's Committees) must not just constitute advisory bodies, but executive organs and should be answerable to the electorate all the time.
>
> Germany's approaching collapse will not be Germany's downfall! Is renaissance can only be the independent democratic Germany on the broadest possible anti-fascist united front — the Germany of the People's Committees!..."

Source: Gerhard Nitzsche, Die Saefkow-Jacob-Bästlein-Gruppe, Berlin, 1957, pp. 201ff.

Document 2. Honecker seeks early release from prison

While in the Brandenburg-Görden prison, Honecker worked as an overseer. He asked his parents to take some initiative:

> It is the most natural thing that, in view of the circumstances, I would be prepared to do my utmost to fulfill my duties, and I

authorize you to declare, also on my behalf, that I would not fall behind those who are ready to defend the peace and the future of the German people with a weapon in my hands.

Source: Martin Sabrow, Erich Honecker. Das Leben davor, 1912–1945, Munich, 2016, p. 346, Barch, NJ7, Bd. 14, Erich Honecker writing to Wilhelm and Caroline Honecker, Oct. 1, 1939.

Document 3. The penitentiary director recommends his release

To the Chief Prosecutor of the People's Court

So far, [prisoner] Honecker has shown good behavior and has worked properly. I have the impression that during his prison term he has come to his senses and that he, who has been brought up and raised in the spirit of communism, is serious and honest when he says that now the ideals of his youth he finds represented in the present state and that he has no greater desire than giving proof before the enemy that his convictions are sincere.

I think that in his case the purpose of the penalty has been achieved and would therefore plead in favor of pardoning him.

(Dr. Thümmler, Senior Civil Servant)
Dec. 12, 1942

Source: Martin Sabrow, Erich Honecker. Das Leben davor, 1912–1945, ibid., XXVIII.

Document 4. Did Ulbricht install a Gestapo spy into the German anti-fascist resistance fighters during the Spanish Civil War?

On the anniversary of the start of the defense of the Spanish Republic against the fascist coup led by General Franco, who was supported by Nazi Germany and fascist Italy, Walter Ulbricht, at a commemoration ceremony, distributed medals for 350 German participants who fought for the freedom of the elected Spanish Republic between 1936 and 1939 and of course also decorated himself, as he had been in Spain on an inspection tour once. The reaction of the anti-fascists present is very telling. One of the participants, the writer Alfred Kantorovicz, who also was in Spain as a member of an International Brigade, later wrote about the incident in his *Deutsches Tagebuch* (German Diary):

The 'Spanish Fighter' Ulbricht

...Something had happened which exposed the prevailing mood among the old resistance fighters. During the official commemoration that morning, not only those German fighters who had survived the fight against the Franco fascists were decorated with medals'; but so were all the others who only had made short visits to the Spanish Republic during the Civil War.

Ulbricht was also one of the recipients. We were given hints in *Neues Deutschland* about his historic role in the Spanish Liberation War. In late 1936, Ulbricht had been on an inspection trip, visiting Barcelona, Valencia, and also the headquarters of the International Brigade in Albacete — a newly created office of the Communist Party of Germany...

At the time when he had come to see how things were going in Spain, we learned from a report published in *Deutsche Volkszeitung*, the paper of our Paris emigrés, that a comrade by the code name of Gerry [i.e., a German — author] had distinguished himself with bravery in the fights near Madrid in November and had therefore been promoted to the rank of captain. There were also rumors that he had received an even higher rank to become an important official at the Albacete headquarters. He was also given special powers for all kinds of issues concerning the German volunteers.

We ourselves did not know the comrade personally, neither did we have any knowledge about who was behind the pseudonym of Gerry. We suspected, however, that he was supposed to be an extremely trustworthy and tried and tested anti-fascist who, due to his merits, had been chosen to play a dominant role now in the war. The fact that the *Volkszeitung* was highlighting his name in such a generous and exemplary fashion seemed to prove just that. For weeks on end, Gerry was praised as a model of courage, fulfillment of duty, and loyalty in the recent issues of the paper. Even as a writer and author, this man of whom we had never heard before, was supposed to have merits, as the paper, in several installments, had also published his Madrid Diaries in a sensational fashion which was also said to be the very first truthful report of an especially commendable and outstanding comrade-in-arms. ...

After Gerry's first article had been published and met with the applause of leading party officials, he himself was promoted major and deputy commander-in-chief at the Albacete base. ...

In the subsequent issue of the Volkszeitung [the paper was sent to the German fighters from Paris — author], you could read the effusive praise for his appearance during a mass meeting under the banner headline of Major Gerry, the Hero of Madrid. He was supposed to be the chosen voice of the international volunteers and had mercilessly settled scores with all those subversive Trotskyite agitators. This report covered several columns on the front page. ...

Up until then, no writer and author had been given such prominence and so much attention by the Party. ...

Then Gerry was exposed by the French police as a crook, a con man and defrauder on whom they had issued an arrest warrant a long time ago. If he was intentionally brought into our ranks as an agent provocateur by the German Gestapo or as a spy and agent, I do not know. Ulbricht was his promoter and I also do not know how Gerry succeeded in passing all the numerous check-ups which the most dedicated and prominent comrades had to undergo and how he could become so friendly with the otherwise extremely suspicious Ulbricht. ...

In the hall the names of the 350 anti-fascists were mechanically announced one after the other in alphabetical order, and, after two hours, the letter "U" was called up. The name of the 'Spanish freedom fighter' Ulbricht was announced. There they were: the gold-braided generals, the field officers of the National People's Army, the members of the Politburo and the Central Committee of the Socialist Unity Party, the minister, the chiefs of the various districts, but the general mood was as such that nobody raised a hand to applaud. There was a deadly silence, no breathtaking.

This way, by keeping quiet in such a devastating manner, the surviving veterans of the Spanish Civil War who had been at the fronts and had risked their lives, showed their disrespect for an apparatchik who had made a career by intriguing and submissiveness inside of office rooms. After 20 or 30 seconds of the defiant silence, the next name was hurriedly called out.

Source: Alfred Kantorowicz, *Deutsches Tagebuch*, Bd. 2, Berlin-West, 1980, entry dated June 30, 1956, pp. 638 ff.

Document 5. "Anti-fascist" Eric Mielke was in the pay of the OSS

Security chief Eric Mielke, No. 3 in the GDR hierarchy, was in the pay of the US secret service OSS in France during the war. After the war he returned from France to East Germany, although in his biography he stated that he had come back home from Russia. A document shows that in 1942 he served as an agent for US intelligence (OSS – Office for Strategic Services, under Alan Dulles, based in Bern, Switzerland, was the forerunner of the CIA). Under the pseudonym of "Leistner" he is listed as a recipient of cash (1,000 francs) from the American spy agency in France. Willi Kreikemeyer, a German communist who also was in France but as a member of the French resistance, brought the list back home to Berlin and handed it over to the executive of the Socialist Unity Party.

Thus the SED leadership knew that Mielke had worked for the Americans as an agent, but later, in 1957, he was nevertheless appointed Head of Security and Minister of the Interior.

FUNDS FOR PEOPLE IN DANGER

Received in early October 1942:

Francs 200,020

Sept. 22, 1942 Mahnke: 500 frs.

Oct. 19, 1942 Leonhard:1,000 frs.

Oct. 20, 1942 Leistner: 1,000 frs,

Oct. 27, 1942 Fritz Lenz:5,000 frs.

...

Sept. 1, 1943 Dudeck and 5 friends: 3,000 frs.

(altogether more than 20 names are listed).

Receipts: 200,020 frs.

Expenses: 200,020

Cash book balanced. The cash book was checked on Jan. 1, 1943 and on Sept. 9, 1943 and found to be in order. All receipts were destroyed by the inspectors for security reasons.

Paris, Oct. 10, 1944...

Source: Wilfriede Otto, Erich Mielke. Biografie, Berlin, 2000, p. 524, excerpt.

Document 6. Stalin's views on a post-war Germany

In a conversation with Georgi Dimitrov, Walter Ulbricht, Wilhelm Pieck and others Stalin proposed a bloc of anti-fascist parties for post-war

Germany. Dimitrov was the former leader of the defunct Communist International. On June 7, 1945, Dimitrov wrote the following in his diary.

> Stalin proposed:
>
> Declare categorically that the path of imposing the Soviet system on Germany is an incorrect one; an anti-fascist democratic parliamentary regime must be installed.
>
> The Communist Party should propose a bloc of anti-fascist parties with a common platform.
>
> Don't speak so glowingly about the Soviet Union, and so on.

Source: The Diary of Georgi Dimitrov, 1933–1949, New Haven & London, 2003, p. 372.

Document 7. The "anti-fascist" Walter Ulbricht disbanding the anti-fascist committees in Berlin

Wolfgang Leonhard, a member of the Ulbricht group brought to Berlin from Moscow to rebuild the Berlin administration and as a witness, describes the way the anti-fascist committees were disbanded in Berlin shortly after the war. In his memoirs he writes:

> Recently various offices, committees, and organizations have emerged, calling themselves Anti-fascist Committees, Anti-Nazi Groups, Socialist Bureaus, National Committees, or otherwise,' Ulbricht declared at one of his briefings. These bureaus I myself had seen again and again when driving through Berlin. I was convinced we would soon get the order from Ulbricht to contact them to support their work.
>
> 'We have evidence,' Ulbricht said, without being more specific, 'that these groups have been established by the Nazis. They're camouflage organizations who are trying to disrupt the democratic process. We must do everything possible to disband them. This is the most important task. Everybody in their district must try and find out where these groups are and dissolve them immediately.'...
>
> For me there was no doubt that they were no 'secret Nazis,' but honest comrades and anti-fascists.

Source: Wolfgang Leonhard, Die Revolution entlässt ihre Kinder, Cologne, Berlin, 1955, pp. 389 f; the revolution releases its children.

Document 8. Ulbrich tells Dimitrov how he dealt with "illegal" German anti-fascists

Ulbricht, having arrived in Berlin after Germany's capitulation in early May 1945, wrote to Georgi Dimitrov in Moscow to tell him about some of the difficulties he was facing in Berlin (reconstructed notes). He claims the law is on his side alone.

> Berlin, May 17, 1945

> ...in the districts of Berlin various committees have been set up who work independently and who have partly established themselves within the district administration. By contrast, our comrades and anti-fascists work separately from them. The communists used to wear red arm bands with the name KPD on them. In some cases, KPD offices were opened with KPD signs.

> We have liquidated this sort of thing and established legal district councils and convinced our comrades that, at this stage, it is not expedient to start founding the KPD. There are lots of illegal groups; some have led an armed struggle against the Nazis...

Source: Gerhard Keiderling, ed., 'Gruppe Ulbricht' in Berlin, April bis Juni 1945, Berlin, 1993, p. 352, excerpt.

Document 9. Pieck asks Soviet General Serov to send German POWs home to assist Ulbricht's mission in Berlin

> To General Colonel Serov,

> On the basis of yesterday's instructions, we would like to suggest that the following prisoners-of-war are released to return to Germany for political work:

> For Berlin:

> • Fritz Rücker, a senior teacher, former Social Democrat. He is a devoted anti-fascist and friend of the communists. He has attended School no. 27; now he in House no. 15;

> • Dr. Günter Kohlmey. He was an assistant lecturer at Berlin University; at present, he is at the School for Prisoners-of-War no. 40. Since he is well-known in the Berlin academia, we need him urgently...

• Dr. Friedrich Krummacher, Oberkonsistorialrat of the Protestant Church; he is a convinced anti-fascist, and we can use him in Berlin for work in the Protestant Church. He is now staying at House 15. He is a member of the advisory council for churches...

For Saxony:

• Ernst Hadermann, a senior teacher and one of the oldest anti-fascist prisoners-of-war who has actively participated in propaganda work among German troops. He resides in House 15.

Source: Gerhard Keiderling, ed., ibid., p. 475, excerpt.

A note on these "anti-fascists":
1. Fritz Rücker joined the German Nazi Party, NSDAP, in October 1940, card number: 8 285 975...
2. Günter Kohlmey joined the Nazi Party on May 1, 1937, card number: 5 585 361...
3. Friedrich-Wilhelm Krummacher joined the Nazi Party on May 1, 1933, card number: 2 916 420...
4. Ernst Hadermann joined the Nazi Party on May 1, 1937, card number: 5 698 532...

Source: Olaf Kappelt, Braunbuch DDR. Nazis in der DDR, Berlin, 1981, pp. 347, 261, 271, 215 f.

Document 10. The 1946 internal crisis of the Socialist Unity Party

Report by B. T. for Comrade Korotkevich on the Situation within the SED in Berlin, bulletin no. 47/51 of the International and Inner-German Information, July 12, 1946. Korotkevich was a co-worker of the Department of International Information at the Central Committee of the CPSU, B.

On the situation of the SED in Berlin

Berlin. From the SMA Inform-Bureau's own correspondents.

"Most recently, in a number of SED organizations some phenomena have been noticed that could worsen the situation and lead to an internal party crisis.

The Inform-Bureau's correspondents have visited numerous meetings of SED organizations and have also spoken to some senior officials and ordinary party members. The outcome of the visits and conversations can be summed up this way:

Participation in party meetings and meetings of party officials is catastrophically low — not more than 30%. We found organizations where less than 10% took part in meetings. To quote an example: one organized by the Weißensee party group was only attended by seven party members, out of a membership of 120. Many other similar instances could be named.

The strong decrease in party activity can also be seen in that even formerly active officials of the Communist Party have now resigned from party life. One former member of the CP of Germany who has been a member since 1925 and is now member of the SED told us that he knows around a hundred people who have once been activists of the Communist Party, but now were no longer prepared to work for the party.

And what is more: in a number of organizations there are certain tendencies to set up opposition groups within the SED. Former members of the "left" leaning Communist Workers' Party have become active. About a month ago, handwritten leaflets were distributed in the district of Rudow (Neukölln — American sector), where it says: 'We don't want to work with traitors of socialism!' Or in another: 'We don't want to have anything to do with them. Fight corruption!' ..."

Source: RCChIDNI.-B.17; Inv. 128; Ak. 157; Bl. 51-55, 57-58, in: Hermann Weber, Ulrich Mählert, eds., Terror. Stalinistische Parteisäuberungen 1936–1953, Paderborn, 1998, p. 312, excerpt; Stalinist party purges.

Document 11. A Soviet officer complains about shortcomings in the democratization effort in the new East German administration

Speech manuscript drafted by a high-ranking SMAD official written in late August or early September of 1947, complaining about grave shortcomings in the democratization effort made in the new East German administration.

"The German Administration.

We have more or less smashed the old fascist propaganda apparatus by our armed forces and also by denazification. We have been trying to establish a new type of democratic administrative machinery based on the support of the few German anti-fascists. After that, we propped up the new apparatus by legal means, introducing provincial constitutions and asked the SED people to draft a new German constitution.

In a resolution for the 2nd Congress of the SED it says that 'the most democratic administration in the history of Germany' has been created in the Soviet Occupation Zone. And this 'most democratic' administrative apparatus in the history of Germany, as we have been told, now attempts to sabotage democratization. In various instances it has acted non-democratically and has tried to sabotage the instructions of the SMAD...

So what kind of administrative machinery do we now have in the provinces of our Zone?

As has been said, the apparatus is new and democratic only in theory. But if you look at its composition and personnel, especially at the majority of the leading staff, with the exception of the political staff, it is still the old Prussian bureaucracy. There is a contradiction here: there is a tiny number of old and experienced anti-fascists, but even they have not yet learned how to govern, and in case they are learning, they are being taught by former Prussian civil servants due to a lack of other instructors. Some of them even support the old Prussian bureaucratic traditions...

The policy of the Soviet Union in Germany, in general, is trying to put the interests of the German working people first. We do not want to divide Germany and to weaken it as an economic power in Europe. We are highly interested in a thorough democratization of the country and want to assist the working people in fighting reaction..." We all know that in our Zone there is a lack of experienced cadres and anti-fascists. Therefore, you will often find dubious people who have kept their posts. What is to be done in these cases?

I think that we have all the means necessary to solve this problem, but we do not provide sufficient assistance to those people who have shown to be honest supporters, leaders, and organizers of the great democratic transformation in our Zone...

The question was asked whether one should reintegrate the old Nazis into the administration who were released in the time of denazification. We think that they should not return, as this would reinforce the position of reaction within the German administrative apparatus...

Source: ZPA NL 36/734-362, in: Rolf Badstübner, Wilfried Loth, eds., Wilhelm Pieck — Aufzeichnungen zur Deutschlandpolitik, 1945–1953, Berlin, 1994, excerpt; notes on German politics.

Document 12. The dismissal of General Tulpanov

Report by the Deputy Chairman of the Political Administration (Head Office) of the Armed Forces of the USSR, S. Shatilov, to the General Committee of the CPSU, B in Moscow.

Case History:

Attn.: the Central Committee of the CPSU, B, Comrade Malenkov, G. M.

I would ask for permission to release Major General Sergei Ivanovich Tulpanov from his duties as Chief of the Information Department of the Soviet Military Administration in Germany and to place him under the orders of the Political Military Administration of the Armed Forces.

It has been established as a fact that Major General Tulpanov's parents were sentenced for espionage: his father in 1938 and his mother in 1940. His brother's wife had contacts to the secretary of one of the embassies in Moscow, to an agent of the British Intelligence Service; her father was sentenced to death as a member of a right-wing Trotskyite organization; his brother and his brother's wife maintained close ties to Major General S. I. Tulpanov's family.

In late 1948, the organs of the MGB (the Soviet Interior Ministry — author) arrested Tulpanov's driver Lukin for traitorous activities and anti-Soviet propaganda. Lukin's father betrayed his fatherland in 1928 and fled to Iran.

Major General Tulpanov kept silent about his father's, his mother's, and his relatives' arrests and sentencing and did not mention these facts in his biography.

A great many employees of the Information Department have recently been arrested for espionage, and some of them have been withdrawn from Germany for reasons of unreliability and sent back to the Soviet Union. Major General Tulpanov made no attempts to instigate legal proceedings against the compromised and said that he was against such measures and did not voice any protests against the way they had acted.

The arrested Lukin, Tulpanov's driver, admitted that he, Tulpanov, had often shown his negative attitude. Feldman, a former collaborator of the Information Department, who has also been arrested, said that Tulpanov was involved in shady dealings with his subordinates, that he conducted usury and profiteering and accepted illegal donations.

A total of 35 books with a fascist content has been found in his apartment and confiscated.

Tulpanov is not very direct and honest. Last year, he became especially nervous and made several attempts to find out what the leading organs in Moscow were thinking of him.

I do not consider it appropriate to keep Major General Tulpanov at his post in Germany and deem it necessary to dismiss him from his post in the interest of the Mission and not to allow him to re-enter Germany. The Political Administration (Head Office) is considering letting Tulpanov work in our country. Comrades Vasilievsky and Chuikov are supporting the proposal to release Major General Tulpanov from his duties in the Soviet Military Administration in Germany.

September 17, 1949
Shatilov

Source: RtsKhIDNI, fond 17, opis 118, delo 567, SVAG Sbornik, pp. 233 ff, collection: Germany in the Cold War, Cold War International History Project, Virtual Archive, at: http://wilsoncenter.org/index.cfm?topic_id=1409&fuseaction=va2.document&identify...

Document 13. Order no. 1, Marshal Zhukov appointing himself chief of SMAD

Soviet Marshal Georgi Zukov appoints himself Supreme Chief of the Soviet Military Administration in Germany. He is later returned to the Soviet Union for theft and disloyalty. He also appoints fellow conspirators against Stalin as his deputies, among them Generals Sokolovsky and Serov.

Order No. 1

Re.: Organization of the Military Administration in the Soviet Occupied Zone in Germany

June 9, 1945 City of Berlin

To carry out the control for the fulfillment of the conditions imposed on Germany after its unconditional surrender and for the administration of the Soviet Occupied Zone in Germany, the Soviet Military Administration has been established.

I have been appointed Supreme Chief of the Soviet Military Administration; Army General V. D. Sokolovsky has been appointed First Deputy of the Supreme Chief of the Military Administration; Major General I. A. Serov has been appointed Deputy Chief in Matters of Civil Administration and Major General V. V. Kurasov Chief of Staff of the Soviet Military Administration.

The Soviet Military Administration's location is the City of Berlin.

Signed by:

The Supreme Chief of the Soviet Military Administration, Supreme Commander of the Soviet Occupation Forces in Germany, Marshal of the Soviet Union G. K. Zhukov,

Chief-of-Staff of the Soviet Military Administration, Major General V. V. Kurasov.

Source: documentArchiv.de (eds); http://www.documentarchiv.de/ddr/1945/ smad-befehl_nr01.html.

Document 14. Zhukov keeps large amounts of German treasure for himself

Soviet Marshal and "Hero of the Soviet Union," Georgi K. Zhukov, who brought Khrushchev to power in a coup on June 26, 1953, had been found guilty of having kept large amounts of looted German treasure for himself. Stalin then demoted Zhukov. Zhukov later brought Nikita Khrushchev to power.

> Top Secret
> THE COUNCIL OF MINISTERS OF THE USSR
> To comrade STALIN J. V.
>
> ...During the night of 8–9 January of this year, a secret search was conducted of Zhukov's dacha which is situated in the village of Rublevo near Moscow.
>
> As a result of this search, it was disclosed that two rooms of the dacha had been converted into storerooms in which a huge quantity of goods and valuables of various kinds are stored.
>
> For example:
>
> Woolen fabrics, silk, brocade, velvet, and other materials — in all, more than 4,000 meters; furs, sable, monkey, fox, sealskin, Astrakhan (fine wool), a total of 323 hides, Kidskin of the best

quality — 35 skins; valuable carpets and Gobelin rugs of very large size from the Potsdam and other palaces and homes of Germany — 44 pieces in all, some of which are laid or hung in various rooms, and the rest in the storeroom.

Especially worthy of note is a carpet of great size placed in one of the rooms of the dacha; valuable paintings of classical landscapes of very large sizes in artistic frames — 55 units in all, hung in various rooms of the dacha and a part of which remain in the storeroom.

Very expensive table and tea services (porcelain with artistic decoration, crystal) — 7 large chests; accordions with rich artistic decoration — 8 units; unique hunting rifles by the firm Gotland — 20 units in all.

This property is kept in 51 trunks and suitcases, and also lies in heaps.

Besides that in all rooms of the dacha, on the windows, staircase, tables and beside tables are placed around great quantities of bronze and porcelain vases and statuettes of artistic work, and also kinds of trinkets and knick-knacks of foreign origin.

I draw attention to the declaration by the workers who carried out the search that Zhukov's dacha is in essence an antique store or museum, with various valuable works of art hanging all around the interior...

There are so many valuable paintings that they could never be suitable for an apartment but should be transferred to the State fund and housed in a museum.

More than 20 large carpets cover the floor of almost all the rooms.

All the objects, beginning with the furniture, carpets, vessels, decorations, up to the curtains on the windows, are foreign, mainly German. There is literally not a single thing of Soviet origin in the dacha...

There is not a single Soviet book in the dacha, but on the other hand on the bookshelves stands a large quantity of books in beautiful bindings with gold embossing, all without exception in the German language.

When you go into the house, it is hard to imagine that one is not in Germany but near Moscow...

Accompanying this letter, please find photographs of some of the valuables, cloth and items we discovered in Zhukov's apartment and dacha.

ABAKUMOV*

January 10, 1948

*Victor Abakumov, former chief of the MGB (Soviet State Security), arrested in 1951 on false charges, was sentenced to death by a military tribunal in 1954 after Khrushchev's rise to power. Beria and Abakumov wanted to arrest Zhukov and put him on trial after they had discovered the war booty in his dacha.

Source: *Voennie Arkhivy Rossi*, 1993, pp. 189–191, at: http://chss.montclair.edu/english/furr/research/zhukovtheft 4648_var93.pdf, see: Grover Furr, *Khrushchev Lied*, Kettering/Ohio/USA, 2011, pp.363 ff.

Document 15. Goodwill telegram by the Communist Party of the Soviet Union sent to the Second Party Conference of the SED

This telegram was sent to the Second Party Conference of the Socialist Unity Party (July 1952) in the hope that the agenda commonly agreed upon by the East Germans and Soviets would not be changed. The Soviet leadership and the SED leaders had agreed on this conference to find ways and means to achieve a united, independent, democratic, and peaceful Germany.

Shortly before the conference took place, Ulbricht and Pieck voluntarily changed the agenda into 'how to build socialism in the GDR.' So building socialism became the chief topic on the agenda and Ulbricht gave an 8-hour speech — a clear breach of trust.

> The Central Committee of the Communist Party of the Soviet Union sends comradely greetings to the 2nd Party Conference of the Socialist Unity Party of Germany, the vanguard of the German working class and all working people...
>
> We express our deep conviction that the working class and all working people of Germany will succeed in carrying out the historical task of creating a united, independent, democratic, peaceful Germany.
>
> Long live the Socialist Unity Party of Germany!

Long live the German people!

Long live the great friendship between the peoples of the Soviet Union and Germany, the guarantee for a long-lasting peace in Europe!

CENTRAL COMMITTEE OF THE COMMUNIST PARTY OF THE SOVIET UNION (BOLSHEVIKS)

Source: Einheit, Zeitschrift für Theorie und Praxis des wissenschaftlichen Sozialismus, ZK der SED, Berlin, August 1952, 7th year, no. 8, excerpt.

Document 16. The Soviet leadership (Malenkov/Beria) sharply criticizes the policy of the SED Politburo

After the implementation of the "socialist" measures adopted at the 2nd Party Conference of the SED, thousands of Germans flee the country, especially farmers, but also many workers and even members of the Socialist Unity Party. The Soviet leadership after Stalin's death (Malenkov/Beria) summoned the SED leaders to Moscow to give them a harsh dressing down and to agree to a "New Course" in East Germany (June 3, 1953) to redress the situation.

Top Secret

On Measures to Stabilize the Political Situation in the German Democratic Republic

Due to the implementation of a wrong political line, an extremely unsatisfactory political and economic situation has been created in the German Democratic Republic.

Among the masses of the population, also including workers and members of the intelligentsia, grave discontent can be noticed with the political and economic measures which have been carried out in the GDR so far.

This finds particular expression in mass flights of GDR inhabitants to West Germany. From January 1951 until April 1953, 447,000 people fled to West Germany, among them 120,000 in the first four months of 1953 alone. An important part of the refugees are members of the working class. Among those who fled in 1953 are

- 18,000 workers;

- 9,600 small and medium-sized peasants;

- 17,000 employees and members of the working intelligentsia;

- 24,000 housewives.

From the police units quartered in barracks 8,000 fled to West Germany. Noticeably, among those who have fled to West Germany during the first four months of 1953, are 2,718 members and candidates of the SED and 2,610 members of the FDJ [Free German Youth — the youth organization of the Socialist Unity Party — author].

The main reason for the present situation: the decisions taken at the 2nd Party Conference of the SED which were approved by the Central Committee of the CPSU. They oriented towards accelerated construction of socialism in East Germany without taking into account that necessary preconditions for such a step, both in the field of foreign and home policy, had not been created.

The social and economic measures taken in that connection, among them the accelerated development of heavy industries without having safe sources of raw materials; the sudden restrictions on private initiative, compromising the interests of a broad section of small proprietors in towns and villages; the denying of ration cards to all private entrepreneurs and free professions and especially the overhasty creation of agricultural producers' cooperatives without the necessary fundamentals in the villages having been laid — all this led to serious shortcomings in the field of the supply of the population with industrial goods and foodstuffs, caused a substantial fall in the exchange rate of the GDR mark and ruined a great number of small proprietors, such as craftsmen, traders, etc., and turned large parts of the population against the regime.

This has even led to 500,000 hectares of agricultural land having been abandoned and left uncultivated, and the thrifty German peasants, who are normally highly attached to their piece of land, are leaving their property and farms and migrating to West Germany...

Source: Peter Przybylski, Tatort Politbüro. Die Akte Honecker, pp. 241 ff, excerpt; crime scene politburo, the Honecker files.

Document 17. Ulbricht speaks to rebellious workers

Professor Alfred Kantorovicz, a communist anti-fascist who fought in Spain during the Civil War against the Franco fascists, was told the following by a participant (named Ewald) in a meeting with General Secretary Ulbricht at the Niles Works . The meeting took place shortly after the workers' rebellion of June 17, 1953:

> "Around 700 workers filled the culture center. Ulbricht came escorted by eight policemen on motorcycles. The police surrounded him when he entered the hall. The workers started whistling, howling, and shouting when the police pushed forward onto the stage:
>
> 'Booh! — Ey, ey...who is that guy escorted by his nannies?! — Police out! — Long live the leader of the working class who comes to his workers under police protection! No police or no Ulbricht!'
>
> Ulbricht whispered something to the police and then they left the stage. He went to the lectern and a chairman of the 'National Front' declared the meeting open. While he was still talking, the police came back into the hall with chairs and sat down in the front row. New protests: 'Now, that's enough!' New booing, many workers rising and leaving. Ulbricht gave a sign to the police and they retreated.
>
> He started his speech without an introduction. Even after one sentence he was interrupted. Around 150–200 workers rose, shuffled their chairs, stamped their feet and left the hall. Others shouted: 'Enough! Stop talking!' One worker stood up and shouted: 'You've given this kind of speech ten times before, haven't you, and we've heard all this nonsense a hundred times over. We now want to talk business.' Another worker shouted: 'It's useless, we don't know what you're talking about anyways. You demand that our youth learn proper German and you yourself haven't learned it yet!'
>
> Ulbricht then shoved his manuscript back into his pocket, saying: 'I'm the son of a working man who the capitalist society has only given four years of education. So forgive me when I sometimes say false sentences, but that's not the point here. You don't understand me because you don't understand what I have to tell you.'
>
> Shouts are heard: 'Ho, ho!'
>
> After more heckling, Ewald stood up in the middle of the hall and shouted: 'Comrade Ulbricht — you are making our job very difficult, I must admit. We as ordinary comrades are standing here among the colleagues and have to answer their questions why you came here with the police.'

Then foreman Wilke stood up, a sixty-year-old highly qualified worker...He then asked Ulbricht: 'Explain this to us: If I do bad work at my boiler, then I'm going to get sacked. You've have openly admitted that you did bad political work, but you are allowed to stay on. What do you intend to do now?' (That hit the nail on the head. Now his position was at stake).

Ullbricht became furious: 'You're lying! It's not true! Bring me evidence that a good worker will get sacked if he makes a mistake at his machine. But it is a different matter if he destroys the machine on purpose. Then he is an enemy. But who says that the government is an enemy of the workers?'

More workers fired their questions at him. One demanded to talk to him on behalf of his department. He said: 'I'm trusted by the workers.' He demanded: 'Remove all the posters and slogans in Weißensee; no more large-sized photos of party bosses, we want to keep our city clean!'

Another worker shouted: 'No more meetings!' And another: '...and not more extra shifts!' Then the trade unionist Wienke, on behalf of his trade union, group number nine, demanded the release of the arrested on June 17th. From the Niles works alone, more than 100 workers had disappeared.

Ulbricht retorted that many workers had fled to West Berlin after the imposition of the state of emergency. One should not assume that all those who had not come back since Wednesday, have been arrested.

Another foreman said: 'We've voiced criticism a hundred times. The outcome was always next to nothing, and about the so-called 'New Way' everybody just says: 'I don't trust it, I can't believe it!'

A party member said: 'We've always wanted free speech and free criticism, but nobody has dared to open his mouth anymore of late.'

And another foreman complained about shortcomings in supplies and the whole mess in work organization, saying: 'It's become unbearable that we keep hearing complaints, that we're not fulfilling the plan, but how are we to fulfill the plan if we don't get any raw material?!'

A friend of Ewald's, a worker called Kreisel, said: 'In my view our functionaries should go through the works for one or two hours and talk to the colleagues rather than sit at their desks and compile reports that don't make any sense at all.'

The restlessness grew, and there was more heckling. In the end Ulbricht ruined all there was left to ruin when he presented a prepared resolution he wanted to get a vote on. Then the storm broke lose. 'Aha! Hooray the SED!' — 'Long live the fuehrer!' — 'Not with us!'

Ulbricht tried to shout louder than they did. Finally, he succeeded in reading out the resolution: the usual declaration of trust for party and government. He put it to a vote. The result: 188 in favor, the rest against. Ulbricht himself estimated: 'So — roughly 500 against.' He declared the meeting closed. A worker said: 'Tomorrow I'll have a look at what they write in the press about it and how they present it.'"

Source: Alfred Kantorowicz, Deutsches Tagebuch, Zweiter Teil, Berlin, 1980, pp. 378 ff.

Document 18. The unconstitutional arrest of Justice Minister Max Fechner

When many people went on strike on June 17, 1953, during the Berlin uprising, Max Fechner, the GDR Justice Minister, told the strikers that they did not have to worry: nobody was going to get punished for that. But after the violent suppression of the uprising, Fechner was suddenly put on trial and was given a long prison sentence for having made this promise. After three years in prison, he was prematurely released. The constitution of the GDR adopted in October 1949 still guaranteed the right to go on strike. Later the article was changed and the right to strike annulled.

CONSTITUTION OF THE GERMAN DEMOCRATIC REPUBLIC (adopted October 1949)

Article 14

(1) The right to belong to associations for the promotion of wage and working conditions is guaranteed for everyone. All agreements and measures designed to limit or hinder his freedom are against the law.

(2) The right of trade unions to strike is guaranteed.

Source: www.documentarchiv.de/ddr/verfddr1949.html, excerpt

Document 19. Ulbricht praises the 20th Congress

In a letter to Khrushchev dated April 1959, Ulbricht raved about the outcomes of the 20th CPSU congress (February 1956):

> It is of great historical significance that at this Congress the Central Committee of the CPSU dealt critically and openly with the dogmatist policy and the violations of the Leninist party norms and socialist legality. This was a courageous act on the part of the Central Committee, and it was Comrade Khrushchev's dynamism playing a large part in it. Only this way was it possible to radically overcome the mistakes and to enable, fully prepare and arm the Party to face the historic problems it has to solve.
>
> The 20th Party Congress enhanced the role of the Party and that of collective leadership and pointed to the necessity to forge even stronger ties with the masses. It made a call to unfold the initiative of all communists, the creative mastering of theory and to abide by the experiences made by the Party. The entire work of Party's organizations — ideological or organizational — was directed by the Party Congress towards carrying out the great practical tasks...
>
> Within the Soviet Union, the implementation of the Leninist course could not prevail without a struggle against those stubbornly insisting on the old, dogmatic stands which are out of touch with life and who, by all means possible, were trying to stop the creative measures that inaugurated a new stage in the development of the international working class movement.
>
> The members of the Anti-Party Group, Malenkov, Molotov, and Kaganovich, resisted those decisions which are critical to mobilize and encourage the initiative of the masses and to enhance the cooperation of the working people. Even after these decisions had been taken, they continued to block their implementation. They opposed the decisions to introduce material incentives for collective farmers and resisted measures to abolish bureaucratic planning and to introduce a new planning regime, opening up more space for mass initiatives. They rejected the great initiative to cultivate virgin land as they did not believe in the power of the masses...

Source: Einheit, 14th year, April 1959, no. 4, pp. 455, 458, excerpt.

Document 20. Ulbricht settles the score with Stalin

At the 6th Congress of the Socialist Unity Party in January 1963 (which adopted the NESPL reforms), Ulbricht declared in front of the delegates:

We, too, the members and the leaders of the Communist Party of Germany, have suffered from the Stalinist personality cult and Stalin's methods of terror. And if some people want to know more about that: our politburo rejected the Stalinist methods and found understanding and support with Soviet comrades and the General Secretary of the Communist International, Comrade Dimitrov.

Source: Carola Stern, Ulbricht — Eine politische Biographie, Cologne and Berlin, 1964, p. 312, note 17; Ulbricht — a political biography.

Document 21. Human trafficking in the GDR

Four "players" were involved in human trafficking that earned foreign currency for the highly indebted East German state: the security apparatus "Stasi," with the Protestant Church (EKD) acting as mediator, the state of the FRG providing the money and the West German taxpayer reimbursing them. By the way: political prisoners were people who had taken part in illegal political activities, who had voiced criticism against the regime or who had applied for emigration. Even members of a Marxist-Leninist organization, the Communist Party of Germany/Marxists-Leninists (KPD/ML), received prison sentences of up to eight years for having spread "propaganda against the state," thus becoming political prisoners and susceptible for human trafficking.

Analysis

Special Business "B," 1964–1985. The transactions are mediated by the Protestant Church and carried out by firms known to us. The following results have been achieved (since 1964):

Year	million DM*
1964	37.9
1965	67.6
1966	24.8
1967	31.4
1968	28.4
1969	44.8
1970	50.6
1971	84.2
1972	69.4

1973	54.0
1974	88.1
1975	104.0
1976	130.0
1977	143.9
1978	168.3
1979	106.9
1980	130.0
1981	178.0
1982	176.9
1983	102.8
1984	387.9
1985	302.0
Total	2,511.9 million DM

(DM = West German currency, Deutschmarks)

Source: Peter Przybylski, Tatort Politbüro. Die Akte Honecker, Berlin, 1991, p. 367.

Document 22. Schalck's decorations for "outstanding services"

Decorations received by Alexander Schalck-Golodkovsky for "outstanding services," according to his Stasi file. After the people's uprising in October–November of 1989, Schalck fled to West Berlin to escape prosecution (December 4). There he spent some time in detention and was then brought to West Germany by the BND, the West German foreign intelligence service.

Position: OibE*, already since October 10, 1966
Rank: Colonel, since October 1975
Name: Schalck-Golodkovsky, first name: Alexander
Member of the SED: since March 3, 1955
Decorations:

10-07-1958   Medal for Excellent Performance, MfAA

05-01-1960	Medal for Excellent Performance, MfAA
10-07-1960	Order of Merit of the GDR
08-18-1961	Medal for Excellent Performance, MfAA
10-07-1964	Order of Merit of the Fighting Brigades
02-08-1965	Order of Merit of the National People's Army (NVA) in silver
05-01-1965	Activist of Outstanding Merit
10-07-1966	Order of Merit of the Fatherland in bronze
07-01-1967	MftrD (Medal for Loyal Services) in bronze
10-07-1968	Order of Merit of the NVA in gold
08-27-1969	Order of Merit of the Fatherland in gold
07-01-1970	MftrD in silver
02-08-1972	Fighting Order in gold
07-01-1975	MftrD in gold
10-01-1975	Order of Karl Marx
10-07-1979	30th Anniversary of the GDR Medal
1979	Outstanding Collaborator of the Ministry for Security
07-01-1980	MftrD in gold, 20 years
04-23-1980	Comrade-in-Arms Medal in gold
07-03-1982	Order of Karl Marx, 2nd time
03-04-1983	Hero of Labor
10-07-1984	Great Star of Friendship Among Nations
02-08-1985	25 Years of Loyal Services Certificate

* OibE = Special Operations' Officer or Special Secret Service Officer

Source: Peter Przybylski, ibid., p. 381.

Document 23. Schalck's connections to West German intelligence

Schalck's personal physician Heinz Wuschech spoke about his connections to the BND (Bundesnachrichtendienst).

> Page 167:...that Schalck-Golodkovsky was chatting with the secret services people for two months — from January to March 1990;

> Page 168: On January 22, the BND brought the fugitive couple to a mountain hut near the Austrian border. The domicile was situated on the Samerberg and was blocked from car traffic;

> Page 170: The talks with the BND often lasted six to eight hours in the vicinity of Lake Schlier and surroundings...in hotel rooms.

The questions Schalck was asked revolved around the economy, finance and politics of the GDR...and especially personnel.

Page 172: The talks ended with a sumptuous dinner in the hotel "Überfahrt" at Lake Tegern on March 16, 1990. The host was BND president Hans-Georg Wieck — a historian by profession and a former diplomat.

Page 173: The BND people offered the Schalck couple a 14-day trip to Italy. Schalck: "We never made use of it."

Source: Frank Schumann, Heinz Wuschech, Schalck-Golodkowski: Der Mann, der die DDR retten wollte, Berlin, 2012, pp. 167–173; the man who tried to rescue the GDR.

Document 24. The GDR selling off its cultural heritage

Since 1977, the West German foreign intelligence service, BND, was kept informed about the GDR's selling off of antiques.

Confidential (classified material)
Date: June 20, 1977
Re.: Sale of antiquities to earn foreign currency/DDR 1935 WENA
Information:

Among GDR art dealers it has become known that "Art dealers in the GDR have been told to sell as many antiquities as possible in the West. A great number of trucks are on their way to the inner-German border. Place of destination: probably Düsseldorf, maybe also Amsterdam. The motive for these transactions: presumably the GDR's constant lack of foreign currency."

Comment:

As early as 1973, the GDR set out to export valuable pieces of art from "the common German past," preferably of the 19th century. For this purpose, artifacts from the museums of Dresden, Berlin (East) and Leipzig were taken into consideration. Prospective customers were art dealers from Switzerland, the US and the Vatican. These intentions, however, were given up due to protests in the Federal Republic of Germany and a lack of understanding within the population of the GDR.

It is suspected that the present case is not a continuation of this kind of art dealing, but an attempt to push exports of antiquities, such as farmhouse furniture, porcelain, clocks, etc. Up to now, deliveries of this kind have been intended to earn foreign currency and were handled mainly via Switzerland, the Netherlands and the United States. We have no exact information about the scope of the trading.

The export trading company Kunst und Antiquitäten GmbH in Berlin (East), founded in January 1973, is responsible for this sort of export. The firm probably is part of the Transisterverband (sales organization) and receives direct instructions from Schalck-Golodkovsky's sector. Chief executive of the company is Horst Schuster."

Source: Egmont R. Koch, Das geheime Kartell. BND, Schalck, Stasi & Co., Hamburg, 1992, appendix, no page given.

Document 25. Werner Krolikovsky on the GDR economy

Werner Krolikovsky's notes on the economic situation of the GDR, dated March 30, 1983, provide evidence that leading officials of the SED were well aware of the economic calamity and the impending bankruptcy of the state. Krolikovsky was Secretary of the Economy until 1976, when Günter Mittag took over and replaced him. K., however, remained a member of the SED Politburo till the end. He kept his criticism to himself, but later published it in his book, Totengräber der DDR (gravedigger of the GDR):

1. The domestic situation of the GDR

Year after year, the imbalance in the national economy between income and expense has been increasing. Calculated on the basis of the GDP, the trend is as follows:

Year	Income	Expense
1971	25.1	74.9
1975	23.8	76.2
1980	22.5	77.5
1982	16.2	83.8
1983	13.4 (as expected)	86.6

Thus it is seen that economic development, purchasing power and the supply of consumer goods are continuously declining.

There is a constant stream of public criticism regarding supply shortages, constituting a permanent phenomenon (enclosure one, showing the fall in supply standards). Growth in industrial performance in the first two months of 1983 is 2.6% (per working day) and the increase in labor productivity in the sector supervised by the industrial ministries is at 1.4%.

In public, however, EH (Eric Honecker — author) is talking about a 4.3% growth in the rate of industrial goods production and about a 3.3% rise in labor productivity in the sector belonging to the industrial ministries, so that statistics are being manipulated by EH and GM (Günter Mittag — author) to gloss things over.

In the enterprises continuous and smooth production is replaced by rushing. Many mechanical engineering plants will only achieve between 50–60% of the targets set for the first twenty days of the monthly production and then must achieve 40–50% during the rest of the month. Lost hours and overtime are a great burden on the national economy.

In 1983, the target increase in industrial performance, scheduled to reach 4.5% according to the law, must be achieved with a 9% decrease in specified utilization of material; in the case of sheet metal even with a decrease of 10%. Up until now, it has become obvious that many combines are not in a position to reach this target. More delays in plan fulfillment are expected in industry...

It must be emphasized and said loud and clear that the GDR's solvency is at stake. At present, efforts are under way to avert such a danger, but there is still no end in sight.

It would be a good thing if EH, in his conversation with Yuri Andropov, will be asked how he intends to master the situation...

Behind EH's permanent offers addressed to the Bonn government lies the GDR's indebtedness to the FRG, amounting to four billion valuta marks, the GDR's dependence on the FRG and its susceptibility to blackmail, lies EH's disloyalty to the Soviet Union's and the Socialist Community's foreign policy towards the FRG, and EH's wish to continue to use the FRG as a sponsor and supplier of goods to heal the wounds of the sick GDR economy. All this is a deviation from Marxism-Leninism, showing that he is bogged down in nationalism...

Source: Peter Przybylski, ibid., pp. 349 ff, 354, excerpts.

Document 26. Two Schürer documents (1989) on the GDR's impending insolvency

Gerhard Schürer	Top Secret
Gerhard Beil	b5 — 1111/89
Alexander Schalck-Golodkovsky	5 copies, sheets 1–7
Herta König	
Werner Polze	

Berlin, September 28, 1989

...

1. The current financial situation of the GDR in trading with the NSW [non-socialist currency area — author] is characterized by the fact that now we have become heavily dependent on capitalist creditors if we want to honor our financial obligations with regard to credits and interest as well as for carrying out our yearly imports.

The GDR's yearly credit-taking stands at 8–10 billion valuta marks [in West German currency — author]. For a country like the GDR this is an extraordinarily large sum that has to be mobilized at 400 banks or so. For further granting of credits, these banks have now set special country limits in their dealings with socialist and developing countries.

Due to the present high degree of credit-taking, these banks are no longer prepared to increase these limits for the GDR substantially.

Source: Peter Przybylski, Tatort Politbüro, Bd. 2., Berlin, 1992, p. 358; crime scene politburo, vol. 2.

The second document

Former SED politburo member Gerhard Schürer, the GDR's planning chief, confirmed the authenticity of the document in his memoirs (see: Gerhard Schürer, Gewagt und verloren, eine deutsche Biografie, Berlin, 1998, pp. 197–202, "Ventured and lost"). There he gives a detailed summary of the contents of the document, but he omits to mention the exact amount of debts incurred by the GDR in the non-socialist currency area: 49 billion valuta marks.

Gerhard Schürer   Top Secret
Gerhard Beil   b 5-1158/89
Alexander Schalck   (to be scrapped Dec. 31, 1989,)
Ernst Höfner   not to be changed
Arno Donda

October 30, 1989

For the Attention of the Politburo of the CC of the SED

Re.: Analysis of the Economic Situation of the GDR, with
conclusions drawn

...

The export targets for the Five-Year Plan 1986–1990 are showing
a deficit of 14 billion marks due to a lack of performance and
insufficient effectiveness, and the indices for imports are surpassed
by around 15 billion marks. This includes imports of machinery
and equipment in the amount of 6.9 billion marks to boost
performance, especially in the metal processing industry as well
as in microelectronics.

Instead of achieving the projected export surplus of 23.1 billion marks,
we are faced with an import surplus of 6 billion marks in 1986–1990.

This is connected to a rapid increase in the debt burden, reaching
49 billion marks in late 1989, amounting to 190% as compared to
1985. This burden is roughly four times as high as the value of our
exports in 1989.

The projected income in foreign currency is only sufficient to
meet 35% of our expenses in foreign currency used for credit and
interest payments, plus imports. So 65% of our expenses will have
to be met by bank credits and other sources. This means that
redemption and interest payments, debt that is, will have to be
paid by incurring new debts. To finance interest payments, more
than half of the budget income growth will have to be made use
of...

If an increase in the total debt burden is to be avoided, a domestic
product worth 30 billion marks will be needed in 1990, equaling
the planned growth of domestic income of three years ago and a
reduction of consumer spending by 25–30% as well.

To avoid a breakdown in solvency, the following export surpluses will have to be achieved:

Billion marks	1990	1991	1992	1993	1994	1995
Export surplus	2.0	4.6	6.7	9.2	10.2	11.3

Under these circumstances, the total amount of the debt burden would be as follows in these years:

Billion marks	1990	1991	1992	1993	1994	1995
Total debt	55.5	62.0	63.0	62.0	60.0	57.0

However: the preconditions for such export surpluses do not exist under the present circumstances...

Source: BArch, DY 30, J IV 2/2A/3252, www.chronik-der-mauer.de/ material/178898/sed-politbuerovorlage-analyse-der-oekonomischen-lage- der-ddr-mit-schlussfolgerungen-30-oktober-1989.

Document 27. Former Stasi officer Ralf Opitz describing the corrupt lifestyle in Wandlitz

The corrupt lifestyle of the GDR's ruling elite in the village of Wandlitz near Berlin: the example of Willi Stoph, long-time member of the SED Politburo, longstanding chairman of the GDR's State Council and at times also Chairman of the Council of Ministers, the GDR government. Ralf Opitz, a Stasi officer, who protected the Politburo members in the closed settlement of Wandlitz, tells the story:

Construction works in the bogs of Birkenheide.

The east bank of the river Müritz was a conservation area, a special hunting ground, being part of the province of Neubrandenburg — a huge forest with marshes and without any strong roads. A timber house of the thirties, belonging to some Nazi type war still there. Mr. Göring [Hitler's right hand, field marshal and interior minister — author] is said to have gone hunting there.

We were given orders to tear down the old hut. The first of the new wooden houses had to be finished by Christmas. We received orders in November, and at Christmas Stoph already wanted to be there! So we built a house within only four and a half weeks, using people from Wandlitz and an entire battalion of the NVA [Nationale Volksarmee, the GDR's army — author]. Paths and roads, leading up to the site and making it passable for heavy vehicles, had to be built as well.

Thirty people were permanently employed who had been given orders to keep the roads in good condition so that the construction vehicles could go there. The building material was driven to the site from all over the district. The house, a type HW 100, was prefabricated in Wernigerode.

On day before Christmas Eve, the furniture was moved in, the roads were ready so that Comrade Stoph with his family could celebrate Christmas there. Downstairs were a living room with a fireplace and a kitchen, upstairs two rooms with a bath.

In the second construction phase which was to begin the following year, the next house, thirty meters away, was built: another HW 100 destined for Stph's kids who were married already. Then one more house was erected diagonally opposite, this time a HW 90 which was destined for Stoph's parents-in-law. We also built garages, a guardhouse, a house for the janitor or a water treatment plant. Getting hold of clean water in the bogs is no easy matter! Later, a special room for his hunting trophies was annexed.

After that, we had to dredge out the canal so that the boats could go from the Müritz to lake Specker. We built bridges and, a little later, even an emergency power plant which became a common installation for all houses built after the year 1975.

Gerhard Schürer in Dierhagen had one, and Günter Kleiber and Konni Neumann in Serwest had one, too, but also those people living in Wilffang, Schluft or Rehluch.

When he was still chairman of the State Council, Stoph spent most of his time in Birkenheide. At that time, he usually stayed there from Tuesday afternoon till Sunday afternoon. When he was chairman of the Council of Ministers, he drove to Birkenheide on a Thursday and stayed there till Sunday. So he only attended a couple of meetings, and that was it. The Politburo meetings were on Tuesday and on Thursday those of the Council of Ministers...

Finally, Stoph expressed his wish to swim in an indoor swimming pool. So a swimming pool was to be built for him which first had to be covered with film; later we added a roof made of acrylic glass, and a heater had to be installed as well...

Fifteen to twenty people were permanently employed in Birkenheide just to look after Stoph's needs and to care for his moods. Even a former head of department was employed as the responsible manager — a lieutenant colonel by rank.

Nobody, virtually nobody, dared to voice any criticism about Stoph's extravaganzas...

Source: Thomas Grimm, Das Politbüro privat. Ulbricht, Honecker, Mielke & Co., aus der Sicht ihrer Angestellten, Berlin, 2004, pp. 146 ff, excerpts; the politburo in private.

4. How Anti-fascist was the German Democratic Republic?

Gerhard Schnehen
An essay written in November 2014

On the occasion of the November events in 1989 in the former GDR, the Communist Initiative, a pro-GDR organization, under the headline of 25 Years of Counterrevolution, wrote the following sentence:

Fascists did not make it to senior positions in the administration, but received a just punishment.[447]

Is this a viable and fair statement, does it stand up to criticism?

Whether this claim, constantly being repeated by the GDR media and the rulers of the GDR, is true or false, mere propaganda and perhaps even falsification of history or an honest and truthful statement, depends on one thing: can it be backed up by hard facts or not? The claims made by a government that was continually trying to justify itself before the own population, but also abroad, is not sufficient proof that this assertion is actually true.

Everybody who is searching the truth should base his or her statements or judgments on concrete, undeniable, verifiable and documented facts. Such a person only trusts her or his own reasoning and always questions cheap slogans or claims made by politicians or the media and then tries to do their own bit of research. Doing ones own research work is not so

---

[447] http://www.kommunistische-initiative.de: 25 years of counterrevolution in the GDR, a contribution by the Communist Initiative, Nov. 2014.

easy, but hard and often painful. One needs a lot of patience and, above all, good pieces of reliable information and a clear mind. It is easier to adopt pronouncements made by people in authority and to believe them, all the more so, if these authorities or these people were or still are like-minded people — people of ones own political "color" as it were.

What strikes you at first sight, when reading the above sentence, is that the claim is presented as a fact. Old Nazis and fascists in the GDR were excluded from senior government jobs and even got their fair share of punishment for what they did during the Nazi era. Punto final. No questions asked.

This already provokes some skepticism and doubts in a critical mind. Was this really the case? But first of all one is tempted to think: former Nazis were rehabilitated in West Germany and given high positions and could even become Chancellor of the Republic when thinking of Kurt-Georg Kiesinger, the West German chancellor between 1966 and 1969; and on the other hand, the GDR was truly anti-fascist and all the leading politicians in the GDR had been anti-fascists in one way or the other during the dark times of German history. Take Eric Honecker, for example, we young communists were told: he was an anti-fascist and even spent ten years in a Brandenburg penitentiary during the "Third Reich" because of his anti-fascist activities. So: fascists there in the FRG and anti-fascists here in the GDR. The past of the leaders says it all.

So at first sight, the above statement seems to hold water. But if you dig a little deeper, some odd things come to light, giving food for thought:

1. In May 1945, Walter Ulbricht, later to become the most powerful East German politician, bans all the anti-fascist committees that have emerged shortly after the war, consisting of thousands of active anti-fascists. He calls them "sectarians" and their organizations, according to Ulbricht, were allegedly set up by the Nazis themselves. High-ranking German Nazis, among them Hitler's personal physician Ferdinand Sauerbruch, are however given leading positions in the new Berlin administration by Ulbricht's group;

2. The same Ulbricht also bans the "Association of Victims of the Nazi Regime" (VVN) some years later and sets up his own rival organization euphemistically called "Committee of Anti-fascist Resistance Fighters." The property of the VVN is confiscated and handed over the East German security police Stasi. The entire archive is now no longer available for research purposes and for tracking former Nazis. In Ulbricht's new organization former Nazis, now called "anti-fascists," are also welcome;

3. The anti-fascists Rudolf Herrnstadt and Wilhelm Zaisser are removed from the SED Politburo. Herrnstadt who used to work many years undercover for Soviet intelligence during the war in Warsaw is no longer allowed to move freely in the GDR and no longer allowed to voice his opinion. Later he is also stripped off his anti-fascist pension even though he is gravely ill. He gets a job in an archive in the town of Merseburg where he becomes an ordinary co-worker. Herrnstadt's crime: after the June 17th events he had voiced harsh criticism against Ulbricht for his mishandling of the crisis and had even secured a majority in the Politburo for becoming Ulbricht's successor. Zaisser, a veteran general of the Spanish anti-fascist resistance, is also banned from the SED and suddenly dies of a "heart attack" in 1958.

4. Eric Apel, former director of the Buchenwald-Dora concentration camp, who was also involved in developing Hitler's wonder weapon "V2" in the village of Peenemünde, is given the post of a chief planner for Ulbricht's "economic reform." Ulbricht co-opts him into the Central Committee and a little later also into the SED Politburo. Together with the other Politburo members he resides in the closed settlement of Wandlitz where he takes part in the numerous hunting events. Apel never was an anti-fascist, but used to be a staunch follower of Adolf Hitler. Eric Honecker, Ulbricht's successor, when asked questions about Apel:

He didn't need to be afraid of anything as everything was disclosed to us and was in his file.[448]

As long as the Stasi was informed, nothing to worry about!

5. After the events of June 17, 1953 when the East German workers came out massively against an unpopular regime, which had put up the work norms by more than 10%, freed prices and cut social spending, Socialist Unity Party, led by the communists Ulbricht and Pieck and by the social democrat Grotewohl, lost hundreds of thousands of members. Many emigrated to West Germany and left everything they owned behind to be save from the SED regime. After the suppression of the revolt by Soviet military, costing the lives of forty people, the Party's gates were widely opened again to attract new members and former members of the Nazi party (NSDAP) were now also welcome. Every fifth member of the newly structured party now had a Nazi past, according to a poll conducted.

---

[448] Eric Honecker interview, in: Reinhold Andert/Wolfgang Herzberg, *Der Sturz*, Berlin/Weimar, 1991, p. 282.

6. GDR politicians in leading positions in the executive or legislature with a solid Nazi past were for instance: Vincenz Mueller, a high Nazi general who was active in Russia (general lieutenant), who became Deputy Minister of the Interior, Deputy Defense Minister and also Deputy President of the People's Chamber (Volkskammer, the GDR's legislature); Willi Stoph, the longstanding chairman of the GDR state council and also at times chairman of the GDR government, during the war wrote a piece in a Nazi paper in which he glorified the Nazi regime, writing, and I quote: "The birthday parade for the Fuehrer (meaning Hitler) left a deep impression on me." Later he received the iron cross for his loyal services in the military. During the war he joined the Nazi Party, but immediately after the war, when the Nazis had been thoroughly defeated by the Red Army, he joined the Communist Party and became one of the rising stars there.

Another example: Arno von Lenski, later decorated by the GDR leaders with the medal "Fighter against Fascism" became an MP in the GDR People's Chamber. Between 1939 and 1942 he had been one of the infamous judges at the so-called Nazi People's Court (also called "blood judges") and had a hand in more than 20 death sentences against German, Polish and Dutch citizens.

Herbert Weiz, Deputy Chairman of the Council of Ministers of the GDR, joined the Nazi Party in 1942. In 1967 Ulbricht made him Deputy Head of the GDR Government. Later he became Minister for Science and Technology. Kurt Blecha became government spokesman. He joined the Nazi Party in 1941. His deputy, Wolfgang Ewert, was an NSDAP member as well. Max Hartwig, in 1960 became Deputy State Secretary for Church Affairs. He joined the infamous "Waffen SS" in 1939, a terror organization responsible for hundreds of thousands of mass murders of Jews, Gipsies, and thousands of Russians, Belorussians and Ukrainians. He also "served" in the Buchenwald concentration camp in the province of Thueringen in East Germany. Ernst Großmann, also a former member of the same organization, had been a member of the Central Committee of the SED for seven years. He used to be an SS guard in the concentration camp of Sachsenhausen in Germany; Prof. Heinrich Homann who joined the Nazi Party in 1933 and became a major in the German army ("Wehrmacht"), both under Ulbricht and later under Honecker was Deputy Chairman of the State Council of the GDR, and the list goes on and on.[449]

It is fair to say that in all spheres of life of the GDR — in politics, in the economy, in the cultural sector, in the health service, in the military,

---

[449] Olaf Kappelt, *Braunbuch DDR. Nazis in der DDR*, Berlin, 1981, p. 238.

in the diplomatic service or at universities — many former active Nazis were welcome if they had disclosed their fascist past to the authorities, especially to the secret service Stasi who kept the files and if they had special qualifications, for example as a scientist. To make a career, they then swore their allegiance to the GDR state or the Socialist Unity Party SED, or both, and everything was fine.

When the war in the Soviet Union was still going on, special retraining schools were set up for German prisoners-of-war, and after some weeks or months, many of the leading generals of the Nazi Wehrmacht who had attended these courses, all of a sudden had become "anti-fascists." Ulbricht, who spent the war in Moscow exile looked after these retraining schools and these generals, and when he later needed some people for his team in Berlin, he just turned to his friend Wilhelm Pieck in Moscow who worked at the Communist International to send him some reliable "anti-fascists" as a counterweight against the many true anti-fascists who had joined the SED.

7. There are a lot more oddities that occurred in the "anti-fascist" GDR, especially in the fifties. Here is the story:

In the mid-fifties the SED leadership around Ulbricht and Pieck started rehabilitating Nazi collaborators from Buchenwald concentration camp — one of the biggest camps in Nazi Germany. The communist overseer Ernst Busse who had committed war crimes against Russian prisoners-of-war by sending them to special commandos where they would never return and were sure to die, and even gave communist camp inmates, who stood in opposition of the collaborators, lethal injections in his capacity as right-hand physician of the camp directorate. After the war a Soviet judge gave this "communist" a life sentence to be served in a Soviet labor camp. Busse made comprehensive confessions and admitted that he had actually committed these crimes at Buchenwald. Ulbricht who must have known his case nevertheless nominated Busse for the post of a Deputy Prime Minister in the province of Thuringen. Busse also became Minister of Agriculture there. While serving his sentence in the Soviet Union, Busse was rehabilitated by the Central Control Commission of the Party (ZPKK) after his death in 1956.[450]

A second camp lieutenant by the name of Erich Reschke who also spent some time in the same concentration camp in a senior position was likewise prematurely rehabilitated by the SED executive board.

---

[450] Lutz Niethammer, ed., *Der ›gesäuberte‹ Antifaschismus. Die SED und die roten Kapos von Buchenwald*, Berlin, 1994, p. 478; the purged antifascism. The Socialist Unity Party and the red overseers of Buchenwald..

Witnesses saw Reschke beating and mistreating prisoners — a behavior for which another Soviet judge sentenced him to life-long imprisonment. Ulbricht who was looking for a chief of police for the province of Thuringen gave him the job on his return to East Germany in 1955. The same commission mentioned above also rehabilitated him and years later Reschke even became a major of the GDR people's militia (Volkspolizei).

A third Nazi collaborator, Willi Seifert, also had a top job in the Buchenwald camp where he was charged with putting together labor commandos. He preferably ordered Russian inmates to serve in these groups who often never returned from their mission. Seifert also convicted of war crimes, later became one of Eric Honecker's right-hand men when the Berlin Wall had to be erected in August of 1961. Having shown exemplary behavior, he was promoted and given a higher position.

Ulbricht who decorated himself with an anti-fascist medal for his one-time inspection tour in Spain during the Civil War, was about to get into trouble in the early fifties: The Soviet leadership, then still under Stalin, sent investigators to East Berlin to look into his dealings with the Field brothers — two American spies who had tried to infiltrate the communist movement in Eastern Europe. Honecker in his interview with Andert and Herzberg in 1990:

As in Hungary and Czechoslovakia the Slánsky trial was ongoing. It was about Ulbricht's person; there was the danger that he could be involved in the trial like the other General Secretaries. We were lucky enough to fend this off. It was still before Stalin's death.[451]

If Stalin and Beria, his most trusted confidant, had lived longer, Ulbricht would certainly have been in deep trouble. Both died an unnatural death in 1953, the first in March and the second probably in December after a show trial, paving the way for Khrushchev's rise to power who was quick to end the investigation.

On the other hand, a camp inmate called Waibel who, as a staunch communist, did not want to collaborate with the Nazis in the Buchenwald camp and rejected any idea of becoming a tool of the SS or right-hand man for the Nazi guards, was later expelled from the SED and called "a Trotskyite element."

8. Another scandal: the case of the euthanasia doctors. To quote just one instance: In 1956, another special rehabilitation commission set up by the SED leadership, among them security chief Eric Mielke, decided on prematurely release Richard von Hegener, one of the main culprits for

---

[451] Reinhold Andert und Wolfgang Herzberg, ibid., p. 232.

the thousand-fold murder of handicapped children and sick grown-ups during the Nazi era. A court in the city of Magdeburg in the province of Saxony-Anhalt in the Western part of the GDR, had ruled in 1952 that Hegener was guilty of war crimes and gave him a life-sentence to be served in a penitentiary. But in 1955 and also in 1956 the GDR Council of Ministers under the chairmanship of Otto Grotewohl passed a special rehabilitation law to prematurely release convicted war criminals and to integrate them into the GDR society. Another special commission, to which also of Eric Mielke belonged, then decided to pardon the euthanasia doctors.[452]

9. Non-prosecution of convicted Nazi war criminals in the GDR and their employment by the GDR security service Stasi: the case of Alfred Hothorn. Hothorn was a member of the Nazi Waffen SS during the war in France when the country was under Nazi occupation. There he took part in war crimes, and after the liberation of France was given a 20-year sentence in absentia by a French court. After the war he returned to the GDR under a new name. In 1952, his identity is disclosed, but as a collaborator of the Stasi he was given protection and had nothing to worry about. Quite the opposite: In 1979 Stasi chief Eric Mielke even decorated him with the "Medal of Loyalty of the NVA in Gold" for his loyal and outstanding services.[453]

10. The case of Heinrich Groth: The former member of the Waffen SS participated in mass murders in Lithuania. Soviet resistance fighters and partisans were his victims. In 1943 he was "honored" with a medal for his "exemplary" work. In late October 1945 Groth returned to East Berlin, joined the Communist Party and became a policeman (1948) and later a commander of the People's Militia (Volkspolizei). Hard luck for him when the Soviet secret service in Berlin checked on his identity, arrested him in 1950, and after that a Soviet court sentenced him to 25 years of hard labor for the crimes he participated in in the Soviet Union. But when Khrushchev came to power he was given a pardon (1955) and was consequently set free, reason enough for him to return to East Germany where he was provisionally rearrested in the city of Bautzen. In 1956, the SED Politburo decided to release him. In July he was recruited by Mielke's security service as an undercover agent to spy on his fellow countrymen and to provide information about the mood in the GDR

---

[452] Henry Leide, NS- Verbrecher und Staatssicherheit, 2006, p. 332; Nazi criminals and state security.
[453] Ibid., p. 129.

population.[454] His expertise as a spy that he had acquired during the Nazi era was obviously needed by Mielke's security people, so it did not matter much that he once was a war criminal.

11. Former high representatives of German industry and commerce who once were members of the Nazi party and even exercised leading positions in the Nazi hierarchy, were reemployed by Ulbricht after the war, instead of handing them over to a court to provide justice for the victims. The former GDR Industry Minister, Guenter Vyshovsky, in an interview with German economists in September 1993:

Yes — Ulbricht kept such people and he even stirred them up against us. It's not so nice when I'm saying this. Take Adolf Thiessen for instance: he used to be director of the Kaiser-Wilhelm-Institut under Hitler. He was one of the big shots of German capital then. Mr. Steenbeck came from Siemens where he was a technical director. He returned from Russia, and in the GDR he became a famous physicist.[455]

Adolf Thiessen, mentioned by Mr. Vyshovsky, even joined the Nazi Party in 1925. Later he left the Nazis, but after the Nazi coup in January 1933 he joined them again and became a member of the NSDAP one more time.

What conclusion can be drawn from this? There is only one left: the claim made by the above-mentioned pro-GDR communist organization that "fascists did not make it to senior positions in the GDR, but received their just punishment" cannot be verified and does not stand up to a closer investigation of the numerous facts nowadays being available to us.

If German fascists who "received their just punishment" were barred from public office in the GDR, how comes that a former head of a concentration camp called Buchenwald-Dora, was charged with drafting NESPL, the most important economic project in the GDR by which capitalist principles were introduced into the East German economy? This project was anti-socialist to the core as I have shown in my above analysis and could not have been drafted by a true communist or a genuine socialist. So obviously other people were needed with a completely different mind-set. How was it possible in the presence of "democracy" — and the GDR called itself one — that Chairman Ulbricht simply co-opted this man Apel into the Politburo — a man who had never been a communist and had only joined the SED in 1957 and then made a steep career.

---

[454] Ibid., pp. 217 ff.
[455] Theo Pirker et al, *Der Plan als Befehl und Fiktion*, Opladen, 1995, p. 190.

If the GDR was truly "anti-fascist," why were Nazi collaborators, who had been exposed and punished by the Soviets stationed in East Berlin — and not by the Germans — pardoned and even allowed to make a career in the GDR and, in some cases, also given medals "for excellent services"? Busse, Reschke, and also the history professor Walter Bartel who, as camp inmates at Buchenwald concentration camp, had already enjoyed privileges in their capacity as overseers, henchmen and collaborators of the Waffen SS, later again enjoyed a privileged life — this time in the "anti-fascist GDR"! Why were these criminals allowed to join the "communist" Socialist Unity Party in the first place if this had been a truly "anti-fascist" and "socialist" party? Was there maybe some common ground between this "socialist" party and the German "national socialists"?

How "socialist" was this party to which also Stasi chief Mielke belonged who had the deputy leader of the West German Communist Party, Kurt Mueller, abducted to Berlin by a squat team, who was then locked up in a Stasi prison cell and tortured to extract confessions from him about his past in the KPD going back twenty years. He had belonged to a faction of the Communist Party in the twenties and thirties that had some issues with another faction to which Ulbricht. Pieck and Mielke belonged. In the early thirties, Mielke and his friend Eric Ziemer murdered two German policemen in front of the headquarters of the German Communist Party and then fled to Mosow to escape punishment — an act of violence condemned by Party leader Ernst Thaelmann in the strongest possible terms as this provocation almost caused the banning of his party.

If the GDR was truly anti-fascist, why did so many upright anti-fascists leave East Germany, especially in the fifties in disillusionment to find a new home in capitalist West Germany where, in some cases, they were also persecuted and vilified? Alfred Kantorovicz, the German anti-fascist who had an excellent record as an upright anti-fascist and as a former participant in the Spanish Liberation War and as a member of an international anti-fascist fighting brigade and who also wrote a diary on the Spanish Civil, was spied upon by Mielke's Stasi and then succeeded to flee the GDR just in time to escape his impending arrest. His Spanish war diaries he was able to smuggle clandestinely into West Germany for fear of confiscation as he writes in his memoirs. The war diaries were banned from publication in the GDR as they contained some critical remarks about Ulbricht and his entourage and their dealings in Spain at that time. Kantorovicz used to be a professor for German literature at Humboldt-University in East Berlin.

So there are a lot of question marks as far as the anti-fascist character of the GDR regime is concerned and especially with regard to Walter Ulbricht who used to be at the helm of the country for decades. Only in 1971 he was removed by some Politburo members, but not because he had been a false anti-fascist. No, no, the reasons were completely different ones. He had become too friendly with the West Germans, and the Soviet leaders (Brezhnev!) wanted someone more loyal at the top of the GDR which they considered their colony. His successor Eric Honecker, who was permanently praised as an anti-fascist by the regime, as we know now, collaborated with the Waffen SS in the penitentiary of Brandenburg-Görden where he was incarcerated instead of joining the resistance group there which was active in the prison underground. The physicist Professor Robert Havemann who had been given a death sentences by the Nazi's highest court, the so-called People's Court, but who was still needed to fulfill some tasks for the Nazis and whose life was spared, had helped the resistance fighters there to do their job, whereas Honecker had taken his distance and became so friendly with a woman overseer called Charlotte Schanuel that he even married her shortly after the war. When he joined the Communists in 1946 he was asked to write a short curriculum vitae and what did he do? He did not mention this marriage but kept silent about it and later married another woman called Edit Baumann, whom he also divorced a little later. Honecker soon rose up to the top of the Free German Youth, the ideal springboard for a promising career in the SED and soon became a Politburo member thanks to Ulbricht's skillful handling of matters of personnel. And what happened to Robert Havenmann who had refused to collaborate with the Nazis in Brandenburg? When he gave some lectures critical of the GDR regime in the early sixties ("Dialectics without a Dogma"), he was first taken into custody and then put under house arrest for years.

The question marks are many and there are so many stories to tell, but it would take far too long to go deeper into them all, to ask more unpleasant questions and to reveal even further oddities about the "anti-fascist bastion" GDR. Even the Berlin Wall built in mid-August of 1961 to prevent the massive flow of emigrants from East Germany towards the West was called an "anti-fascist protection wall" by the SED leaders. People were told in all earnest that this wall was built only because West German fascists wanted to invade the GDR and to take over the reins there. Later the propaganda was changed a little and then the Wall had supposedly been built to "rescue peace in Central Europe" because the Americans wanted to start a nuclear war in Germany. Did President Kennedy really want war in Central Europe? I seriously doubt that.

I told Professor Wolfram Triller, a leading theoretician of the German Communist Party, about my findings and also of my analysis of the Buchenwald myth which did not correspond to the legend that the camp inmates had liberated themselves under the leadership of people like Busse, Reschke, and Bartel before the US army had arrived in the surroundings of the camp. I suggested to enter into a debate and to exchange letters. First he agreed, but soon, when I had confronted him with more and more cases of Nazi collaboration he got fed up writing to me and then suggested to end the correspondence. Here is what he wrote in his last letter:

If we cannot come to an understanding that the GDR was the greatest achievement in the history of the German workers' movement then there is no need to continue our discussion...Maybe we should now make a break in our debate.[456]

He also accused me of having depicted the GDR as "a Nazi republic."

Out of curiosity I visited the website of the German Communist Party (DKP) which has now shrunk to only 2,800 members. When I was still a member before leaving the party, the organization had almost 50,000 members who were also very actively involved in politics. Anyway: there I found a piece on the Berlin Wall and, alas, again the old story: It was still being described as an "anti-fascist protection wall" by the writer of the article and he added that the GDR as a whole had been such an anti-fascist fortress...

But facts speak louder than ideology.

Gerhard Schnehen

---

[456] Prof. Wolfram Triller, writing to me in early February of 2006.

Printed in the United States
by Baker & Taylor Publisher Services